8312696716

*f***P**

The Secret

Lives of Girls

What Good Girls Really Do—Sex Play,
Aggression, and Their Guilt

Sharon Lamb, Ed.D.

THE FREE PRESS
New York   London   Toronto   Sydney   Singapore

THE FREE PRESS
A Division of Simon & Schuster Inc.
1230 Avenue of the Americas
New York, NY 10020

THE FREE PRESS and colophon are trademarks
of Simon & Schuster Inc.

Manufactured in the United States of America

10   9   8   7   6   5   4   3   2   1

Library of Congress Cataloging-in-Publication Data is available

Lamb, Sharon.
    The secret lives of girls : what good girls really do—sex play, aggression,
and their guilt / Sharon Lamb.
            p.   cm.
    Includes bibliographical references and index.
        1. Girls.   2. Girls—Psychology.   3. Girls—Sexual behavior.   4. Aggressiveness
in children.   I. Title.

HQ777 .L35 2002
305.23—dc21   2001054755

ISBN 0-7432-0107-8

To my teacher and friend, Rachel Hare-Mustin

Acknowledgments

W hen the time is right for an exploration of girls' sexuality or girls' aggression, an author is not alone. She works in a community of scholars, some of whom she knows, some of whom she doesn't, some whose work has gone unnoticed, and some whose work is more thorough or incisive than her own. I thank these scholars, poets, and authors.

I consider myself lucky to have found a home at Saint Michael's College, where faculty colleagues, staff, students, and the administration have supported my work in every way, through friendship, funding, warmth, reading of the manuscript, and their sensible spirituality. While many are mentioned below for specific help they gave, the community as a whole has my grateful thanks. There were several students who helped me in the beginning of this work: Kate Hanley, Jennifer Courtemanche, Jason Becker, Chrissie Venerus, Kate Colistra, and Heather Watters. I thank them and Herb Kessel, Kristin Novotny, Christina Walulik, Pauline Beaulieu, Meghan Carhart, Padraic Springuel, and Lizz Green, also at St. Mike's, for the practical assistance they gave. The Saint Michael's Faculty Development Committee as well as the Social Science Research Consortium helped support the cost of some travel and interviewing. Kristen Hindes, clever seeker of obscure references, made me feel as if I had access to my very own personal interlibrary loan shark. Vince Bolduc, Kyle Dodson, Bill Garrett, Adrie Kusserow, Sue Kuntz, Susan Ouellette, Trish Siplon, and Lorrie Smith read chapters or loaned crucial books. Buff Lindau's intelligent reading of the proposal helped shape the book itself.

The following friends and family outside of Saint Mike's helped through earlier work in this area, timely suggestions, loaning of books, or reading the manuscript at some point in the process: Diane Anstadt, Larry Blum, Lyn Mikel Brown, Peter Chubinsky, Mary Coakley, Crow Cohen, Bill Downs, Susan Edgar-Smith, Lisa Fontes, Janice Haaken, Gary Lamb, Leanne Leahy, Judith Levine, Shannon Longcore, Jeanne Marecek, Joanne McGee, Paul Okami, Doris Orgel, Shelley Orgel, Edie Raskin, and Sarah Sappington. Mary Theresa Struck and Jay Munane, amazing people, helped me to reach more African-American girls and women. Special thanks also to Laura Orgel, who interviewed some West Coast women for me as part of her doctoral work.

I am indebted to those friends and colleagues who went out of their way to help me find girls and women to interview: Andrew Garrod, Nona Lyons, Amy and Lois Bodnick, Joanne McGee, Bill and Nadine Downs, Rit Devenere, and Robin Koestner. Bill Puka's generosity, in particular, has overwhelmed me.

I also passionately thank my friend Bev Colston, because of her interviewing, her energy, her intelligence, the talks we had, the hugs, and her help in working through all the emotions associated with doing these interviews. She is a goddess.

Thanks to Doris Orgel and Judith Wallerstein for introducing me to my agent, Carol Mann. Thanks to my transcriber, Irma Gifford, whose competence and accuracy were phenomenal. Jennifer Kemp, with her baby name books, and Kathie Balutansky, with her collection of world literature, helped me find aliases for the 122 women interviewed. Sometimes I also borrowed the names of people I knew, and hope that no one will think the stories here actually are stories of these friends and neighbors. I am also grateful for Nancy Keyes, who approved of the wild girl, and Barbara Torpie, who helped to civilize her.

Rachel Hare-Mustin, Jerome Kagan, Catherine Snow, and Carol Gilligan at Harvard Graduate School of Education have been major influences. And I am thankful for those phone and e-mail conversations with friends that keep me on track and intellectually alive—Larry Blum, Judith Levine, Jeffrie Murphy, and Janice Haaken, as well as for my connections with the good people at the Association for Moral Education. Conversations with Jan Haaken and Judith Levine always helped me to clarify my thinking, and I am especially indebted to Jan for her thoughts on lower-class girls and their lack of a "protected space," as well as Shelley Orgel for his thoughts on women's aggression and creativity.

Carol Mann, my agent and wise woman, helped shape the book early on by asking important questions and sending me away to rewrite. My editor, Philip Rappaport, had tremendous enthusiasm for "girl books" and was keenly aware of the moral dimension of this work. Beth Haymaker, who also edited the book, became for me the epitome of that smart, enthusiastic, and totally engaged reader every author dreams of.

While I wrote this book, my all-male family went on and lived their lives, unconcerned with the secrets this girl kept. They loved me and put up with my moodiness and deserve thanks for that. Memories of my parents, Martha and Tracy Lamb, their encouragement, generosity, and my dad's love of "Oprah" were always with me.

The women and girls I interviewed are to be thanked and thanked again. I appreciate wholeheartedly their willingness to share what secrets they could and understand what secrets they maybe couldn't.

Contents

Preface

This book celebrates two aspects of girls' lives that they try hard to keep secret: sex and aggression. After years of studying girls' reactions to victimization and women's memories of both sexual victimization and sexual play at Harvard, Children's, and Massachusetts General hospitals in Boston, Bryn Mawr College in Pennsylvania, and now Saint Michael's College in Vermont, I've learned that girls and women have amazing strengths and clever, if hidden, ways of acknowledging feelings of sexual agency as well as anger and aggression. Although I have learned to welcome these forces in the lives of girls, I haven't always felt this way. I initially came to this work with a guilty conscience.

When I was a child I had played sexual games with other girls and was deeply concerned for many years after about what I had done. I had even had sexual feelings during these games. For many years I believed I had seduced another girl into playing with me, although years later I found out that she didn't see it that way at all. The games I played were delightful games of heterosexual romance where a handsome young "man" would seduce or trap a young "woman" into sharing his bed and rubbing up against him. But I felt so terribly guilty for years about these games that I sought out therapists and social workers in high school to tell me if there was something wrong with me.

By the time I began working on this book, however, I had sufficiently dealt with those issues in my life, through coursework as I trained to become a psychologist, through therapy in my twenties and thirties, and through my work as a feminist, a professor, a therapist, and a researcher of sexual abuse and victimization. In my earlier books, *The Trouble with Blame* and *New Versions of Victims*, I easily disclosed that I had been molested at the age of six by a neighborhood adolescent boy, and although it was a scary and confusing experience at the time, I emerged relatively unscathed and consider myself lucky compared to the many victims of sexual abuse who experienced so much more—penetration, threats, bribes, assaults to their very being. What I think is so interesting and also sets the stage for this research about girls and women that I have done is that an experience of sexual pleasure (the games I played) was so much more life-defining, threatening to my ego, shameful, and disruptive than that experience of abuse.

Another defining experience was my work with Carol Gilligan, who taught me how to listen and direct my attention to the words of the girls and women I interviewed. But the body of work that arose after her original brave book, *In a Different Voice*, pushed me in a different direction. In the 1980s I wanted so much to join the crowd of believers in women's caring natures and their deep strivings for connection, but I felt that I didn't belong. As a woman who experienced anger, wishes for vengeance, who could be sexual, mean, bad, and as a woman who grew up in a lower class family where some forms of aggression were valued, I felt at odds with the glowing image of girls and women that became a popularized version of the ethic of care. And as Carol's original and political message became reduced in the public arena to the simple thought that women are both caring and more caring than men, I felt uncomfortable with the model of girlhood that seemed to be emerging. Redefining my sexual urges and needs for vengeance as deep-seated strivings for connectedness did not ring true to my own experiences. They had a life separate from my wishes to be known and loved and even to be "good."

That is why I think I have a new perspective to offer readers on the development of girls and women, a perspective that gives girls' sexuality and aggression their due and doesn't subsume it under a blanket of caring nor as a defense against oppression. This is a perspective that returns us to a more complicated version of girls, that understands sexual and aggressive feelings as "normal." Hopefully, it's a perspective that will help girls to integrate these acts into their definitions of who they are and how girls are "supposed" to be.

For those readers who might want to know a little about the research I did, I interviewed women from over twenty-five states, using family trips and trips to conferences in other states as opportunities to find women and girls to interview. Friends and family helped me to find parents who would allow me to interview their daughters. A student with connections to an elementary school in New York City introduced me to low-income Puerto Rican women so that I could explore a group of women rarely tapped by researchers for a focus on healthy development. A friend who consulted with an after-school program situated in a housing project helped me to bring into my sample low-income African-American girls and women as well as low-income white girls so that I might write a book that reached out beyond middle-class white readers alone.

Concerned that African-American women and girls might not open up to me, I trained Bev Colston, a middle-class Black woman with Caribbean roots, to do some of these interviews. Her warmth, intelligence, and love of the topic produced some of the best interviews. Also, an older doctoral student in Oregon, Laura Orgel, who had great energy for the topic, interviewed some West Coast women for me. Students at Saint Michael's College did some initial interviewing as we developed the interview questions. I am the interviewer for the rest, the majority of the interviews, that follow.

Listening to these women and girls was an incredibly powerful experience. They were from different racial and ethnic backgrounds, from different parts of the country, different socioeconomic classes. I worried about how much truth they were sharing and the limits to that sharing; about whether I influenced or led women down paths they may not have followed on their own; and whether I might have made them too vulnerable or accidentally shut them up. I had concerns about how other psychologists would see this kind of work, data which would always remain incomplete; that is, we would never know the whole "truth." And I had feelings myself when memories came back that I needed to confront.

Of the 122 women and girls interviewed, 29 are African American, 21 Latina (primarily Puerto Rican-American), and 3 Asian American. Of the 122, about 30 are children or teens. I reached them all through word of mouth and through friends who had friends in churches, schools, colleges, and housing projects. In the stories that follow I may have changed around characteristics or descriptions of individuals to preserve their anonymity, but not their words, which ring clear and true.

Perhaps the reader will want to know whether I believe I got at "the truth." My answer is that I got at some truths, and not the whole story. Many women and girls are not ready to tell the whole story.

Still, I don't believe people made up stories to impress me. Perhaps there were untruths that aren't lies—stories that became distorted over time. These stories arise in a culture and context that cannot be ignored. For example, how many times did women erroneously remember someone else initiating a game of sexual play instead of herself because our culture has taught her that good girls do not "ask for" that sort of thing. I suspect that when involving desire or the initiation of sexual games, the stories may have emerged distorted.

And sexual feelings. This is another area where the full story may be hidden. For some interviews it was difficult to even ask the question, "Do you think you had sexual feelings while playing the game?" If a woman answered yes, it was almost always tentative. If I felt bold enough to ask, "Did you experience orgasms?" and if the woman replied that she did, she would almost always ask whether I thought this was "normal."

Shame is a funny emotion, making people want to hide their faces, their selves, and their stories. It also makes people want to confess in order to find some relief. I tried to bring out the shameful as well as the delightful. I welcomed the hearty, joyful stories of childhood power, sexuality, and aggression, and tried to make room for the scarier, more tentative childhood feelings. My hope was to begin a dialogue about such taboo topics.

I hope these stories will change the way people talk about girls and raise their daughters. Truths or partial truths, I think these stories can offer that.

The book is divided into two parts: The first focuses on sex (the sexual play and games in childhood) and the second focuses on aggression (power, anger, and aggression, to be exact). Feelings of guilt and shame are woven throughout the stories presented in both halves of this book, yet so are feelings of delight and wonder. Interspersed between chapters the reader will note sections or minichapters I label "Zeroing In On. . . ." These are reflections or summaries of research or background information on smaller topics that are aimed at preparing the reader for stories to come.

Through the stories and reflections I hope to offer a more complex understanding of female development than is currently offered to parents by psychologists, one that allows for a wide range of human desires, emotions, and actions. While common notions of "girlness" influence girls in ways that protect and oppress them, making them feel shame and guilt for their ungirlish acts, the girls in the stories to come challenge these notions. With honor and integrity, many find a way to stay "good" while incorporating their secret urges for sexuality, power, and aggression.

Introduction: Good Girls versus Real Girls

As Sarah, naked and vulnerable, struggles to free herself from the imaginary bonds that tie her hands to the bed frame, Lisa bends down over Sarah's naked body and slowly but gently places a kiss on the top of her bare vagina. Because they hear footsteps in the hall, this electrifying act signals the end of the game, and both girls, seven years old, hasten to get their clothes back on before Lisa's mother knocks on the closed and locked door of her bedroom. They are now satisfied and silly but still hopeful that tomorrow or the next day they will find another time to reenact this powerful game as well as switch roles. Next time Sarah will be the man, Lisa the woman.

Lisa is a Jewish white girl and Sarah is a Christian Japanese American. Both do well in school, are their teachers' pets, and they are best friends. It is 1962, long before children were likely to be exposed to semipornographic magazines, TV shows, movies, or videos, and long before these children could read well enough to learn about the erotic traditions of romance novels. Yet at some time during their imaginative play, a game developed, secret and even unspoken between these two, that reproduced one of the most sexually thrilling scenes of female imagination for the time—to be captured, stripped, and then, not degraded or humiliated, but adored.

This is not an unusual story of two oversexed seven-year-olds who found each other, but a story more common than not in the secret lives of girls. Like Sarah and Lisa, there are other girls who play these games and games like them with other girls as well as with boys. There is Chrissie, who loved to kiss the boys on the playground when she caught them. Abbie played mermaids and rubbed her naked top against her friend's as part of the game. So many other girls play "I'll show you mine if you show me yours," usually with boys. Some enjoy getting together with friends to play "naked Barbies."

There are also typical stories of girls whose secrets are about pleasurable aggression. Leah, for example, got a "kick" out of kicking the boys in the crotch and running away as they doubled over in pain. Chanelle beat up a girl in her school who had nice clothes, and enjoyed it.

The following pages hold many stories from girls and women I interviewed about the sexual play and games of their childhood as well as the moments of aggression and sometimes evil they committed. These interviews about the secrets they've kept have shown me a few things about what goes on behind closed doors, and what sorts of behaviors have been hidden by women and girls to preserve their outer image of goodness. Two themes stand out: sex and aggression. Girls hide their sexual acts and feelings as well as their aggressive impulses because girls are not supposed to have these. But sexual feelings and aggressive impulses are a part of human nature. They can be about power as well as self-discovery. Their narratives show that

- many girls play sexually, not just out of curiosity. Many have sexual feelings and pursue these feelings. They teach themselves and their friends (boys and girls) about their perceptions of adult sexuality. Even at early ages, they incorporate into their sexual styles images of what they think adult female sexuality is really about.
- many girls do aggressive things to other people, and not always to retaliate or out of frustration or because they were losing a connection to someone. Some enjoy their aggression, and especially if they have grown up in poverty or in dangerous neighborhoods, they wear their aggression as a badge of honor. Middle-class girls live with life-long secrets of what they see as inexplicable outbursts or furtive evil done to another, badness they have never been able to explain to themselves.
- many girls crave power and seek it in their relationships with others, not only to connect, but because power over another is sometimes pleasurable.

There are an amazingly wide variety of sexual and aggressive behaviors in childhood, but most girls and women see the incidents from their own lives as outside the range of "normal."

I interviewed girls ages six to eighteen and women from eighteen to seventy. They came from over twenty-five different states, a variety of upbringings, poor, low income, working class, middle class, and wealthy. Some grew up on farms, some in housing projects, some in high-rises, and some in suburban houses. And what I found traveling around the country is that many girls and women have secrets, secrets of sexual play and games, and secrets of aggressive acts that surprised and sometimes scared them. It's not my intention to shock the reader with raw sex and pure aggression in the lives of girls; instead, after reading story after story and learning about the meaning of sex and aggression in girls' lives, I hope that for some this behavior will look a little more "normal" than it did at first glance.

"Normal" is something that we as a culture construct. In America today, we can look at a girl's sexual talk and games and call her prematurely slutty or, using a more clinical word, oversexualized. We can look at her plans to play sexually with another girl, the sexual feelings she has with another girl, and we might call her a lesbian. Or, we might simply say "this is what children do," "they have bodies, they have sexual feelings; the exploration and expression of both are *normal*" no matter whom they are with.

Some people would say that we shouldn't even use the word "normal" and they might be right. It's hurt too many people and gives special power to the word "abnormal." But the one question that girls and women asked me over and over when I was interviewing them was "Am I normal?" Usually what I told them was that I had heard many stories like theirs already, and that answer seemed to satisfy. What they really wanted to know was: Am I different? Should I be ashamed? And more often than not, Should I continue to be ashamed? Rather than encouraging the self-condemnation, secrecy, and shaming of these girls, I wanted them to see that what they did was more or less typical of girls growing up, that sex and aggression are a part of human experience, and even sometimes sources of pleasure. To see sex and aggression as part of life and even a source of pleasure doesn't mean we ought to abandon all efforts to treat these as moral acts, but that we base our moral judgments on issues of harm and caring, justice and individual rights, rather than on conventions of purity and outdated stereotypes of women and girls.

After sitting with and listening to over 120 women and girls across the country I know a little bit about what goes on in the privacy of children's bedrooms and backyard playhouses. And after reading this book, so will many others. In knowing this, maybe we all will look at girls a little differently, and maybe we will reframe our own pasts, reclaiming some lost parts of ourselves that were discovered in the basements and closets of girlhood, in the spots where teachers and parents weren't looking.

Good Girls and Guilt

This book tries to undo the image of the good girl that I think has been unnecessarily harmful to girls as they grow up. And this book tries to take a second look at all this moral language, such as "good" and "bad," when it gets applied to sex or aggression. The word "good," when used to describe girls, has little to do with real morality and lots to do with social norms. I think of social norms as rules about what's "proper" or acceptable, rather than rules about what's morally right. These rules rein in women and girls and restrict their development in important ways.

While the exaggerated guilt and shame that little girls carry around with them for their secret acts of sexual pleasure or aggression is a burden, it is the hemming in of girls through the rules of "niceness" that hurts girls most and causes the guilt and shame. The girls whose stories are told are all too aware that they act in ways not befitting a girl or young woman, and as acting like a girl gets merged in their minds with being good, they grow up with a nagging guilt that they are never good enough, nice enough.

How could so much be going on behind the scenes while still so many girls and women continue to think they have done something perverted, abnormal, or horribly cruel? There is some greater social force teaching girls and women how to interpret their acts and impulses. On the one hand society suggests these impulses to them, for where else but from our culture (parents, movies, peers, advertisements, and more) do ideas about sex and aggression come from? And then, on the other hand, societal norms aimed at girls make them feel bad about it, bad and immoral. This is a real shame. It's a shame that women and girls have to learn about themselves and their potential for both sexuality and aggression in a secret and shame-evoking manner. I want this book to free up women and girls to acknowledge all aspects of being human and to take off the shimmering costume of a femininity that equals goodness.

But the point of this book is *not* to find yet another area in which girls are victims of the culture. (In some cases it certainly is true, yet women, who were once girls themselves, are key shapers of girl culture.) The larger purpose is to expose all of these acts that are going on in secrecy so that girls and women can feel less guilty about their sexual desires as well as their aggressive impulses, can learn to accept these as part of themselves and still love and honor themselves for them. It is so that the goodness of women and girls can be defined in terms of a more universal morality, grounded in justice and caring, instead of in terms of their ability to sit still in a classroom or restrain themselves from the human desires for revenge or sexual pleasure.

You might think that feminism has done a lot already to change this popular image of the good girl. But, in some ways, it's probably helped it along a little bit. What popular feminism has taught us about girls over the past twenty years (after the sixties, that is, when anger and rebellion were celebrated) is that girls are more caring and more vulnerable, more likely to be victimized by the culture and more likely to nurture, more likely to suppress their anger so that they don't hurt others and more likely to try to please. While there also has been a tradition rewarding girls' spunkiness and resistance to images of purity, psychologists have for the most part told parents that these qualities in girls of caring and sensitivity are to be admired.

But they are also qualities that confirm a stereotype that works against girls feeling powerful. Readers have come to know the rebellious lost teens of *Reviving Ophelia* as really and truly empathic, caring girls who have lost their grounding connections with adults. Mary Pipher, who wrote *Reviving Ophelia,* is so like the good nurturant mother who has come to pluck out the treasured adolescent soul, preserve it, and cherish its goodness for all time. Many will also remember the voices of caring, nurturing women who were ignored by male psychologists who valued independence and rational decision-making. Women psychologists gave these women's voices a hearing. But are these pure and caring voices so different from the good girl of yesterday? Whether or not these voices box girls in or recognize a reality of girls' development, psychologists continue to re-create them on the covers of best-selling psychology books to the exclusion of other parts of girls and girls' development. The point is, we all would so much rather look like the lovely lost souls found by Mary Pipher than the bad girls we suspect we really are.

Not so long ago, girls and women were viewed as evil temptresses, seductive witches, and manipulative matriarchs, but even when these images flourished, there was always the opposite image of the pure and good girl, as in a fairy tale, set beside them for comparison. It's time to take a look at the fantasies that we all keep repressing—those fantasies of women as insatiable, angry witches and bitches, oversexed, with monstrous appetites, women who actually want power over another person, who want to dominate, and women who find pleasure in sexual feelings and aggression against another. And when we allow them into our lives, they may not feel so exaggeratedly wrong.

Creating an "Other"

Little girls' attempts at being active, angry, and sexual are pushed away by the culture and by themselves. They hide these from us or we don't see them for what they are. And when they are aggressive or sexual, they "other" the experience—someone else made them do it or they see it as something outside of themselves, a strange and weird occurrence. In fact, in these pages you will hear the words "weird," "strange," and "not me" used over and over to describe these experiences.

Another way of "othering" the experience is to project it onto women and girls who really are considered others in our culture, for example, African-American and Puerto Rican girls. Because when we conjure up the image of the good girl who "minds" her parents, does well in school, and doesn't dirty herself, we do not usually picture her Black or Latina. It's easier for society to see aggression and sexuality in, as well as project them onto, these girls. It fits the stereotypes and allows white girls to feel superior in comparison. While it is difficult for African-American and Latina girls to project an image of the "good girl," given the culture's unwillingness to see them that way, there still is a lot at stake for these girls if they embrace sexuality or aggression.

In this book I include stories from Puerto Rican and African-American women as girls growing up in a culture in which they are othered. The scope of the study did not allow me to collect enough stories to explore other groups who are treated as others, such as other Latina groups, Native Americans, or Asian Americans. Even as I tried to integrate the Puerto Rican and African-American girls' and women's experience into these chapters I was acutely aware of the intersection of class, race, and ethnicity and how these complexities are difficult to do justice to within one short book. On the other hand, I also was aware of how at times I may be treating "whiteness" as some monolithic term without reference to the variations in class, ethnicity, and experience within this group.

Yet while the realities of many white girls' lives do not conform to the stereotype of the white middle-class girl, as the realities of the lives of African-American or Puerto Rican girls do not conform to the culture's stereotypes of them, there is still an image of a girl, a good girl, that is internalized for all girls. This stereotypical ideal may indeed loom larger in the lives of white girls than in those girls whose lives become other to the stereotype. Girls growing up in situations that make such a stereotype seem less attainable will in some way be freed from the stereotype, but they will be hurt in other ways. This othering brings about harmful counterimages of sexual and aggressive girls that they accept or resist to their detriment.

The general kind of othering (the other girl started it) that is so much a part of how middle-class girls explain sexuality and aggression is done out of guilt and shame. But in the following pages we will take apart this guilt. Some of it is appropriate, and we would wish that all people might feel the sense of guilt and remorse that many girls feel when they've hurt another by acting out aggressively. Even so, because these acts are forbidden, they carry with them an unrealistic burden of guilt for girls. And they try to hide the fact that these are human impulses we all share—the taste for revenge, the sexual urges of the body, the desire to dominate another.

Girl Power

Finally, someone reading this book is bound to ask, What about "girl power"? Aren't girls today more powerful than ever thanks to those early feminists who fought for the empowerment of women and girls? Don't girls today have better self-esteem? Can't they do everything boys do? In sports, for example? And even sexually, aren't they worlds apart from the white-gloved Mommy's helper of the fifties? Many have commented on how high school girls today seem unashamedly raunchy in their discussions of sex and bodies.

Teenage girls today engage in sex earlier and speak more freely about their sexual exploits. These acts frequently do not derive from a love of their bodies or an urge to express and understand themselves sexually, but from a desire to garner male attention and define themselves as desirable, even if "wild," in the eyes of boys. They don't divorce themselves from the image of the "good girl" but evaluate their behavior against the backdrop of this image, which makes them feel somewhat ashamed. If recent reports on teen sexuality are accurate, sexually active teens frequently regret their early sex, wishing they could do their teen years over again. The raucous, in-your-face teen sexuality of today is not a sexuality that leaves them feeling powerful.

But what about "girl power," the media slogan that focuses on the preteen as well as the teen? Even the new movement about girl power plays into this image of goodness and sets up unrealistic images. For white middle-class girls, the image of "supergirl" is evoked by shouts of "Girls rule!" This is the girl who can achieve well in school and pursue a career when she grows up. Girls knew, even before these slogans appeared, that they did better than boys in school and were well loved by teachers for their achievements. But Valerie Walkerdine, a British sociologist and feminist, points out that the image of the supergirl that "Girls rule" and "girl power" suggest sets up an opposing image of the girl of color or from a low-income family who is the other and not given the opportunities to achieve superwoman status. And it ignores the privilege that helps only *certain* girls become supergirls and makes them suffer when they come close to achieving this status, working as hard as they do for some perfection or recognition that is often unattainable.

Girls love these slogans, though: Girls rule! Girl power! And why? Because so many girls seem to love power and love to win. And girls have been deprived of that exuberance for a long time. Boys in our culture have greater freedom to engage in transgressive activities and call them their own. They are free to explore, rage, experiment—free to be ravenous, sexual, and outrageous. Their secrets are of a different kind and deserve their own treatment elsewhere.

When boys act "bad," a different kind of distancing from their acts occurs, perpetuated by the boys themselves, their parents, educators, and the media. Rather than othering (projecting their badness onto others), boys are *excused* quite publicly for the sexual and aggressive acts they commit. Unless the boys take guns to their high schools or rape another student, adults in the United States will tend to see their aggressive or sexual acts as typical, and in some cases, biological—a part of who they "really" are. When we hear of a sexual game or an aggressive act of a boy we say that *all* boys are like this; we say "boys will be boys."

Who Are the "Real Girls"?

It would be tempting to tell you that the stories ahead show what *"real girls"* do, just as William Pollack asserts about "real boys" in his book of the same name. Any such truism would mislead just as much as the prevailing stereotypes of girl and boy behavior do. Biological urges get shaped by the social expectations of specific cultures and specific times. The "sexual girl" is no more real than the pure and innocent girl, for both potentials are in us and our children. Still, recognizing the potential for sexuality and aggression in our girls affords them a little more privilege in this world, helps them to lead more fulfilling lives in our current culture, protects them from self-destructive acts, and encourages them to be "good" in truly moral (seeking peace, justice, and care) rather than in merely conventional ways.

If parents want their daughters to be full and moral people, aware of all aspects of their humanity, good and bad, they need to accept certain impulses in girls that up until now they may not have wanted to see. Girls, like boys, are deeply sexual, deeply aggressive creatures. And these impulses exist alongside their sweetness, competence, and ability to love and care for others. Real girls are morally complex, interesting, and interested creatures, and while the culture may do its best to simplify and codify their "girlness," box them in so to speak, they do their best to resist, rebel, redefine, and explore this girlness through the secret games they play and the secrets they keep.

Part I

The Sexual Lives of Girls

Both women and girls told me sexual stories—truths, partial truths, memories, but stories nonetheless. Storytelling is community building, the cultural theorist Ken Plummer tells us. In the 1960s, after centuries of silence, women began to tell their stories of coercion and rape, in books, consciousness-raising groups, and "Take Back the Night" rallies. These individual stories created one large historical narrative about the lives of women. It served to bring women and girls together, together in their victimization.

Storytelling can also be subversive. It can change the way we view the past and it can overthrow what we think is normal to create new norms. The public form of storytelling takes individual acts of rebellion and unruliness, brings them together as a body of stories, and by virtue of making them "women's stories" (rather than Judy's or Mary's or Ling's story) gives them a power all their own.

But there is no larger story about women's passions and sexual energy. In sex education classrooms, in girls' and women's novels, and in our conversations with one another, the sexual stories shared most easily are those about victimization and restraint rather than about pleasure and desire. Telling sexual stories of childhood addresses this lack from the bottom up. Sexuality does not begin at thirteen. And if we tell these beginning stories aloud, we give energy and space to a hidden part of the lives of girls and women. Because sexual play and games are acts of resistance, experiments in "girlness" and sexuality, sharing these narratives liberates all women.

What do we reform by telling these sexual stories of girlhood?

- We make it okay for girls to have human feelings of sex and aggression.
- We encourage them to develop spaces in which they feel powerful.
- We allow them to find spaces in which they feel sexual, even as children, especially as girls.

Who would deny our daughters this power? Who would deny them this knowledge? We would. We deny them this understanding almost unconsciously as we preserve some ideal of childhood innocence, treat sex as something shameful and dirty, and write sex education curricula to focus on victimization, disease, and pregnancy. Despite these structures, girls seek out knowledge to make themselves more powerful personally and interpersonally. They mostly do so, though, behind closed doors.

These are secret stories, stories rarely told, and as such, their telling brings with it a certain power. The African-American poet feminist Audré Lorde wrote, "[K]nowledge is power. Our erotic knowledge empowers us, becomes a lens through which we scrutinize all aspects of our existence, forcing us to evaluate those aspects honestly in terms of their relative meaning within our own lives."

Marie Howe, in her poem "Practicing" (cited in full following), writes of the power of the erotic, even in seventh-grade girls. In this poem, with her use of the words "love poem," "hymn," "song," we learn that what might have been called "practicing" was more than "just" practice. In somebody's "parents' house," that is, the house that heterosexual romance built, there are some things that go unsaid. And what remains unsaid is not a story of lesbian romance (though many girls fear that it is). It is a story of girls' bodies and girls' pleasure, their sense of power in that pleasure, a story rarely told. Part One of this book wants to tell that story.

Practicing

By Marie Howe

I want to write a love poem for the girls I kissed in seventh grade,
a song for what we did on the floor of the basement

of somebody's parents' house, a hymn for what we didn't say but
   thought:
That feels good or *I like that*, when we learned how to open each
   others' mouths

how to move our tongues to make somebody moan. We called it
   practicing, and
one was the boy, and we paired off—maybe six or eight girls—and
   turned out

the lights and kissed and kissed until we were stoned on kisses,
   and lifted our
nightgowns or let the straps drop, and Now you be the boy.

Concrete floor, sleeping bag or couch, playroom, game room,
   train room, laundry.
Linda's basement was like a boat with booths and portholes

instead of windows. Gloria's father had a bar downstairs with
   stools that spun,
plush carpeting. We kissed each other's throats.

We sucked each other's breasts, and we left marks, and never
   spoke of it upstairs
outdoors, in daylight, not once. We did it, and it was

practicing, and slept, sprawled so our legs still locked or crossed, a
   hand still lost
in someone's hair . . . and we grew up and hardly mentioned who

the first kiss really was—a girl like us, still sticky with the
   moisturizer we'd
shared in the bathroom. I want to write a song

for that thick silence in the dark, and the first pure thrill of
   unreluctant desire,
just before we made ourselves stop.

Chapter 1

*"I'll Show You Mine
If You Show Me Yours"*

"If somebody saw us doing this, they would think it was very, very wrong."
—Lynn, African American, 41

Why do children pull down their pants for one another? Curiosity is one reason. Girls want to see what's "down there" if the other child is a boy. And girls want to see other girls to compare them to themselves. They wonder, Does it look different? Has a friend started growing pubic hair yet? Another reason is that they're show-offs! Girls try to show their panties to the boys on the playground by hanging upside down on the monkey bars, while boys may surprise girls by whipping it out in the most unusual places. "I'll show you mine" games are exhibitionistic, like the girls' games of striptease played at slumber parties. "Playing doctor" is generally an excuse to examine the other person's private areas. The main reason, though, that exhibitionism gives the exposer as well as the viewer such a thrill is because private parts are supposed to be private. These acts are forbidden.

"Playing doctor" and "I'll show you mine" are only sexual games to the extent that parents and the culture give body parts an aura of sexuality. And they are only forbidden games to the extent that a culture sees sex as something naughty or bad. One woman who grew up in New York City has a memory of playing doctor on a rock in a lot behind her backyard. What she remembered, though, is her mother coming out of the house screaming at her. Another woman, an African American who grew up in the sixties, also knew that playing doctor was bad. It was "a sin":

> It wasn't a game but it was really like intense curiosity and like having to see absolutely everything. . . . It was something having to do with um, health and investigation. [laughing] Pure science and health. . . . We were aware somehow that if somebody saw us doing this, they would think it was very, very wrong, and we thought we'd get in a lot of trouble and that it was probably a sin too. . . . Even though it was all couched in this doctor medical thing. I don't think we fooled ourselves in the least.

These games are not all sexual in the way that some of the more exciting games of the next few chapters are. In other words, they are not games that always involve feeling sexy, feeling sexual feelings, or even exploring sexual activity, although some children do get a thrill from them. Instead, they reflect the first thing that children are taught about their private parts—that they are "private" for a mysterious reason they don't know yet. Still, they intuit that if their privates are private, the exhibition of them must be something deliciously forbidden.

While more and more parents see these games as an outgrowth of natural childhood curiosity, both parents and professionals set limits outside of which such curiosity is verboten. In a study of over three hundred professionals, Jeffrey Haugaard, a psychologist of human development and family studies at Cornell University, asked social workers and doctoral-level psychotherapists what they thought about four-year-olds undressing together, showing each other their genitals, and "fondling" genital and nongenital areas. Despite questions raised by Haugaard's terminology (How does someone "fondle" a nongenital area?), professionals generally thought most of these acts were acceptable among four-year-olds. Touching another child's genitals, however, even at this young age, was strictly forbidden.

Researchers are being suggestive, though, when they use abuse-evocative terms such as "fondling," especially since many of the professionals whom they surveyed already have been keyed in to the dangers of child-to-child sexual abuse. There is indeed strong documentation showing that children who have been molested by an adult sometimes "act out" that abuse on other children, introducing to the new child "adult" forms of sexuality too soon. It is little surprise, then, that when Haugaard asked professionals about eight-year-olds, they answered even more conservatively. About half of the female professionals thought it was still okay for eight-year-old children to undress together, while only a third of the male professionals did. About 40 percent of the female professionals thought it was still okay for the eight-year-olds to show each other their private parts, while about 25 percent of the male professionals did. However, very few thought touching was fine (16 percent females; 6 percent males).

For the majority of Americans, not just professionals, nakedness is a sexual act, and we convey this to children. Unlike countries that have nude beaches or where families sauna together, we teach our children that nakedness is sexual. Because there are pedophiles who do view children's naked bodies for sexual pleasure, it would appear that all viewing of such is suspect (as in the controversy over Sally Mann's beautiful photographs of her naked children). Because the parts of the human body deemed sexual are clothed specially (in bathing suits) and sometimes clothed and flaunted provocatively (as in Wonderbras), they become sexually charged in a visual way.

If it were acceptable for children to see each other naked, there would be little interest in "show-me" games. In places where children's nudity is acceptable, such as some U.S. preschools where girls and boys are allowed to share a bathroom, there is no need to hide behind a bush, pull down pants, and ogle. These ogling games are mildly forbidden by adults (more strongly forbidden twenty and thirty years ago) because they indicate to adults an unnatural or dangerous interest in sex. For girls especially, such an interest is considered immodest and unfeminine.

Parents also discourage their girls from expressing too strong an interest in their genitals, confirming the feeling that boys have "something" there, girls have "nothing," a feeling Freud wrote leads to penis envy. If a girl shows an interest in such matters, the adults around her usually wonder whether she was abused or if she is growing up "wild," and whether or not this behavior indicates that she will be a promiscuous teen. Boys defined by the culture as having a greater sex drive, have greater leeway and receive greater understanding from parents in their wishes to play the show-me games.

For Aidee, a seventeen-year-old Puerto Rican girl, sparkly and tomboyish even at seventeen, her "doctor" game confirms to her that she is not "really" a girl. After she played it with a little boy, she thought about this game "a lot of times." She would picture in her head what her mother might say to her, if she only knew:

I'm a bad girl. Like, I don't deserve to be a girl . . . like "you're not re-
ally a good girl and you're gonna be a little hot thing!"

It is interesting to see Aidee associate sexual goodness with being a girl.
She imagines her mother will not only see her as bad, but as not a girl at
all. Being "hot" is not only opposed to being a good girl, but to being a girl,
period.

If guilt does not weigh down the girls, when they do expose themselves
they often feel a wild exuberance rather than more intimate sexual feelings. Marilyn, for example, felt pure joy when her baby-sitter came to her
house and she and her sister got to play the game "Nastigators." That's
what the baby-sitter dubbed the game, laughing, but making sure that the
girls knew they were being "nasty":

We were little. We used to wear shortie pajamas. You know those? And
we would pull the side over and dance around chanting, "See my popo.
See my popo." And Lana, the baby-sitter, had a big booming voice,
called it nasty. "She's nastigating."

In many women's memories, it was shocking and fun to expose oneself.
In fact, the joy was more about exposing oneself rather than about being
looked at, an important distinction to make when looking at the relation
between girls and power. It might be too easy to call these girls' acts a form
of becoming passive objects for boys' gaze, when their true experience of
the event may be more akin to the rebel or sexual provocateur.

One adult woman remembered that she and her brothers invited her
best friend to join them in what they called

a "naked parade." I think my friend was shocked to see it and I think to
be included in it.

Another remembered taking a "naked shower" with a boy when his
family was visiting.

And we had a great time. Totally hilarious. And then everybody found
out we were in there. And everybody just laughed and chuckled, and
you know we were getting away with it, that was the thing. Whenever
there was some kind of transgression, I kind of wanted to be discovered.
That was, like, part of the fun.

Girls today and in past years have played "truth or dare" games in which they or a friend would have to run around naked outside, or dash into someone's parents' bedroom in her underwear in the middle of the night. Six-year-old Madeleine, who is chatty and opinionated and adorable, described a dare where the girls all had to pull down their pants, put their underpants *over* their pants, and then run out of her bedroom flashing her dad their underwear. As she related her story, it changed a little, and she confessed they actually *exchanged* underwear! They also had to do a little dance in front of the dad of the house.

It was as if these girls were rebelling against what they have been told for years, that these are private parts. In Madeleine's story the girls recognize that the issue of privacy in America extends into the family, where brothers and fathers are to be kept separate from daughters and mothers. A father may bathe his infant or toddler daughter as well as change her diaper, but as a girl grows up there will be a gradual wall built around this physical intimacy, restricting it to hugs and kisses by the elementary school years. There may be good reasons for such separation, but it raises questions and anxieties about these boundaries and what is private about oneself and one's body?

Most exhibition games are between peers—boys to girls, girls to boys. An eighteen-year-old African-American girl, Jennifer, laughing and embarrassed, described a game she played when she was younger with a bunch of kids after school at her baby-sitter's house. The boys and girls together would play a game where the girls would go into a room and strip and then call out, "Okay we're ready," and then the boys would come in and look at them. Then they would switch, and the boys would go into a room and take off all their clothes and the girls would come in when they were ready and look at them. "And we were like, 'Oh my gosh!'" said Jennifer. The boys would make the game more exciting by pretending that the baby-sitter was going to walk in at any moment, "Watch the lady. I hear her coming," they would call out, and the girls would scramble to get dressed.

Susan, a quiet woman who grew up in upstate New York in the sixties and now works as an assistant to a college administrator, remembered

> being with a bunch of girls. We would go over to the monkey bars and hang upside down so the boys could see our underwear, which is kind of odd . . . they'd stand around and watch.

In some ways it is surprising that these games are labeled "odd" or "weird" by the girls who play them. They're not even unusual. It is as if they think it is wholly unacceptable for a child, a girl, to want to show off her body. One little girl I interviewed showed horror at the question. When I asked her if she ever, when she was younger, might have played a game with another child like "I'll show you mine if you show me yours," she responded quickly, "Oh no! Never!!!"

The fact that such games are seen as odd or weird speaks to how rarely women have shared such stories, in spite of a public acknowledgment that children "play doctor." It also suggests that these girls assume that such behavior will mark them as sexual rather than as good girls.

In fact, when girls expose themselves to each other, the games sometimes turn into more intricate explorations, and sometimes become integrated into fantasy games. Helen, a baby boomer who grew up in the late 1950s, didn't remember this sexual incident until the day after the interview and called back to tell all:

> My cousin and I, when she was about six and I was about eight, . . . used to take baths together at the end of the day. And I do know that we used to sit in the bathtub, and we would kind of sit crossways and look down into our bottom area, and we would pretend that the little piece of tissue that's down there that's probably where our urethra [surely she meant clitoris?] is in between the labia, that kind of sticks out there, we would pretend those were our babies, and we would show each other our babies, you know, and talk about our babies while we were in the bathtub.

Helen and her cousin take a sensitive, sexual body part and find some way to make it acceptable to play with. Mothers are never made to be "sexy" in society's view, not in movies, TV, or advertising, but these girls found a way to incorporate the sexual into a more typical game of being moms!

Freud thought that girls, when they looked down at their bodies and compared what they had to what boys had, discovered they had nothing, a great lack, an absence of a penis. One of the first feminist psychoanalysts, Karen Horney, laughingly pointed out in her essay "Womb Envy" that this is exactly the way a little boy thinks when he sees a girl. The French feminist writer Irigaray has since pointed out, in her essay "The Sex Which Is Not One," the intricacies of women's genitals, our understanding of them, and how what's "down there" affects women's psyches. Girls see stuff down there. Like Helen and her cousin, even girls in the fifties saw it, but they didn't know what to call it or all the different parts of "it," thus also explaining her mistake of calling a clitoris a urethra. In their game these girls called that part of their vaginal area their babies, allowing them perhaps to play with it and stroke it, and thus transforming codes of sexual behavior to work toward their goal of sexual pleasure.

In the less imaginative games of show, most women remember exchanges with boys. More often than not they remember the boys as initiators of these games. And while girls are curious about themselves and their sexual feelings, as we see in so many of the fantasy games that are in later chapters, they are not (as Freud would have wished) so curious about boys' penises. These "show-me" exchanges are fun and shocking but lack the intensity and strong emotion that the other games have. They're not remembered with much guilt because they mimic, in a sense, adult heterosexuality. Many of the memories are vague, quite possibly because they are usually one-time events and over very quickly.

I do remember a brief incident with a neighborhood boy behind his garage. I think I had been hanging upside down on the monkey bars and I had a skirt on and he was, "If you do that again I'll show you what I have in my pants." That's all I remember. (Linda, white, 53)

We were standing outside in the backyard, and it was, like, "I'll show you mine if you show me yours." . . . I don't remember being apprehensive about it. I just know that it did happen and I just looked at it . . . I think I probably wanted to show. I felt almost honored to be enlightening somebody in that way. "Look at me!" (Jody, white, 21)

I remember being about five and being with a friend of my mother's who had this little boy, and we went in his room and we pretended we were married and what we did was, we kissed. We pulled down our pants and we kissed, although we didn't touch each other. For some reason that's what we thought that you did if you were married, and we gave each other a peck with our pants around our ankles and we pulled our pants up and we went. (Laura, white, 33)

One day Paul said to me, "I want to show you my beetle." And I'm thinking he had a pet beetle and the next thing I know he's got his pants open with a flashlight down his pants. I didn't feel like returning the favor. . . . I think I was just too shocked to do anything. I wasn't expecting that. (Karen, white, 39)

"Honored," shocked, interested—these are the feelings of girls who have these exchanges with boys. Few are caught. All are "enlightened." Most know they are doing something sneaky and possibly wrong. But in retrospect, these are fun memories and delightful experiences. The guilt did not last into adulthood. None have memories that haunt them. They can explain away these experiences as a form of curiosity or just plain fun.

Playing Doctor

Playing doctor is much the same for girls. These "doctor" experiences are like "real life" and are not as sexually provocative as fantasy games. The point isn't even to play "doctor," usually; it is a useful entry to acquiring knowledge, making comparisons, getting "checked out," and doing some "checking" oneself. Perhaps these games are sexually stimulating for the boys, but for the girls the games of dress-up, fantasy, and horror that will appear later in the book capture their sexual excitement so much more completely.

Boy cousins are frequent players in girls' doctor games, sometimes as initiators. Eleanora, a Puerto Rican woman who had been a sickly child, knew how to be a good patient. Even though she described herself as a "goody-two-shoes," she also played doctor with her cousins.

> It was the three of us, but it turned out that I was the guinea pig . . . basically all that I can recall is that I was laying down and they had lifted, I guess, my dress. . . . He said that he was the doctor and he was going to examine me, and I was used to being examined because I was always asthmatic, and so I was like the volunteer. Sure. You know. I'm a good girl, I know how to be examined without crying. . . . It was just a lifting up the dress and you feel cold sort of. It wasn't anything beyond that.

Another woman who played doctor with her two male cousins was caught. Her mom and aunt walked in and saw them and told them to stop: " 'What are you doing?' It wasn't as if they got mad; they were mainly trying to convey 'That's not a thing to do.' "

Some boys tried to talk little girls into exposing themselves:

> One time they tried to get me. They invited me into this pup tent and, I think, I don't know what was going on, but, so I went into the tent and

all three of these little boys said, "Okay, we want to play doctor and nurse and we'll be the doctors and you be the nurse and we'll go first. And so they all dropped their pants. I stood there and looked at them, and they said, "Okay, now it's your turn." And I just left. I wasn't gonna drop my pants in front of those three boys. (Maura, white, 47)

Sometimes there was a little guilt. Marilyn, the "nastigator," for example, worried about corrupting her younger sister:

We took baths together and there were three in the tub. We would explore. We found holes, a little thing that looked like a penis, and it was all very fascinating. And later, much later . . . my friend Callie and I, we used to play doctor with my little sister, and she was the patient and the exploree, and we did wondrous things with her. We did. I'm glad that this interview gave me an opportunity to ask my sister what her memories were of the times we played doctor upon her and how she felt about that. And she didn't remember any ill feelings or have any ill feelings about that. Because that was the one thing I was a little concerned about.

Carol also felt guilt. Carol, a Jewish woman living in New York City who grew up in the suburbs in the fifties said:

In his front yard we had built [a fort] so it wasn't, like, for everybody driving by to watch us. I remember he was the doctor and I was the patient. I guess that's true. We didn't have women doctors in those days. I remember I pulled down my [under] pants. I had on a dress. . . . Sometime years later I heard a conversation about this playing doctor, and you know, and that children do this, and I was like, Oh my God, that's what Jack and I did that day and I didn't know that's what it was . . . I don't remember that I ever told anyone about it. . . . when I heard about it afterwards, it was sort of the sense of relief about it, "Oh. That's all it was!!!" I guess somehow I just knew that it was, you know, it was something that nobody should know about.

What makes these doctor games "sexual" after all? The nudity? Because boys show girls their penises? Because girls show boys their vaginas? These are more than sexual parts. To a child these games are just as much forbidden as they are sexual. They are not always about sexual feelings or thrills. They are not really about learning about sexual responsiveness, except for the thrill of being admired.

When the girls hang upside down on the monkey bars, they're not pretending to be sexual objects for men, as they do when they dress up as stripteasers or pose as models. They are doing something forbidden—showing their panties to boys. While they may have an awareness that adults call these acts sexual and therefore immodest, to them they don't feel sexy. They feel bold and risqué.

These games are permitted by the culture in a way that sexual feelings in children are not. If we stopped our exploration of childhood sexuality here, with games of show-and-tell and doctor, we wouldn't have found out much about the secrets girls keep. If these are secrets that girls keep they are easily disclosed and more about curiosity than sex. For some girls, especially the little ones I interviewed, these were the only kinds of secrets they could tell me about; adult women remember and tell much more.

Zeroing In On: Play. What Is Play? What Is Sexual Play?

What is play? While some have examined the content of girls' play, few researchers have studied the spirit of play—their experiments and their development as sexual beings through the games they play. As a play therapist and a mother I have thought a lot about the healing power of play and the secrets it reveals. D. W. Winnicott, the famous English psychoanalyst, describes certain special qualities about play that I paraphrase below.

1. Play involves fantasy and, because of this, reaches down into the unconscious to bring out secret desires, wishes, and fears.
2. Play involves the mind as well as the body. The child absorbed in play is present both mentally and physically.
3. Play is both real and unreal at the same time.
4. Play is fun as well as utterly serious to the child engaged in it.
5. Play creates a space that is both "me" and "not-me," and in this way reminds the child of the teddy bear or other transitional object that was both a part of her and separate from her. It also is reminiscent of earlier development, when her mother was both a part of her and yet not her.
6. There are no consequences for acts done in play. Or, consequences are "play" consequences. According to Winnicott, a child can walk away from play and not be bothered by what occurred. She can leave the feelings and thoughts that were a part of play there on the playroom floor.

7. Thus, what is secret or hidden can become external. It no longer has to exist only in fantasy in a child's mind; however, because it is play, a girl doesn't have to take responsibility for it.

This is why play is deeply satisfying, as well as why sexual and aggressive parts of the person can materialize in play, especially as parts that are different from the public persona. It is precisely this doubleness that allows play to be fun and exciting—stimulating—at the same time.

The following chapters show many instances of play that is mutually enjoyable and utterly delightful. They also show some play that becomes deeply disturbing to girls, making them feel lifelong guilt. Sometimes play gets too real. Sometimes wishes and fears are brought too close to the surface, and when brought to the surface they contrast too vividly with societal expectations regarding what's proper and befitting a young girl.

Sex is in the mind, researchers have told us for a long time. And play gives us indirect access to the mind of a child. But because it is part real it can disturb, it can make a person feel guilty.

It is difficult to determine the borders of play. When real bodily excitement happens, is it no longer play? When it is a girl from a low-income neighborhood, is it no longer play? There may be cultural expectations that play a role here. When a girl acts sexy, is it still play? When she acts tough? These are questions that the stories of mutual play may help answer.

Girls need to and sometimes succeed at acting out their sexual curiosity. Sometimes it is with great bravado and wildness, leading to some very risky behavior in adolescence, and sometimes it is gradual and furtive and behind closed doors. Most of the play experiences of the girls and women interviewed for this book are overwhelmingly positive, except when they punish themselves through guilt or believe that they are "abnormal."

Chapter 2

Just Practicing: It's in Her Kiss

"You must remember this: A kiss is just a kiss."
—Sam, "As Time Goes By," in the movie Casablanca; lyrics by Herman Hopfeld

A kiss may not be "just" a kiss in two of the more common games of childhood. Children kiss in "chase-and-kiss" games, where children chase each other in order to grab and kiss the captured. Girls also kiss each other directly, or each others' hands (which are placed strategically over their mouths), or even sometimes their pillows (while pretending that they are on girl-boy dates). Many children in late elementary school years play structured kissing games such as "Spin the Bottle" and "Truth or Dare," which are meant to introduce them to "real" kissing. They make this distinction between "real" and "practicing"; we may not.

Chase and Kiss

There are three important observations I have about the chase-and-kiss games of childhood:

- Chase-and-kiss games give girls a sense of the power of their sexuality.
- Girls chase, trap, pinch, and pin down boys as frequently as vice versa.

- "Chase and kiss" solidifies a transition for girls, from having boys as friends to seeing them as the "enemy" in a "battle of the sexes."

The sociologist Barrie Thorne sees a copy of the imbalanced gender relations of adulthood in the "chase-and-kiss" playground games. Through these games, she notes that girls are "marked" as sexual beings and boys are meant to avoid being "contaminated" by them. Girls have cooties or see boys as having cooties, and the message is clear: cross-gender contact is potentially dangerous. As Madeleine, that chatty six-year-old who ran around with her underpants outside of her pants, told me, "Boys give cooties; girls give frooties." On her playground, even the words differentiate the germs.

Many women and girls played and play these chase-and-kiss games, and adults remember them fondly; whether it's the girls who chase the boys or the boys who chase the girls varies from school to school. We like to think that in today's world girls are more forward and assertive, but girls chased the boys just as often thirty years ago as they do today. In the interviews, girls and women alike became more lively when they remembered themselves as part of a group of girls who were the aggressors. Their eyes lit up; they laughed as they thought about sharing in the chase.

In some schools the game is one of hostile competition, with tackling and jailing rather than smooches and tickles. For example, in one elementary school in Chicago they jailed a boy; in another elementary school in California they tried to force him into the girl's bathroom—a different kind of boundary violation than kissing! In several schools the object of the game was to touch the butt of the other person rather than to kiss them. This occurred both in lower income city schools and middle-class suburban schools.

Avery, eleven years old, described a game the other girls play on her playground:

Well, there was like a whole bunch of girls and one boy, and they were holding him down and they were like pulling at his clothes and stuff. [Was the boy upset? I asked.] He wasn't very upset. He was trying to get away. But he was, like, not laughing. But he wasn't really upset. He was, he's a popular boy, but he wasn't really upset, like helpless like that. He was just trying to get away because there was two boys and he got caught. It was nothing like he was being abused or something.

It is important for Avery to reassure me that they weren't really doing any-thing bad to the boy. She told me three or four times that he wasn't upset, which would mean, in her words, that he wasn't "helpless." I think that she means that as long as there was a "fight," it was still a game.

The idea of hostile competition is so ingrained that at Caitlyn's school, when a boy fell down and a girl helped him up, all the girls thought this was "weird":

> One time he fell in the wood chips and she helped him up and everybody was, like, "Oh my gosh!" Why would you help a boy up? And it was like really weird.

When I asked why a girl wouldn't do something like that, she answered:

> I just think they'd be really embarrassed, and I know that I really wouldn't want to be embarrassed, so I'd kind of stay away from boys.

What's so interesting is that obviously the girls are not staying away from boys merely because the boys are chasing them on the playground or they are definitionally the "enemy." To do something friendly with a boy would be seen by one's friends as having a romantic interest in him, an interest they would be teased about and that would set them apart from their boy-hating friends. This fear interferes with girls and boys becoming friends, learning from one another, and sharing interests. Here, ten-year-old Cait-lyn described a friend, Terry, she had when she was younger:

> He was so fun. He'd always think of these great ideas to do during recess and he was like a brain. . . . So I thought that it was just really great to have a friend that was a boy, you know? It was kind of different and no-body really had a friend that was a boy . . . and then in third grade everybody would make fun of me, and I was kind of like uncomfortable, and I didn't think it was good anymore. I thought it was really weird.

Children, for better or worse, socialize each other, making it uncom-fortable for each other to have cross-gender contact unless it's in the form of a hostile competition or a sexualized game like chase and kiss. I say un-fortunately because girls and boys could be so much more to each other, as Caitlyn said. This boy was a "brain" and would help her with math. "He wouldn't just say figure it out. He would actually explain it to you three or four times till you got it." But the other children made her feel "weird."

So when a game of chase isn't actually about hostile competition between the boys and the girls, it shows the other side of this dilemma: Girls do like boys and want to relate to them.

Maya, now eleven, remembered a first-grade game with a "designated kisser":

> *In first grade we used to play chase and kiss. . . . You would bring them to the fence and my friend Frances would kiss them. [Why Frances? I asked.] I don't know. She was just elected for that job. She didn't really mind.*

At her current school the girls chase the boys but don't kiss them. They form a tight circle around a boy and the game is that he tries to escape from it.

To adults, kissing might be cute. But to children it is serious, grown-up stuff. Madeleine, the chatty six-year-old from Chicago, told me that her teacher announced to the class, "If she finds out that anybody is trying to kiss somebody, they will *literally* be sent to the principal's office and be suspended from school." She emphasized the word "literally" to let me know how serious her teacher is. This reminded me of six-year-old Jonathan Prevette in North Carolina, who made national news when he was suspended from school for kissing the girl next to him at lunch.

Madeleine's teacher doesn't sound so harsh when we consider what actually went on in her school. The kissing games got a little rough in this lower-middle-class Chicago neighborhood. As Madeleine described it:

> *Colette, Meagan, and Dara were playing with Pablo and chasing him around the park. They chased him and pushed him and he slid on the rocks facedown. I saw it and I told on them to the teacher. And then they lied and said they didn't do it. And then she [Dara] found out that I liked Pablo, and she told him she liked him too, just to get me mad. And he told her that he didn't like her anymore. . . . She gave me the biggest, ugliest, dirty look in the world.*

This kissing part of the game was about who liked whom on the playground, and Dara, "when she liked Pablo, literally made them [Colette and Meagan] chase him, pull him back, and hold him" and then Colette and Meagan "made them [Dara and Pablo] kiss." Dara, according to Madeleine, was the boss of this game, rounding up friends to hold Pablo down so the two of them could kiss. She would show Madeleine who "owned" Pablo! This example also presents girls in a more active role than we usually picture them in "chase and kiss." It isn't the only example like that.

On another "violent" playground, in a Vermont suburb, Grace remembered second-grade playground games where one of the boys she liked got pinned down

> by several girls. So, like, I kissed him, but I didn't feel very happy about that, because it wasn't very fun to kiss someone who had been pinned down and who obviously did not want to be kissed. . . . It wasn't serious stuff, but I remember thinking, "He probably doesn't like that."

It is interesting to consider whether when girls chase the boys they feel a kind of sexual power. Are they living up to age-old images of women as seductresses, evil temptresses to be avoided? Miranda embraced such archetypal images.

Miranda, a white twelve-year-old from a middle-class suburban neighborhood, loves to play "Crazy Licking Ladies" on the playground. The boys dubbed the girls this wonderfully descriptive name. On their school playground outside of Boston, the girls run after the boys and lick them when they catch them. Though they make the game less sexual by calling it a licking game rather than a kissing game, they make it more sexual because the girls are now "ladies." By chasing the boys they are more grown-up than girls, like the wild Bacchae of ancient Greek myth who make boys their slaves.

Bacchae, witches, vampires, and licking ladies. Kissing is not always cute but can be an act of wild abandon for children, an act that threatens a girl's equilibrium by pushing her into an adult role she might not feel ready for. Miranda had a dream about vampires and kisses that she shared with me. A boy she had a crush on in school was a vampire in her dream.

> It was gross. Well, I won't tell you the whole thing, but it was. I was a vampire and he was a vampire and . . . I said, Oh, who cares! I'll tell you the whole dream . . . But it was weird and it was true, but I made up the ending. And, um—first he was my brother. I had known him, like I was split up from him for a really long time, but I don't really know him, know him, like now I do. But I lived next door to him when I was a baby . . . and I had this dream where we were brother and sister and

; just like this weird snake guy, and he came on like, and I'm like,
like remembering it. It was bad now that I know who he is, and I
....m so much. Well, sort of I do but, see, I don't like his personality,
but he's cute. He's really cute.

The dream was about a boy she had known since infancy. Like girls and
boys who play together from an early age, they were like brother and sister,
a closeness manifested in the dream story. But things change. Now she
hates him, she said, but doesn't really. You can hear in her voice how she
feels two ways about him. She doesn't like his personality, but he's cute.
She's known him since he was a child but now he's different, changed.

He kept on saying, "Kiss me. Kiss me," and I was like, "No, why?"
And he was like this weird snake, cobra, vampire guy, and he kept on
saying, like, "Kiss me, kiss me" and I'm like, "No, because I know that
you're just going to bite me and you're going to kill me and whatnot,"
and then I wake up, woke up, and that was annoying.

There was also "this old lady and this old man who were, like, friends
of ours, but not the snake, too" and they were "trying to save me from
him because they saved themselves from him and 'cause he was a weird
snake guy."

In Miranda's dream she is being seduced, but she resists. The boy who
was a friend from childhood reappears as a person with a snake (as a sexual
being with a penis, a Freudian might add), and in this way is now dangerous to her. As a child he was like a brother. But as a teen he is a weird, vampire snake. She is attracted to him (he's "cute"), but also repelled. Kissing
him means the death of childhood, and she resists. There to help her resist
are the old man and old lady (her parents, I presume) who she imagines
have escaped him. Children rarely believe in their parents' sexuality, and
in her dream she makes them old to insure their asexuality.

As a preadolescent dream, this is a nightmare. It both frightens and
excites her. And it also marks kissing as a boundary between childhood
and high school. This border is particularly salient for white suburban girls,
where sexual knowledge is acquired in a step-by-step manner (e.g., first
base, second base, third) as opposed to urban girls, who sometimes cross a
boundary before they even get a chance to think about it. Where girls are
protected by parents (symbolized by the old man and old woman in her
dream who are her friends), she has time and space to resist.

Like the chase-and-kiss games, Miranda's dream pits girl against boy.

The idea of "girls against boys," which they re-enact in school for games, teams, and projects, confirms to children that the differences between boys and girls must be immense. Many adult women remember playing in cross-gender groups. Children today still do play in cross-gender groups. But something happens around the age of five that changes their "public" presentation of themselves and whom they can be friends with. Candace Feiring and Michael Lewis, developmental psychologists at the child development laboratories at Rutgers University, call it the "birthday party effect" because beginning around age five, only same-sex peers are invited to one's birthday party.

The public separation goes on throughout middle-class neighborhoods and schools, making cross-gender contact even more fraught with danger. It is a shame when children are made to feel embarrassed because their wish to play with someone of the other gender is interpreted as a sexual wish. It's also a shame that when children do wish to experiment with sexual girl-boy contact it can only be represented in the hostile disguise of chase and kiss. This means that from early on sex and cross-gender contact are connected with shame and hostility, and these fractures in cross-gender friendship carry over to adult cross-gender misunderstandings. When girls play with other girls, much of this hostile disguise is missing or projected onto the one who plays the "guy."

Practice Kissing

Practice kissing is altogether different from "chase and kiss." Practice kissing introduces girls to sexual desire in a safe and limited way. Furthermore, practicing on each other is usually seen by the girls doing it as practice for heterosexual romance, but the fact that it's girl to girl also brings up guilt and self-doubts. As I listened to girls and women describing these games it occurred to me that many if not all of them describe the "other girl" as more "into it" than themselves.

While practice kissing, as in the Marie Howe poem cited earlier, girls frequently role-play boy-girl kissing. While many stories involve girls kissing girls for "practice," a few of the stories involve boys. One girl taught her little brother how to "French" kiss: touching tongues. In fifth and sixth grades in a school in California, the girls and boys would pair up after school into girlfriend-and-boyfriend pairs, then kiss each other in the playground, timing each other with a stopwatch.

In another boy-girl scenario of a kissing game, Rachel, who grew up in the Philadelphia area, remembered that a boy in the neighborhood, Josh, had a clubhouse, and to be a member you had to kiss the president, Josh himself.

Another practice kisser, Jeanine, took full responsibility for the kissing and the pleasure in her game with the son of her mother's best friend. Though she is a twenty-eight-year-old African-American woman today, she vividly remembered when her mother's friend would come over with her four children. She and the youngest son, who was Jeanine's age, would go off and kiss. At the beginning, they did it in front of the others, "like, 'Look what we can do. We can kiss.' But it was really innocent." Then, when they got a bit older, they would still go off by themselves. It "just didn't stop," she said.

> We would sit in the closet and kiss. We really did. And we would just practice kissing, and it was just like we were six, seven, eight years old. Always kissing. I guess until just before adolescence, because right about that time we were, like, it got more meaningful. But at that time we would just kiss and we were, like, this is fun!

Jeanine and her friend probably knew that this was forbidden, since they hid in the closet. But she also didn't feel much guilt because it was "practicing" even though the practice lasted at least four years.

Most "practice kissing," however, takes place between girls. In a sense, that's what makes it "practice" instead of "real." Often girls kiss themselves (their own hands or a pillow) in the game, and this is a way they remain true to the idea that the kissing is just "practice." This is also a way they assure themselves that it is not lesbian practice. Leah played a game like this with a bunch of girls at a fifth-grade birthday party.

> We all pretended we were going out on dates, and we'd take turns going into the closet, like by ourselves, but pretending like we were going into the closet with our dates. And pretending like making out with someone, either with a pillow or with something "pretend" that represented your date there with you. . . . And I remember somebody opened the door when Tara was in there, and she'd gotten very much into this game, and like she had her shirt off and all of us were like [makes shocked face]. It was really funny.

Why do many women remember the "other" girl getting "into it" more than she herself did? Is it too shameful to remember or simply to tell about the time when you were the one experiencing desire? Gina had a similar memory, where for her the play was just "practice," but for the "other girl," it was more. There was a kiss that was more than a kiss.

> I do recall that we would play make-out games, where you kind of pre-tend you're kissing, you know and you're hugging in the dark of the closet, you kiss necks. And you kind of pretend. Now this is something I never told my parents. A couple of times she did kind of get close to kissing me. And I thought, Well this is a little strange, but you know, she just did it for the make-out game. So she would play the boy or I would play the boy and we would do this. But I sensed already something different, but I thought, you know, Oh well, what the heck. Then one time, it meant more. It wasn't just a game for her. I really sensed that.

The feeling she described for herself was a "benign kind of interest." But it seemed as though her friend Kim felt something more. And then one time,

> [w]e were sitting in the bedroom playing dolls, and out of the blue she laid one on me, you know. She kissed me. She leaned over on her bed and she just kissed me, very tenderly, very sweetly, and I thought, "Oh my!" And I don't even know if I at that time registered the word "les-bian," but I'm sure I did by then. "She's a lesbian. She likes me. She _likes_ me, likes me. Yeah."

Gina sensed something different about her friend's kiss, something that crossed a boundary and made it real. When it was "just a game" for Gina and her friends, there was nothing personal and rarely the presence of de-sire. Her friend Kim made it personal and revealed herself to be a desiring individual, not desiring to learn more about sex and boys and kissing, but desire as in desiring someone sexually. Gina, however, felt a border was crossed and pulled back.

In contrast to Gina's "benign kind of interest," May and her friends were in it whole hog, together. For long periods of time they would do sen-suality experiments on each other's backs and arms, especially on the backs of their hands, moving their fingers lightly around in circles "a hundred times" for the pleasure of it: "It just felt lovely!" she recalled. May remem-bered being alone with her best friend.

> One time we wanted to know what kissing was like, so I remember I kissed her—we kissed each other.

If we stop her story here for a moment, we notice how she corrected herself. Maybe it actually is more accurate to say that they kissed each other, but if she hadn't changed her words, it would have been one of the only times in a narrative where a woman telling a story about her childhood sexual game made such a direct statement about kissing or doing something to another girl. Among the women and girls interviewed, desire is something hard for a woman, let alone a girl, to claim for herself, even amid the sensual pleasure May described. May recalled

> thinking that was so bad. But, and that was it. It was like we were wondering, what was that? It was like in second grade or something . . . and I remember thinking that was bad, and again when I look back on it, it's like no big deal. But at the time . . . I think even then I was thinking it was two girls and that I had never kissed someone before, so even the notion of just sexuality in general. I don't know how I learned that as something that is sort of taboo or bad, but I remember thinking that back then.

I wonder how many other "first kisses" are actually kisses between girls. The idea that kisses are practice for adult "dating" makes these first kisses "not count" to us as adults. The women who remember them discount them in this way too: "no big deal." But for May, a real sensualist who loved to have her back rubbed and who would confess to her mother her love of masturbation, this kiss did mean something sexual. It *was* a big deal.

Karen, like others before her, claimed that "Ann and Jessica were the instigators" of the games she played in the basement of her friends' homes. But she also admitted that, in turn, she "would also instigate Lissy," the youngest of her friends. She began:

> You know. Touching ourselves and pretending to kiss each other. We were never really kissing each other. That was taboo. . . . When we would pretend to kiss each other it would be like one of us would pretend to be the guy and somebody would pretend to be the girl.

They would kiss with one hand over their mouths and one hand on their own private parts. Karen said she felt some "sexual excitement. Yeah, I guess it was sexual excitement, and then maybe thinking, well, one day I'll have a boyfriend and do this for real, sort of feeling."

The game went on for several months, and so it became a stronger part of Karen's history than some of the games other girls play. Quite possibly, it was the sexual excitement that she felt that made her timid about revealing the game. This truly was a "secret" game, in the sense that whenever parents "came downstairs [they] would stop what they were doing." And also in the sense that she never had talked about it until I asked her about it. It wasn't exactly "real" in the way children think of what is real, and yet from the way it was so hard for Karen to tell this story, I wonder if it was more than "just practicing."

Miranda, the twelve-year-old girl with the dream, told me:

Well, like I pretend to make out with my friends and stuff, but it's just, I just hug them and go "wa wa wa" [kissing noises]. I don't really kiss them. I mean, I kiss my friends but . . .

But with Miranda there's not much of a boundary between kissing when you're pretending to be a boyfriend and girlfriend and feeling close to her friends for real.

I also just, like, if we're wrestling and I find myself in a weird position, I just, "Oh, I love you!" and stuff like that.

What does she mean? Does she mean, for example, that when she pins her friend and finds herself on top of her, she just spontaneously says, "I love you"? Maybe. In that way, wrestling is an excuse for two girls to get close, and feel close, without actually making out themselves.

No other young girl told me about practice kissing. Madeleine, the chatty six-year-old from Chicago, reassured me that she would never play a game like that:

They were making me play this game. I don't know what it was. But they said that you had to kiss somebody. And I said, I don't really feel like playing, and then they told me I was chicken. And I said, I think it's really gross that you guys want to kiss somebody.

The game itself has an element of coercion, so that even the people who did want to be kissed could pretend as if they didn't.

Avery observed a game at a slumber party where the girls kissed each other but put their hands over their mouths; "That's sick!" she said. "We were too young to be doing that." She added, however, that the girls were having lots of fun.

Were these girls presenting me with the "good girl" perspective? The version they imagined their mothers would tell? They were some of the youngest girls, and thus perhaps did not have the distance from their stories they would need to place the games in a "childhood" context. No doubt they did feel uncomfortable, but only Avery sees two sides. It is "sick" and also a lot of fun, but not for her. For her it might have seemed too "real."

What's Real?

There's an enormous variety in sexual interest in the elementary school years. And when a girl growing up has this interest, when she wants to know what kissing is all about, what it feels like to rub against another person, she is lucky if she can find a friend who will discover this with her and who won't make her feel "weird."

But because American culture doesn't acknowledge the possibility of childhood sexuality, when children do this, it isn't called "kissing" or "sex." It's called "practice" or "play." And why? Because by calling it practice or play we make a space for it and give children some time to act in a way that does not label them or define them in a permanent manner. It's also called practice so that girls don't have to admit to the strong feelings of attraction they may feel for other girls, so they can "successfully" move on to boys in their teen years without worrying that they are gay. You might even say that we help to guarantee heterosexuality by allowing girls to dismiss these games.

In middle school and teen years girls can begin to talk about "real kisses" and "first kisses." Are they not still practicing? Games like "Spin the Bottle" and "Seven Minutes in Heaven" bridge the gap between play and real. They initiate girls into the world of heterosexual and "real" kisses. These are not "secret" games. They are very public ways to prepare girls for "adult," "real," and heterosexual sex.

Chapter 3

Feminine Ideals: Make-up, Midriffs, and the Pleasures of Being Objectified

"One is not born a woman—one becomes one."
—*Simone de Beauvoir*, The Second Sex

Britney Spears's popular video for her hit song "Hit Me Baby One More Time" shows her in a schoolgirl uniform with a short plaid skirt and a white button-down shirt tied up to show her midriff. Little girls love this look; they love Britney. I was recently in the stereo component section of a superstore and noticed a girl not more than three staring up at a poster of the blonde and smiling Britney. When the mother came to get the little girl, she said, "Isn't she pretty?" "Yes, she is pretty," said the mother. The little girl already senses the appeal and attraction of a Britney Spears, a cross between Barbie and her little sister, Skipper. The girl's mother gives her approval that Britney Spears is indeed pretty and to be admired.

American culture now knows the dangers of girls' excessive preoccupation with looking pretty (in terms of eating disorders and low self-esteem, not to mention the way such preoccupations draw girls away from mind- and skill-enhancing alternative endeavors). Generally, cultural critics agree that this "lookism" and excessive control over women's appearance by the media derives from a male power base that seeks to keep women infantilized, working to please men and spend money on products. Few have analyzed the appeal of these images for women and what aspects may reach women and girls in a less sexist way. These images may not only be about giving pleasure to a male audience but about experiencing it themselves.

Just a few years ago, girls in the nineties liked to play Spice Girls. Dressing up like "Spices," girls put on high heels, tucked their shirts up high to bare their midriffs, and then put on music and danced. They danced for each other, and they took turns posing and dancing in front of a mirror to look at themselves being Spice Girls.

Serena, who is nine, told me she likes to play "rock stars" with her friends: "We do the belly button thingie." They tuck their T-shirts up so that their belly buttons show. Sometimes they do a kind of play, where they layer their clothes and "throw off pieces until we just had like a little tiny skirt, like something very little, and a little bra." Serena said playing this game made her feel "weird." Weird bad or weird excited? She didn't elaborate and I did not take the conversation in that direction with so young a person. It may be that a nine-year-old cannot distinguish between weird and sexually exciting, given the strangeness of these feelings for which children are given no names. It might have been exciting to be dressed up like a rock star, wearing sexy clothing and performing for one another. Or it might have made her feel guilty weird.

Mothers and fathers are in collusion with girls' self-objectification in so far as it means dressing up to look pretty. If you asked for their opinions, they probably wouldn't say that a Spice Girl or a Britney Spears is a good role model for a young girl. But they would approve of their daughters' dreams of stardom, wealth, and glamour, just as some feminist moms bemoan the fact that their daughters will only wear pink dresses while simultaneously understanding that it gives their daughters pleasure.

Girl power posters rarely show girls dressing up like the Spice Girls and prancing around with their midriffs showing, preferring instead to show girls doing science behind test tubes or girls on the soccer field celebrating a goal. The girls most prized by adults advocating "girl power" are not the ones who are "growing up too soon," as the media has put it, but those who are considered to be "natural."

But what is a "natural" girl? A lot of thought, resources, and planning go into creating the "natural" look. Teens and young women believe the "natural" look most closely matches what is real about the girl, what is inside of her, her very true, private self; that's why fashion magazines can use this look to sell clothing. Girls both want to be loved for who they truly are and to also aspire to a kind of beauty that is breathtaking, "natural," and unattainable.

The idea of a private self is one that we all share in Western society but becomes especially important to adolescents who hope to find, express, or hide their true selves. But even a true self is a presentation a girl makes to herself. For example, the diaries girls keep are active attempts to construct the self to an imagined reader. There is always an imagined audience to a secret diary, and maybe even an audience to the secret thoughts of a young girl, even if only in her head.

The idea of a natural (or true) self actually is anything but natural and springs from stereotypes used to control girls' behavior. Like the idea of modesty in the forties and fifties, "natural" is a term of control, one that the term "spice" seeks to overturn or rebel against.

But it's even more complicated than that. Today we might assume, as many feminists do, that makeup and heels are a male invention to make women objects for their viewing, to make them ridiculous and powerless. Regardless, many girls see these items as having special power. Why else would their mothers forbid their wearing them? Why else would highly made up, fashionable women get so much attention?

There was a time when the power of such artifice was acknowledged: the Middle Ages. Church fathers from medieval times on have argued that wearing makeup, dying hair, and donning fancy clothing are all wicked arts designed to seduce men. One church father, Clement of Alexandria, wrote that the woman who wears makeup and decorates herself in fine clothing both hides her soul and practices deceit; the real woman in this case is the one behind the makeup. Clement further elaborated that women who adorn themselves too much distract men and tempt them toward sin.

Feminists of the seventies and eighties agreed in part. They, like the church fathers, saw the artifices of makeup and clothing as degrading. But they saw this artifice as designed *by men* and *for men* to make women and girls into the objects of desire that would please men—not women—best. For them, women's power was in sisterhood, working against all the man-made aspects of being a woman; they celebrated as natural all that was deemed not male-influenced.

The outcome of feminism's attack on man-created fashion was support of the "natural girl." Today, even in the fashion industry, the natural girl is a much celebrated creation supported by parents. For decades mothers have fought with their daughters not to wear makeup too early, not to wear skirts too short or shirts too skimpy. My son's middle school has a policy that girls are not to wear tops with spaghetti straps, because if they do their bra straps would show. These rules are applied equally to boys, who are not allowed to wear T-shirts with beer or drug advertisements on them. But the rules seem to be more of a burden on the girls, many of whose lives to some extent revolve around shopping and clothes when they leave school. Boys aren't that interested in beer- and drug-emblem shirts per se (even if they are interested in beer and drugs); but girls are the ones who have to make an effort to conscientiously adjust their wardrobe every morning and reject or manipulate the items they truly do want to wear. Through rules such as "no skirts or shorts that don't come down below your fingertips when your arms are at your side," the school unwittingly helps girls to see dressing to appear sexy, and even sexuality, as a form of resistance.

The rules, however, are dropped for concert nights, which is a spectacle in and of itself. When the mostly girl pop chorus, in cartoonlike high heels and wedged shoes, teeters up onto the movable stands to sing their tunes, these girls look absurdly glamorous. They are eleven- and twelve-year-olds in three-inch heels, with thick blue eye shadow, spaghetti straps and bra straps entwined, long and leggy with short black dresses. They are silly and adorable, sexy and marvelous all at once. They are good girls dressed up "bad" or "sexy" and they are playing dress-up to represent an image of a seductive grown-up woman that the culture has shown them, an image not reflected back by the mothers in the audience. By sexualizing themselves, they both differentiate themselves from their mothers and celebrate their objectification.

Before middle school, girls often "do girl-ness" by dressing in clothes considered feminine, choosing pink and lace. Laura, whose mother was a lesbian feminist, took karate and played cards and Legos with boys, yet she still longed for the pink and the lace. Growing up as she did she had fewer expectations of being a "girly" girl than most other girls who grew up in the sixties. But still she yearned for it. Her best friend, Prudence, lived in a wealthy, traditional family, with a maid and a country house that the family would go to on the weekends to escape New York City. To Laura, though, Prudence's mother embodied ideal femininity. She even wore white gloves! When they played the card game "Bullshit!" at Prudence's house, the girls had to be careful because they couldn't swear in front of Prudence's mother. Meanwhile, Laura could swear as much as she wanted to at home. Laura wanted nothing more than to have a pink polyester nightgown like Prudence's with lace on the collar and cuffs: "It represented normalcy to me . . . the Brady Bunch or whatever." When Laura's mother tried to respond to her budding sexuality by buying her a purple, lacy bra,

Laura "was horrified." Laura's mother was trying to make becoming a woman fun and sexual for Laura, but Laura wanted to be like all the other girls whose mothers were teaching them about modesty and decorum. She had absorbed social prescriptions for female behavior and, finding that her own mother didn't "fit," invested her fantasies with so-called "normal" visions of femininity.

Mothers teach daughters that if a girl presents the right kind of femininity, she will attract romantic interest and respect from boys and men. In the fifties and sixties, being taken care of in life was an important future goal. But in the seventies, eighties, and nineties, being a good girl was protection against being abused and raped. So mothers thought.

In aspiring to femininity girls are encouraged to seek power through their appearance and their manners. The ideal of femininity is pretty, nice, desirable, and popular. Truth be told, there really is power in this ideal, but it is a borrowed power, a granted power—granted by men who benefit most from girls' niceness. When girls are encouraged to seek power through their actions and accomplishments, something that the girl-power movement aims for, there usually follows an outcry that boys are being displaced. This response has already begun with Christina Hoff Sommers's new book, _The War Against Boys_, and the onslaught of boys' books (_Real Boys_, _Lost Boys_, _Raising Cain_) that seek to refocus our attention on boys after, it would seem, girls have had enough.

Ideals of femininity insure that girls will not be too sexual or too aggressive, staying away from areas presumed to belong to boys. They exert a control on girls that mothers and fathers enforce and that girls support in their rejection and exclusion of other girls for being too tough, rough, or wild. Nevertheless, girls resist this good girl ideal. While they are conforming to men's objectification of women they also could be resisting it.

Girls resist when they play lovely little games in high heels, stripteasing, flouncing, and jutting their chests out in great amusement. When they dress up with boas and heels and red lipstick, and put socks in their play bras, they are aspiring to be like sophisticated grown-up women and, at the same time, they know that they are exaggerating. They become caricatures of real women. They totally embrace and invest in the idea that a woman is constructed—constructed of pretty, sexy, and lacy things.

In their wholehearted belief in sexuality as power, girls resist the idea that they should be asexual, modest, and polite little girls. They are outrageous. They break the rules. Like men in drag, they play at being sexy and sexual, desired and ogled. They are their own best audiences and use mirrors to watch themselves be transformed into sexy grown-ups. In these mirrors they sense the power of the sexual. That's why these games are private and usually halt when a parent or other adult enters the room.

The Power of Being an Object:
Stripteasers, Super Models, Spice Girls

"Did you ever play at being a sexy grown-up?" I asked the women and girls I interviewed. Most knew exactly what I meant. Sexy for some meant sophisticated. For others it meant being a star. For some it meant being a stripper or seductress. Many, many girls and women play and played dress up, choosing the sexiest of their mothers' clothing and imagining themselves as all sorts of slutty and glamorous women.

Joan Riviere, one of the early American female psychoanalysts, used the word "masquerade" to describe flashy women. She said that there is an inclination in women to flash their femininity to signal they are not really very threatening to men, that their power is a charade. The psychoanalytic literary theorist Jacques Lacan also understood the trappings of femininity as fetishism. The flashy costuming of womanhood, he believes, is meant to make up for what a woman lacks—a penis. Some modern psychoanalysts might interpret these girls' dress-up games in this way. They might see the costuming and feminine flashiness as a power display, but also as defensive: Girls are trying to make up for their lack of the greater social power that is granted to those with penises. But I don't think they would be telling the whole story. The power in these games is more than defensive. These girls are exhibitionists of a kind of power they see all around them, every day—the power of being an object.

There are two kinds of power in being an object. In one sense, the power is in the gaze of the other. In adulthood, many women yield such power to others by depending on their gaze and evaluation for their self-worth. But in another sense, when girls dress up and dance in front of a mirror, as they do, they also become the looker, the one with the eyes, the one desiring and approving of themselves. Their gaze can't be reduced to a male's gaze. To say that they look at themselves as they imagine a man would suggests that a woman can't look at herself as a sexual being without pretending to be a heterosexual man. It makes her sexuality only a gift derived from male attention.

The power one feels from being a subject of one's own desires and not only the object of someone else's desires is more profound and upsetting than being an object for a boy or a man. It upsets the way things are supposed to be. In point of fact, women and girls are only supposed to feel sexy and sexual due to male attention. Finding oneself sexual feels unnatural, perverse. That's why girls hide this kind of response and are ashamed of it.

But isn't there something natural or, to use a better word, fundamentally human about wanting to be seductive? About wanting to be an object, taking oneself as an object? Like the infant who claps at herself and says 'Look at me!' Isn't there something delightful in painting one's face into something alluring or changing one's hair with the fashion? Brianna, a ten-year-old growing up in the Chicago suburbs, told me, "Sometimes I put on big black shoes with heels, and I say, 'Oh, look at me!! I'm Ginger Spice!' " And can't we adults respond to her in a way that acknowledges how lovely it is that she is not ashamed to say "Oh look at me!"

Couldn't we also ask why men deprive themselves of this pleasure? It wasn't until about two hundred years ago that there began to be a sharp differentiation in the way men and women dress. Men stopped dressing decoratively, with ruffles and plumes, while female clothes remained imaginative and fanciful. When I teach my gender issues in psychology class, I like to ask the men in the class if they ever feel deprived because of the colors and textures that women can wear? Do you ever want to wear feathers? I ask. Have you felt how nice a silk scarf is?

Girls who dress up are indeed acting out two-dimensional images of what a grown-up woman is, the striptease, the model, the ultrafeminine girl, the prostitute, but they do so with such energy and love and creativity that we can't deny the pure pleasure in being fancy and in being watched.

The adult women I interviewed spoke of these games with joy and openness. In contrast, many of the little girls I talked to seemed hesitant, unsure if this is a bad sort of game to play. Madeleine, who is only seven, described what other girls do: "They pretend they are taking off their clothes. . . . That's why they don't have any friends." Kelly, a ten-year-old, also was hesitant: "We get high-heeled shoes and then we get some skirts on and we just walk around." When asked how she feels when she does this, she replies, "Embarrassed. . . . Because she makes me do it. She's like p-l-e-a-s-e, can we play Spice Girls?" Although Kelly played this game, she others the desire. It is her friend who made her do it. She intuits that the vamp is not a proper role.

Play that involves being a "bad" woman is exciting because it is play.

That which isn't permitted in real life can be enacted and enjoyed. Strip-pers and prostitutes and "sluts" are bad women. The girls might not know what they are called, but these images are present enough in the culture for these girls to notice and wonder about their power.

The beauty pageant is an acceptable form of striptease because their stripping (the swimsuit competition) is regulated. But Bethany's friend re-worked the game so that the beauty pageant ran out of control. Her friend invented a new part of the game where the two girls would line up the chairs in her basement to represent the line of the judges, and then her friend would seductively go over to a chair and pretend to sit on the judge's lap doing sexual things to him and exposing parts of her body, so that the judge would vote for her. Bethany was always quite uncomfortable with how far her friend went with this game: "She would really get into it." Thus, even the game at being a "good" object of desire (beauty contestant) was turned into a "bad" object (slut).

Aidee, the seventeen-year-old tomboy who grew up part-time in the projects of New York and part-time in Puerto Rico, played at being a pros-titute

> once or twice with my friends. And we would dress up in like sexy clothes and pretend to be like not perverts, but like prostitutes. I don't know why. . . . It was fun because like we would laugh, like, "Yeah, give me a penny and I'll give you my body." But it was weird 'cause, like, I didn't know the meaning of what it was.

It is "weird" and she doesn't know why she played it. I asked if it made her feel powerful, and she said, "Yeah, cool."

Bad woman images are indeed inviting. In the sixth grade Marilyn took a walk down Bourbon Street in the city of New Orleans. There the strippers and prostitutes hung out on the streets, waving and smiling at the little girls. They had long feather boas and high heels. Their dresses were long and studded with thousands of sequins. Her mother said to her as they passed these women, "I want you to promise me you won't do that when you grow up." So, of course, said Marilyn, she used to pretend to be a strip-per for hours at a time, prancing around her room with a boa and high heels.

Linda remembered a slumber party at age twelve where the greatest fun of the evening was a striptease show that each girl had to perform. Marilyn and Linda, both adults today, look back on these memories with no shame and a lot of pleasure. This is because as an adult looking back, the meaning of these games is clear—it was about fun, pretend.

Many other women remembered the pleasure of dressing provocatively. Although May is an adult now, she remembered the luscious feeling of crossing a "boundary that you shouldn't" when she dressed up in lipstick and a miniskirt and walked around "acting sexual." One woman called it wearing "trashy" clothes. Another called it wearing "sexual, seductive clothes." As girls these women knew that "clothes make the woman." But they didn't yet know what kind of woman they would become; they were in the process of developing. Like girls today who mimic Spice Girls and Britney Spears, they had mixed feelings about who they wanted to turn out to be, but could play out these feelings in their games.

The child absorbed in play takes what she is doing utterly seriously, yet knows at the same time that it doesn't count. The grown-ups, who of course were children once, have for the most part lost or forgotten that serious aspect of their experience. They look back and say, "It was just play." The children know that it is not "just" play, that play affects your mind and soul and could send you in directions you don't want to go. It's great fun and it's totally serious.

These stories show that the way popular culture and sentiment get into the hearts and minds of little girls is not through direct force. Somewhere along the line, through the barrage of images, girls take over, regulating themselves and other girls according to certain ways of being a woman. The twin ideals of being a modest feminine girl and also a glamorous object aren't images that are forced down their throats by one monolithic media. If they are victims, they are willing victims. Girls play an active role in taking in these images, rearranging them somewhat, and creating new expectations for themselves. But while they obey the images and re-create them, they also undermine them. Herein lies the potential for becoming a sexual person, a sexual agent (not just a desired object) for all girls.

Chapter 4

Naked Barbies

"I was scared of Barbies. They were so sexual. . . . when I wanted to play Barbies it was like, let's get to the good stuff . . . and they had sex."
—Chrissie, white, 21

Though the namesake of Mattel Toys was a man named Matt Elliot, it was his wife, Ruth Handler, who masterminded the creation and marketing of its biggest seller: Barbie. She pushed the executives there to create the first Barbie doll. In Susan Stern's film *Barbie Nation: An Authorized Tour,* Handler remembers aloud why she wanted a Barbie doll. As a developing pre-teen, when her breasts began to show she had felt self-conscious, and would walk around stoop-shouldered. Handler wanted girls to be proud of how they look, not ashamed or embarrassed. Barbie was a doll with boobs and fantastic posture.

First advertised as a teenage fashion model, Barbie was made purposely bland in face and personality so that girls could project their grown-up longings onto her. She was modeled after a German "sex doll" (literally, a doll men could buy in sex shops) called Lilli. When Handler and her husband brought the model of Barbie to the factory workers, the men in the factory refused to do it; they said that there was no way they could make a doll with breasts. Sid Kahn, the marketing executive for Mattel at the time said, "I could not believe this doll was going to be marketed to kids." Marketing knew that mothers would hate Barbie, and so, using the new media, TV, Barbie was marketed directly to the children.

Barbie is sexually provocative. Everything about Barbie says, "Undress me," "fondle me." This is a little hard for me to admit, because as a feminist I don't want to be saying that the way a woman dresses has anything to do with what you can or can't do to her. One woman quoted in Mary Rogers's book *Barbie Culture* agrees, saying, "I think dolls shouldn't have that kind of body. It sometimes makes children do bad things to her." Imagine what it is like to be a six-year-old living in a presumably sexless society and to have in your hands every day a little woman whose breasts jut out at you, whose clothing fits so tightly you have to stretch the shirts over those firm, pointy breasts. Imagine the turn of her heel and, in the late fifties and sixties, what could only be called Barbie's "bedroom eyes." It has to be said: Barbie turned kids on.

Adult men too! In Barbie's early years, the 1960s, she was seen as a threat to men. In a 1964 issue of *The Nation* magazine, one man wrote, "Barbie threatens to make a generation of vipers that will cause men to plead for the return to monism." In 1965, in the magazine *Ramparts,* another man wrote, "Mattel wants little girls to realize the American feminine ideal, growing up to be a big-spending, busy, powerful, frigid woman." It's funny how the second author equates powerful with frigid, but both men see the downfall of womankind as existing in the power that the very sexual Barbie exudes. This is in keeping with thought from one hundred years ago that characterized the good woman as someone who will be ruled by the superior judgment of her husband. It's also ironic how today we ignore the sexuality of Barbie and only see her as an unattainably perfect body; we condemn Barbie for disempowering little girls, preoccupying them with concerns about their appearance.

Mary Rogers, also in the book *Barbie Culture*, calls Barbie a "fantastic icon" because she contributes to our lives by exaggerating what is "actual, possible, or conceivable." But for girls, what is conceivable is so much more than the Barbie figure. It is the possibility, or promise, of sexuality. Stephen Kline, in *Out of the Garden*, wrote that "Barbie was intentionally crafted to invoke a specific kind of imaginary role-playing that went beyond the mothering and family scripts that had until then defined doll play." This new script equaled a kind of power for girls not easily found in games of wife and mother.

One of my most fun experiences in interviewing women about their memories of sexual play and games was asking them if they ever played "naked Barbies." So many of them would react with shock and glee: "How could you know?" It was as if I were the omnipotent parent of childhood whose knowing glare they couldn't escape. Only in my case, the delightful stories would follow.

For example, Laura had Barbie and Ken "humping": "We would put Ken on top of Barbie and there'd be a lot of heavy breathing." Grace strung her Barbie up naked in a game about children seeking revenge on an evil baby-sitter. Grace claimed that her Barbie game was more about straight humiliation than sexual humiliation. However, this opinion is hard to buy wholesale, for she did tie Barbie up naked.

In contrast, Leah's Barbie had an active sex life:

Every time my mom would open the door, Ken and Barbie would be naked . . . and we, it was like there was one Ken doll, and whenever you could, you would buy a Barbie. You always wanted to get the pretty Barbie. You didn't want to waste your money on Ken 'cause they all looked the same. So there was one Ken to go around. So, you know, Ken made it with a lot of Barbies, and we'd, like—we'd put them in the bedroom and we'd take off their clothes and roll them around on the bed and make little kissing sounds and stuff. . . . And I remember Barbie and Ken would make it on a horse (naked). . . . And the two of them were riding this horse naked, and I remember my Mom thinking [aloud], "Hmmmmm. Should I be worried about this?"

Mothers did worry. Abbie's mother, for example, like many modern-day mothers, wouldn't allow her to play with Barbies. Whenever she went to her friend Mary Jane's house, the two of them would take out the Barbies:

Yeah, we enacted a lot of sex with the Barbie dolls. Mary Jane taught me what "69" meant when we were in seventh grade. We did that with Bar-bie dolls. We were still playing with Barbie dolls then. You know. Ken and Barbie would copulate.

When children played naked Barbies together, the sexual aspects took on a more daring and mutually delightful quality. Alone, children won-dered, once again, whether they were normal. Caroline's first confession as a Catholic involved Barbie. Her Barbie and Ken play was no different from many other girls'. She stripped her Barbie and Ken, put them next to each other, and made kissing noises. However, this was around the time when she was supposed to make her first confession, right around age seven.

It was my first confession, in a dark church in the sixties, and, you know, I said, "I committed adultery." And the priest was, I don't know if he thought I was being a smart aleck or what, but he got really angry with me. . . . He repeated the word, "You committed adultery? What do you mean? What are you talking about?" . . . At the time I didn't, I thought it was such a horrible sin that he . . . And he got really mad, and it just scared me so much. . . . I ran out of that confessional and it was years before I got back.

In most Barbie and Ken play, there is an element of practicing for dates. The TV commercials originally encouraged this kind of play as well, labeling some of Barbie's outfits as outfits for a "date" and suggesting that Barbie had a date with Ken that night. Although some girls borrowed their brothers' GI Joes, most used Ken for what he was created for, Barbie's date.

Having Barbie and Ken date was a very safe way to play at being a heterosexual teenager. When girls practiced kissing with each other instead of Barbies, problems could arise. Sometimes one girl got more "into it" than the other. Sometimes a girl actually would get stimulated by kissing another girl. There was always the worry that if this happened, then the two girls weren't really "practicing," they were experiencing, and if they were experiencing, then they might be lesbians.

Psychologists who do play therapy with children know the usefulness of doll play as a form of distancing. When children have strong emotions, sometimes it is too difficult for them to express the emotions directly, so the therapist, through doll play, can watch how the dolls interact and what they do and say as a clue to the unconscious or hidden feelings of the child. As the child attributes these feelings to the doll, she or he doesn't have to own them as her or his own. Also, when children don't have the words yet for how they are feeling, doll play can help them enact that which they can't express. In both ways, Barbie dolls help girls express what they don't have words for yet, chiefly their sexual interest, which helps them to distance themselves from it at the same time. They can remain good girls while Barbie is the slut.

The practice for dating isn't the only way Barbies introduce girls to heterosexuality. I noticed that in all of the stories about Ken and Barbie and their antics, Ken was always on top of Barbie. Did they pick this out from TV programs or from romantic book covers? Did they translate their romantic fantasies of being swept away into the sexual activities of Barbie and Ken? Did Ken hold for them the idea of sexual longing while Barbie became the passive beautiful object? Was Ken always the initiator, or did Barbie's outfits, in some not so subtle way, tell Ken that she wanted to "get naked?"

Erica Rand, in her book *Barbie's Queer Accessories*, points out the irony that Barbie is a female doll that excites girls. Girls dress and undress her, "fondle and obsess" over her. They show no real interest in Ken's body. Granted, Ken has no genitalia, but from early on, girls learn to sexualize the adult female body. Do they translate that to their own bodies? Or do they come to see other women as sexual bodies, sexual beings, as they get older? In Rand's view, Barbie play promotes girls' sexual feelings toward other girls.

Whether or not Barbies encourage lesbian feelings may depend on how girls feel about who they are when they are playing Barbies. Who is the subject of the desire? If they feel excitement, and they feel it as though they are the Barbie dating Ken, then, in a sense, they embody the heterosexual fantasy. If they feel the excitement in the handling and dressing of the Barbie, if they acknowledge it in themselves, we can't deny it is a woman-to-woman kind of excitement.

It is not so hard for heterosexual women to imagine that they could have been gay. Many older heterosexual women say jokingly to their friends that when their husbands are dead, they'll go off and live with them in an all-women's house. Many teen girls will tell each other that they love each other, sometimes adding, "Don't think I'm a lesbian." Little girls hold hands and kiss their girlfriends on the lips. Adrienne Rich, over thirty years ago, said these acts exist on what she called the "lesbian continuum." She tried to remove from the idea of "lesbian" the notion of it only meaning women having sex with other women, and tried to broaden the idea to include women loving other women in a variety of ways.

A number of psychoanalytic theorists suggest that everyone's first love story is with their mother, whether you are female or male. The richness of girls' connections to other girls, some have argued, comes from the fact that they are nurtured and cared for by a woman in their early years. Some pop psychologists go further by arguing that women are disappointed with their husbands (in heterosexual relationships) because they expect their husband to be more like their first love, their mother—more like a woman. In my teaching of young adult women about gender and sexuality, many have confessed that they are attracted to "sexy" adult women. Some interpret this as a sign of their bisexuality; some see this as the end product of being taught by the culture to respond to stereotyped images of what is "sexy."

If Barbie represents to young girls the possibilities of their bodies, then ambivalence will most certainly come out. Researchers and journalists have paid a lot of critical attention to Barbie and her looks. The problems they see are related to her large breasts, her small waist, and the fact that she always walks around on tiptoes. Blonde, white Barbies are the most popular items among a wide variety of dolls. The "multicultural Barbies" or "ethnic Barbies," when they first came out, simply looked like white Barbie with brown skin.

Mary Rogers has argued in *Barbie Culture* that Barbie takes the stuff that most girls become preoccupied with (being nice, having an attractive body) and turns it into fun, glamour, and excitement. Stories of Barbie "torture" on the other hand, suggest the limits of such play, as well as girls' ambivalence toward what Barbie stands for. One girl humiliated the naked Barbie baby-sitter. Another rubbed Vaseline on her Barbies' vaginas and tortured them in what she created and called a "zombie chamber" (not the "barbie dreamhouse"). A Catholic girl from Indiana played a game with her best friend in which they tied up Barbie and pretended to pluck her pubic hairs out, one by one. The torturing of Barbies expresses fear, hostility, and anger, which we'll say more about in the chapter on anxiety about bodily changes. However, if doll play expresses unconscious feelings, we can safely assume that girls did not simply want to grow up and look like Barbie. They resisted such transformation as well.

Zeroing In On: Childhood Innocence and the Shaming of Sexuality

When the Grimm brothers rewrote the fairy tales they had collected, although they acknowledged some of the eroticism and aggression of children that occur in many of these stories, they cleaned up others. Sleeping Beauty, in earlier versions, gave birth to twins, whereas today we know her only to have been kissed. Marianne Warner, the English essayist who analyzes this and other fairy tales and myths brilliantly, states that "the belief that there's a proper childlike way for children to be has deep roots" and warns that the way we treat children "really tests who we are, fundamentally conveys who we hope to be." There is an expectation that children should be innocent, and that girls especially should be innocent of sexuality.

The Puritans thought that children went astray as soon as they were born. One New England preacher in 1689 claimed Satan got them to be "proud, profane, reviling, and revengeful as young as they are." In the eighteenth century, although there was a fight to show that the newborn child was born innocent, the philosopher Locke noted that in addition to their love of freedom, children also loved power and domination, and that these two traits showed themselves very early. Romanticism and its desire to discover the lost paradise of childhood innocence had a huge influence on our understanding of childhood as we see it today. Children were seen as closer to nature, and in that closeness, girls were seen as quite sexual and in need of education for modesty. The Victorians made rules about sexuality that were antisensual, placing reason over emotion. And the modern citizens of the twentieth century strove to undo the hypocrisy of Victorian times by speaking openly about what they believed had been repressed earlier.

Freud's so-called "discovery" of childhood sexuality in the early twentieth century shocked his contemporaries and revolutionized the way we see children today. He argued that children experience sexual pleasure throughout their body and throughout their early years. That children, and for that matter, all of us, have sexual and aggressive feelings that are both natural and unacceptable to us is basic Freud.

Anti-Freudians place the seat of sexuality as outside the child and see adults as corrupting influences. At the turn of the twentieth century, parents were warned about governesses who oversexualized children and taught them to masturbate. In the 1920s parents were warned about overstimulating their children themselves. In the 1980s and 1990s parents continued to be warned about the pedophile. Also, in the last few years, parents and professionals alike see children's sexual expression as a direct result of media images that sexualize them unnaturally.

Children are well aware of our expectations about their innocence. One of the college students I interviewed said it well:

We were supposed to be playing with our dolls. We weren't supposed to be knowing that you could have sex with boys. We were in third grade.

Another girl felt all alone in the world because she thought often about sex. It was constantly on her mind, but she was confused about those feelings, felt guilty about them: "It never occurred to me that anyone else would be thinking about those feelings."

Patty, an adult who grew up in an Irish Catholic household, also had sexual feelings, and remembered playing with herself in bed at night when she was young, until one night her mother discovered her and said, "Don't do that!" Another woman discovered sexual feelings rolling around on a hassock. When her mother saw her, she said, "Good girls don't do that." A Puerto Rican woman who grew up in New York in the 1960s kissed a boy and got punished for it.

Researchers still know very little about children's sexuality. The famous sex researcher Alfred Kinsey, despite his many other discoveries about human sexuality, did not notice that girls play erotic games with each other. More recently, researchers have taken to asking parents (!) about the sexual lives of their children (rather than asking the children themselves—or asking adults about their own childhoods). In a study of Irish parents, about 36 percent answered that their children had had some form of sexual play with each other, while only 3 percent actually had seen their children simulate intercourse by lying on top of each other. Reporting of explicit sexual behaviors was unusual, but then, this would be difficult for a parent to see. In another study, William Friedrich, a professor of psychology at the Mayo Clinic, and his colleagues gave questionnaires to over eight hundred middle-class mothers. They found that about 38 percent had caught their children engaging in some kind of sex play. Only 8 percent had seen their children or knew that their children had engaged in some sexual touching (direct genital contact).

But there's more. In their book *Sexual Abuse and Consensual Sex: Women's Developmental Patterns and Outcomes,* Gail Wyatt and her colleagues at UCLA count about one in five children as engaging in some sexual play in childhood but write that there is no adequate information about ethnic differences in childhood sexual practices. In the early 1990s they conducted a major survey and interview to learn more about the sexual experiences of African-American girls and women compared to white girls and women. Because they were interested in all kinds of experiences, they did not look very carefully at children's games and lumped together in their analysis all kinds of childhood sexual experiences, from the mutually delightful to the uncomfortable harassment, as well as social and individual masturbation. They found that childhood and adolescent sexual involvement was unrelated to adult psychological well-being. They did find quite a bit of sexual experience in the lives of children.

These researchers and others have found that sexual activities do not decline in the latency years, ages six to eleven, as Freud had suggested. Instead, sexual activities continue with increasing frequency. Mutual sex play is common among children, and in most studies it's the atmosphere of the home that determines how this sex play is perceived by parents and children. In these studies and others, even those investigating abusive adult–child sex, it is the blaming and the repressive atmosphere in the home that contribute to long-term feelings of guilt.

The only place where we find a lot of information about girls and sex is in anthropology research. Anthropologists have learned that children can have orgasms and that some parents stimulate the genitals to please or pacify a young child. In some Muslim and American Indian cultures, boys are allowed sexual play and intercourse in childhood. In Melanesia, while boys and girls can play naked with one another, they cannot touch each other. In contrast, boys *are* allowed to play sexually together. In some cultures on the Hawaiian Islands, girls would have their vaginal areas rubbed with coconut oil and their labia and clitoris stretched orally by their aunts to make them more beautiful. Despite the sexual overtones some westerners might read into this, neither the adults nor the children perceived it as sexual. Furthermore, the girls enjoyed it. Sexual exploration among children was encouraged however, and children often observed adults having sex.

Even in the anthropological literature, not all things are equal. Boys' sex education seems to take precedence over girls in that most anthropologists writing about sexuality were much more interested in occurrences of intercourse rather than sexual play. Thus there is a bias in their writing, reflecting their own ideas of what is a topic of sexuality worth writing about and what questions are worth asking a resident of a culture. Most anthropologists occupied themselves with studying sexual initiations and rites of passage, obscuring the practices that go on among children by not seeing children as full participants in a culture.

In the United States a wide range of evidence suggests that sexual freedom has its good points. Unfortunately, we tend to ignore it and harp on the harmfulness of the media in portraying sexuality to kids. In families where children and parents are less self-conscious of being nude in front of one another, children grow up to have better body images. Conversely, we know that sexual perpetrators are sorely lacking in sex education, often getting most of it from pornography or their own prior abuse.

Sweden is the first country to require a comprehensive sex education program that starts in elementary school. In Scandinavia and much of Europe, the idea that sex in itself could be harmful to children is absent. Children's right to sexual play and games as well as sexual freedom is recognized in Scandinavian countries, and the practice of lovemaking is even taught. These are countries that, by the way, do much better than our own in preventing and recognizing abuse as well as keeping rates of abortion and venereal disease low.

Shame

While sex can be a source of energy and creativity, it can also, especially in the United States, be a source of shame. In a culture where children are supposed to be innocent and girls are supposed to be good, where sex is considered bad or dirty, girls are not allowed to have sexual feelings. Sexual shame is what drives girls to do such things in closets and behind closed doors.

In a society where play is for children and sex is for adults, what happens when the two meet? Sex becomes the province of the Other. Diana Gittins writes in *The Child in Question* that the "bad child . . . has tended to be played down and/or denied at the same time as it is projected outside, located elsewhere, in others and in the Other." While the intense interest of (usually Western) anthropologists in the sexual lives of children has furthered common understanding of children's lives and culture, it has served to displace that youthful sexuality from the West to the Other, the so-called "native" peoples, thereby demonizing it. It is high time to claim this sexuality as common to all of us—and nothing to be ashamed of.

Chapter 5

Bodies and Pleasure: If It Feels Good, Why Is It So Bad?

"And that is how we became 'best vagina pals!' instead of 'bosom buddies.' "
—Abbie, white, 42

Sexually pleasurable feelings are a part of some of the games girls play—games that are specifically about sex, games that are sexy, and games that arouse and excite. Adult women looking back over their childhoods think these games were great fun at the time. But even when they seemed fun and natural, they still often worry about certain aspects. Sometimes they worry whether they might have hurt another child, a younger one, by playing these games with them. Other times they wonder about a specific game of torture or "evil" involving sex—was this normal? Sometimes they worry about whether they were lesbians. They search for normal.

But the idea of normal is constantly shifting. Even anthropologists, who've seen and read about a wider range of human experience than most of us, were blown away in the late 1970s when anthropologist Gilbert Herdt returned from his stay with a New Guinea tribe which he called the Sambia. He shocked the academic world with the reports he brought back of male sexual initiation and development in this culture. While there he learned that little boys ages seven to ten were taken from their mothers and put through a ritual that lasted ten to fifteen years, a ritual in which they performed oral sex on the older boys of the tribe on a daily basis and then became the older boys upon whom oral sex was performed by the younger males. They were called "Guardians of the Flute," and the men of this tribe believed that swallowing semen created biological maleness and maintained masculinity. After their "teen" years these boys rejoined the community, married, and became "bisexual" until they had children. Then all homosexual activity stopped. This ritual shocked the West simply because it showed a culture in which homosexual practices involving children had been normalized; furthermore, it showed that the practice of such acts didn't necessarily make a young boy homosexual for life.

In contrast, American girls' sexual play is not at all acceptable or part of regular public life for girls. Nevertheless, they like to "practice" with each other, play with each other in sexual ways, and find some sexual pleasure in their games. Though this differentiates them from the Sambian boys, like them most of these girls do not go on to conclude that such play makes them gay. In point of fact, while some of the grown women I interviewed are presently or had been at some point in their lives lesbians, they were no more likely than heterosexual women to have played girl-to-girl sexual games as a child.

In cultures where children are allowed to be sexual, there is still often a differentiation between child and adult sex and a differentiation by gender, too. For example, an anthropologist studying Hawaiian cultures was amazed to see that the part of the vaginal area called the mons is rubbed regularly with coconut oil by the girls' mothers or aunts. These women and those on other islands also pull at the labia of girls with their fingers and mouths to make the lips of their vaginas longer. They massage and knead girls' butts to make them rounder and more attractive. Although this culture may no longer carry out such practices after missionaries proselytized against them, sexual exploration between children during this time was encouraged, and at puberty a child was expected to be skilled sexually. There was even a word for the child's orgasm, which translates into either "joy" or "fun."

In Africa, among the Baganda, an anthropologist, to his embarrassment, observed girls playing a game of pulling at each other's clitorises to lengthen them. The girls experience sexual pleasure in such games, and adult women claim great benefits from such practice.

There is something about this cultural practice that seems refreshingly pro-women. Lately there has been a lot of media interest in the practice of clitoridectomy in Africa, a practice in which the clitoris of a girl, either the hood or the whole thing, is cut off in a terrifying ritual. Many feminists and anthropologists have made the case that this only happens in cultures that also show hatred for women in other ways, and that this practice serves to keep women in line, taking away her pleasure at intercourse. With the Baganda, however, the opposite is encouraged: The clitoris is enhanced, teaching young girls about this pleasure center of their bodies. It is interesting, and perhaps significant, that there has been little media interest in such practices.

When I wrote the word "mons" a couple of paragraphs back, it gave me pause. I used that word because that was the word used in the book where I read about this practice, but what exactly is this place and will my readers know about it? To further complicate an investigation of girls' sexual lives, we simply don't talk about these different parts of the vaginal area. Most young girls in our own culture don't even know what a clitoris is, let alone the name for it. What might this say about our capacity for pleasure?

The stories that follow are about pleasure, the way girls teach each other that sex can be fun and erotic, but also about the shame and guilt that unfortunately go along with these pleasurable experiences. Sexual games make girls feel like sexual beings. They involve moments when girls can share the wonder and mischievous fun of playing around with sex. Sadly, in bringing pleasure to young girls, the games also bring out a lot of anxiety.

Marilyn was one of those women who seemed to have had a lot of sexual fun in childhood. At forty-five, she recalled how she and her friends discovered and shared erotic secrets. At "an early age," she and her friend Randi, she remembered, discussed how each of them had "rubbed their bottoms," and then confided in one another, "That feels good, doesn't it?" Then they went on to talk about other things. Marilyn also recalled that once she saw her cousin stimulate herself by leaning

> against the little table where we did art. It came at just the practical level for her and we [the other girls] noticed it, and we said, "Oh, this is how I do it" and then we all proceeded to lie on the floor and show her our various styles. And it was the time my mother walked in and we all stopped, but we were embarrassed and she understood that, and she just said, you know, "Don't do anything that embarrasses you," and left.

Abbie, a white middle-class girl from outside of New York City, also felt sexual pleasure as a child and was able to talk about it:

> I think I got excited with my "best vagina pal," Renee Segal. At the time I learned the phrase "best bosom friends" and Renee and I decided that

*we were "best vagina pals" . . . and the main thing I remember in con-
nection to that is that we used to go to the beach and we used to create
sort of sand sculptures by pressing a lot of sand into our crotch with our
legs spread out so that we could make a kind of a mound that represented
our genitals somehow, and that is how we became "best vagina pals."
[Was this sexually stimulating?] I think I got sexually excited. . . .
What else could we have been doing? Just like shoving sand into our
crotches. My God!*

Abbie also played a game at summer camp with a little girl she adored:
"I thought she was beautiful and I wanted to touch her":

*We would pretend that we were Greek goddesses and I would call her
Dernida, and I can't remember what she would call me, but I would just
sort of jump on her, and the goal was to get both of our shirts off and to
like lie on top of her and kiss her and embrace her with no shirts on. And
I was definitely the leader. She was always wanting me to cut it out and
never do it again, and I was always wanting to do it again, but she also
enjoyed it. I think she felt guilty and bad and wanted me to stop initiating this thing.*

This game was quite sexually arousing to Abbie: "Well, we kissed, you
know? And then I'd lay on top of her with our naked chests. I don't think
we got into our pants." Abbie was one of the few women who admitted to
initiating a game like this. Like the others she worried about the fact that
she enjoyed it.

*Well, at the time I felt that this was a very exhilarating thing to be doing.
And yet I could see her point, that this was maybe not quite the right
thing to be doing spending our time at camp. I needed to distance myself
from the lesbian aspect and not the sexual aspect is what I remember.*

For other girls, these kinds of games were thrilling or "exhilarating"
too, but even more secret. Devin, a twenty-year-old student, remembered
having sleepovers with her cousin who was the same age. They'd see each
other about twice a year and sleep together in a big double bed, "for conve-
nience's sake."

*And I remember when at night they'd put us to bed, and I think this was
when I was very young, like between the ages of six and ten. . . . I re-*

member this is kind of weird. I don't know what, why we did what we did or what it meant. I think it was just curious, curious about sex and, just, you know, our sexuality. And we didn't even know that it was or didn't realize that it was; we were both females. That didn't really matter to us. We'd sleep back to back, you know so our bottoms would touch. And we found that very exciting. And at the time we didn't talk about it either. I don't know how, I don't know how we initiated it, or I don't remember the details, but I remember it being dark and us being sneaky and you know, sleeping with our butts touching. . . . It was something with our bottoms! It was very thrilling! Even now we don't talk about it, but I'm fairly sure she would remember it.

Devin took a long time to get to her confession of this small but exciting sexual act. Is it so small? To a child, it is an enormously sneaky and guilty pleasure. And until she told me, she had never told anyone about it: "Maybe the lasting feeling of naughtiness has carried over. I still feel that way when I think about it." This must have been a powerful sexual feeling for a child if the guilt and pleasure are so tangible years later as she speaks about it for the first time out loud.

Another girl reminded me of Devin. This was Marissa, an African-American college student, who grew up on the West Coast in a very religious family. The family would pray together before breakfast every morning. Marissa was a "good girl," in her own words, and even belonged to a club of good little girls affiliated with the church called "Glory Girls" who on their thirteenth birthday would wear a crown, dress in white, and walk down a ceremonial aisle to receive a rose. Although Marissa was good, she did one small sexual thing that had a lasting effect. Like Devin, this occurred during sleepovers with a cousin:

We were doing nothing, and like we were in my room, and then I turned off the lights and we were supposed to go to bed, and for some reason or other we both like felt the urge to like take off our clothes. And we were just sitting there. And I like just prayed that she wouldn't tell her parents, you know what I mean? 'Cause then like they probably would tell my parents, and I'm like a year older than her so I like felt responsible, and I was so afraid that after she left my house that like my parents would find out.

As I tried in the interview to find out what exactly she felt guilty about, it emerged that it is only the guilty pleasure of sitting naked next to someone.

For some reason or other, like I don't even remember what happened, but like I felt so responsible. I almost felt I'm the one who initiated. I'm not sure . . . I think it was pretty out of character for me . . . and I felt guilty for a long time, and I was like scared for a couple of years that my parents would find out.

Scared for a couple of years? The guilt over such a small act as this or Devin's rubbing of bottoms seems extraordinary. But if you imagine that the thrill was also incredibly big, like the excitement of crossing a boundary into the unknown world of sexuality expressed by so many little girls, it makes more sense. As one adult woman remembered about camp, a girl yelled out, "Let's have an orgy!" and all the girls fell upon one another kissing!

This wild exuberance seems to be more possible when there is a whole group of girls. Today's gender psychologists are fond of saying how wild boys are when they get together, that boys like to hang out in groups (they run in packs!), and that when boys get together in a group they give themselves permission to lose control. By saying this only about boys, though, they reinforce the stereotype that girls are always good, no matter what the social situation. But girls, when in groups, also egg each other on to do things they might never do alone or in a pair. Abbie remembered one night:

I went to this slumber party where the girl lived next to a graveyard, and we went in the graveyard and played truth or dare. And it was very sexy. And we had to do things like take off our underpants and sit on— straddle—the gravestones and stuff like that . . . there was some kissing of each other and taking off clothing. Mostly I remember that the most outrageous thing was having to straddle these gravestones with no pants on. No underwear on. . . . It was great fun, and I felt guilty. . . . It was very, you know, intoxicating . . . very arousing. I didn't know what it really meant at the time, but I know I was very excited.

What many of these girls who played these games with sexual excitement didn't know, was that other girls were also playing these games. Over and over I heard from adult women remembering back, "We knew we weren't supposed to be doing this stage yet" or "We knew we weren't supposed to know this yet" and "I was always pretty much the good girl." And then sometimes, they recalled, they would find out that someone else had done the same thing. In eighth grade, Heather, who in a game had had long kisses with a girlfriend, later exchanged secrets with another friend who told her about her own games, and Heather exclaimed, "I did the exact same thing!" Heather told me, "As soon as someone told me that, it was fine, it was like over." The guilt had evaporated, and with it the worry that she was different and weird.

Who would deny children these small sexual thrills? Unfortunately many people would, thinking that bottoms should stay covered, that cousins shouldn't touch, that girls shouldn't experience pleasure with each other, and that children should ignore sexual feelings rather than pursue them. With all these shouldn'ts, it is understandable why Devin felt guilty and Marissa worried for years about her small act. Rather than worrying about children becoming too sexual too soon, we might instead turn our attention to the burden of guilt our expectations place on these very good girls and on how we might be teaching them that sexual pleasure is wrong or bad. How will we then unteach this guilt later? And if we do try, can we?

Chapter 6

Playing Dead but Feeling Tingly

"Just ignore it and it will go away."
—*A mother*

Not all the girls were able to feel the wild exuberance of Abbie, who straddled tombstones in the moonlight with her friends. Girls like Marissa and Devin had to pretend they weren't doing anything to allow sexual feelings and play to emerge: the exquisite torture of only putting your butt against another girl's, of *only* sitting naked next to her. This form of play was taken to its extreme in games where, in the game plan, girls needed to play dead or remain totally still to add to the feeling of danger and thrill while other children did the dirty work.

In some ways these games interested me most because they point out the contradiction in girls' lives. Girls want to be desiring individuals, they have desires, but to own these desires, to make them their own, makes them feel slutty or unnatural or unfeminine. It makes them bad girls. These games, then, like many group games, take away the responsibility of the individual girl. She can lie there passive, unrequesting, with no desire, perfectly still, like Sleeping Beauty, yet anticipating and experiencing the secret excitement and thrill of sexual feeling.

Dorothy Jean and her cousins had a game called "Playing Dead," where one girl would be posed seductively and scantily dressed as the murder victim, and the other girls would enter the room one by one as spectators, commenting on how beautiful she was. It was always wonderful for

Dorothy Jean to play the part of the dead woman, and the sexual thrill would come when an onlooker would say "Oh, isn't she beautiful." But to be beautiful and, more importantly, to be sexual, she would have to be dead.

Leah remembered a game she didn't want her parents to find out about that she played with her sister, Sherry, and two boys. Her dad's friend would bring over his two sons when he visited to play with Leah and her sister, and the four of them would play "The Skeleton Game."

> The skeleton was the bad guy, and he lived in Castle Grey Skull or something, and we used to pretend . . . we pretended we were like prisoners of his and that he had this machine that hooked up to our private parts, and we would be giggling a lot, and then our parents would come in and we would pretend to be asleep.

Using strings and toys, the victims would lie still as his or her genitals were tortured or stimulated. Like "playing dead," this game conveys the message that sexual feeling is something forced upon you rather than something you might actively pursue.

"Playing doctor," one of the most common images of childhood sexual experimentation, incorporates the role of the passive "victim." In Connie's experience, growing up in Chicago in the sixties, "playing doctor" required total stillness of the patient. I was the first person Connie had ever told about her doctor game, and she felt quite guilty about it. Where Connie lived, all the girls on the street played together, almost every day after school and on the weekends.

> We started playing doctor with each other, but with only the girls in the basement, like behind this built-in bar we had. Mom and Dad never knew about it . . . we didn't realize what we were doing. It got us aroused, I can remember it happening. . . . But we didn't know what was going on or why we were feeling that way. We had to go to the bathroom when we were finished. "I've got to go to the bathroom now," and so each girl would have their turn.

It would happen every time the girls in the neighborhood got together, and they played it "quite often" over a period of two years. One girl would take a turn as the patient and lie naked as the other girls would explore her body, touching, rubbing, and poking. Connie speculates that as they got older, maybe this game was part of the reason why they didn't remain friends.

> *Looking back, I'm thinking, well, I don't know how those girls feel about it, and I kind of feel guilty that maybe we shouldn't have been doing that, and the older I got, I thought, and then you learn about lesbianism and, well, maybe we were. And I'm not a lesbian, but why did we do those things? What possessed us to do those things?*

As I talked further with Connie she said that she thinks all of them were experiencing orgasms too, but

> *we didn't know what we were feeling because it was our first experiences with that. [And when they went to the bathroom afterward it was as though they thought] "Okay, I'm satisfied. I can leave now."*

These games of pleasure mimic adult female sexual experience in many ways. It's not that these girls think they know what adult sex is and copy it—the woman lies still while the man does the work? It would have been rare for any of them to have seen sex portrayed in so stark and strange a way. Their doctor game instead shows a more implicit understanding of the role women are supposed to play sexually. They understand this from everything they are taught about being a woman and a "lady" in spite of all the progress women have made vis-à-vis these sex roles in society.

Sexual Feelings Are Good Feelings

Why are we so uncomfortable with the thought that our children have sexual feelings? So much so that our daughters have to play dead to experience them? Recently a mother told me that when her son was six, she and he were watching a sexy scene in a movie, when he said, "Look, Mom. My penis is sticking up!" She said embarrassedly, "That's nice. Just ignore it and it will go away." This same message is given implicitly to girls. Implicit because it is the unusual girl who asks about physical sensations she has around her vaginal area.

A particular instance of such a discussion stands out in my memory. I supervise college students who work at a residential home for out-of-control children. Many of the children there have been abused sexually.

Most have been neglected and physically abused, too. One student told me of a girl, Frannie, about eleven years old, who shocked a group of children and counselors while they were all watching a romantic movie by saying, "My private parts feel all tingly and wet." She was told not to talk about this out loud, and the counselors exchanged glances as if to say, "Look how sexualized she is!" This is a girl who had been abused several times in her short life.

Somebody needed to talk to this girl and confirm that this is a good feeling, and that even though we don't want her to announce it, this is the feeling we would want her to have when she is with someone safe and respectful in the future. Instead, the sexual feeling is seen as bad, a product of the abuse rather than a natural part of growing up to be a sexual person.

Granted, if a boy in this home were to have said something similar, he too would probably have been hushed. But I suspect that the counselors were that much more shocked by the girl's statement than they would have been by the "oversexualized" boys who talk about their erect penises.

It is rare when a girl says to her mother, like this girl in the residential home, "Mom, my vagina is feeling all tingly." By the time they can say this they already know that they shouldn't say it, or feel it. I think that for boys the message we give them is to hush up about it, but that it's okay and normal to experience it—a part of growing up. This may not have always been the case, given the strenuous attacks on boys and masturbation at the turn of the century (involving even straightjackets to keep a sleeping boy's hands away from his private parts), but today, girls are taught to straitjacket themselves. What must not be spoken about, must not be felt.

Particularly for girls, and perhaps in response to our growing awareness of sexual abuse, the idea of private parts has been taken way too far in U.S. culture. It is meant to convey that these parts are private even to oneself. It alienates girls from their bodies. This is part of a wider cultural response to women and their bodies that contributes to disorders such as anorexia and bulimia. Shouldn't girls learn a little bit about "down there" before they reach puberty? This certainly would be a way to undo some of the body anxiety of the teen years before our girls reach them.

Chapter 7

Wanting It and Not Wanting It

"I think I felt something really twisted."
—*Heather, white, 18*

Women and girls buy into an idea of romantic love that means that it is fine to be sexual as long as you are passionately in love with someone and he sweeps you off your feet. Carol Cassell in her book *Swept Away* explains this feeling as a coping mechanism women develop that permits them to be sexual in this society. We "hand our sexuality over to the men in our lives, make them responsible for our submission to them. . . . We won't have sex unless we are seduced, driven, out of control."

Heather and her friend, when they were preteens, would read the *Sweet Valley High* books and act out some of the scenes. "We didn't understand concepts like lesbianism," she said, when they pretended to be boyfriend and girlfriend. One time her mother came into the room while they were naked together in bed. "We were naked all the time," said Heather. When her mother asked "What are you doing?" she answered, "Playing house," so her mother left them alone. In one particular book, *Playing with Fire*, there was a scene at a beach that alluded to a rape. This was the scene that Heather loved best to reenact because the boy was gorgeous and popular. Reflecting back as an adult, she sees that the author was trying to describe a date rape. But as a child reading the book, it was thrilling to enact first the struggle and then the yielding to the popular boy who wanted the girl.

Some women may learn to feel most sexual when they are in this passive position, like a sleeping beauty awakened by a prince. Their fantasies may be of being tied up and forced to submit to someone else's sexual desires, or of being carried off to some dark place where they are made to have sex with someone, or even of being admired and ogled at from afar because they look so sexy. I'm not denying that there is real sexual feeling in this passive position. But it does get women into trouble sexually. Women's fantasies of a man who will come along and actually do all the sexual work might not come true. And after the fantasy, in the nitty-gritty act of sex, women might not find themselves feeling much pleasure unless they know their bodies and know how to pursue it. Although the fantasy is that passionate love will bring with it sexual feeling, the best sexual feelings these girls might have are when they take the time, as they did with their childhood playmates.

It is interesting to hear how adult women, looking back on their childhood experiences, simultaneously use words depicting abuse and pleasure. Leah described how she purposely would sit between two boys on the bus home from school in seventh grade, two boys who would play a game with her by putting their hands on her leg, moving their hands a little bit higher until she would swat each hand away:

So here in the back of the bus are two boys, I'm in between like the two most popular boys in the school. . . . So I would sit in between them and they would basically just sexually harass me. I should have been offended, but I was, like, it's kind of more of a game. They'd put their hand on my knee and then fly it away, and then I'd put my hand on their knee or whatever. [So it was mutual?] Yeah, basically, like I was never upset about it. It was the kind of thing that if an adult had seen it, it would have been inappropriate behavior, and like as an adult woman, if a guy did that I would have probably completely . . . they'd just like try to get like as close as possible, like tight next to my body, 'cause they had my leg going on, and they could get closer and closer like to my thigh or to my chest or whatever. And it was mutual in the sense that there was two of them and only one of me, so like they had the upper hand. [Did it ever get serious?] No, but this was a total game, like we both, and it was kind of like the sexual behavior you get in seventh grade.

Leah said it was both a game and "sexual harassment" of a sort. As a smart, hip college student, she certainly knows about sexual harassment of girls in the schools and also about boys' entitlement and girls' victimization. But in all her education she hasn't been taught about women's ambivalence. It has been easier to teach our daughters to fear sexual victimization than it has been to teach them about the desires they have that make them vulnerable to putting themselves in situations that they may not feel entirely comfortable in. As a college student looking back on this experience, Leah thinks these boys were "belittling her" and "objectifying her," but she also remembers liking it.

It was a game. Just like the games of tying up Barbie dolls or playing dead. In order to feel some sort of sexual pleasure, and to feel wanted by the popular boys, she entered into a game of chase and kiss, only it had more to do with her legs than her lips. In this game, she became the pursued and they the pursuers, which is a lot like the games little girls are taught about anyway, concerning sexual response: The boy pursues, the girl resists but really wants it. It's a dangerous game, I might add, as it will confuse boys about how to read girls' desires.

But it's also not just a game, because a game is usually played among equals. Leah recognized the danger in playing a game that denied boys sexual access while also showing her desire. It taught both the boys and Leah about her position as ambivalent naysayer, encouraging them and putting them off. It also reflected the impossibility of the fact that she could not be in the instigating position without being labeled a "bad" girl.

The fact that she did want it made her feel guilty. She thinks now it may have been even "sick" because she was enjoying being "sexually harassed." In labeling this as sexual harassment rather than as a gender game, a scenario played many times in boy-girl romances, Leah labels herself as a "bad" girl. Did she want to be raped? Something must be terribly wrong with her, she thinks.

Was it still sexual harassment if she enjoyed it? The elements were there. Leah was trapped between them in the bus (though she chose to sit there); there were two against one (though she liked the attention); they were trying to push her to let them feel up her leg (though wasn't she really the one in power as she swatted them away); they really were thinking of her just as a conquest or as a loose girl (though she was aware of that and continued); and finally, she enjoyed it. How should girls reconcile the pleasure of being treated as a sexual object with the codes governing good girl behavior?

Take, for example, Toni. Toni grew up in New York City in what can only be called a chaotic house that her mother tried to hold together in every way she could. Toni's father was a drug addict and her parents would fight constantly about money—her father wanting it for drugs, and her mother keeping it for food. The kids in the family fought constantly, too: "We wasn't going to sit there and let him do that, so we was all in there." The family violence carried her to the streets, where she was in a group called "The Sweet Seven," who would go around beating people up, "just to be beating them up."

Despite this background, Toni's story here is not about violence or drugs. It's about a small amount of pleasure she had growing up with her cousin, who was a couple years older. This cousin lived with her, and would visit her at night, when she was in bed pretending to be asleep. He would feel her up and down and eventually had sex with her. In relating these events Toni vacillated between the grown-up view she holds now, that she was responsible because she allowed it to happen and enjoyed it, and the child's view she held then, that she had nothing to do with it because she was "asleep."

She told me, "When we were little we actually had sex. It was about maybe age seven. . . . I was sleeping, actually, and he came and he was feeling on me, and I was about seven or eight years old and it felt good, so I continued to act like I was asleep but I wasn't asleep." I asked her if this was because she enjoyed it, and she said, "Right, but I never told anybody. And he did it a lot, several times." When I asked if she felt any guilt about this, she said, "No, because I was asleep." Then she laughed. I asked if her enjoyment had to do with sexual feelings and she explained, "I did have sexual feelings at the time. All I know is that it felt good and I didn't want him to know that I was feeling good about it so I didn't wake up. And so I didn't say anything about it. And we never discussed it." I wanted to know more about her pretending to be asleep, worried that this was a form of sexual abuse. I asked, "What do you think stopped you from actually fully participating?" She replied:

> Because if I let him know that I liked it, then I would have to participate and, then he's supposed to be my cousin, and even though he wasn't really my cousin, we were supposed to have a tie. . . . [That made it] more taboo, right?

Later in the interview I asked her why she didn't consider what she did with her cousin to be "sex" (somewhere in a discussion of other things she had said that it wasn't). Toni answered, "It wasn't sex! I didn't participate

. . . I wasn't involved in it. I know penetration is considered sex, but I didn't consider it sex at the time."

Pretending to be asleep, like the girls who pretended to be dead or tied up, allowed Toni to feel her sexual pleasure but to not be responsible for it, to "other" it, and to not have to acknowledge herself as a sexual being. Today we might call this act abuse, thinking that she was young and couldn't speak up for herself, and believing that whether or not she felt pleasure, she was "seduced" by an older, more experienced cousin into learning about sexual feelings that she had no business learning about at that age. But it's unclear whether this is abusive or not. If it were an adult who came in the middle of the night, even if Toni enjoyed it and pretended to be asleep, we would know this was abuse. And we wouldn't hold her responsible for telling him to stop. We would consider her too young to be able to judge that this might hurt her in the long run, and too young to be able to stick up for herself with an authority figure. Both of these reasons don't address the complexity of the situation.

The fact that it is another child, her "cousin," who is doing this to her, makes it a little different. In Toni's memory she feels a clear sense of being able to stop it if she wanted to, but she doesn't stop it and doesn't want to. Neither does she call this experience abuse. In fact, she clearly differentiates it from a rape that happened when she was a few years older. Even in retrospect, Toni said, the overall feeling was enjoyment.

Moving from New York City to a New England suburb, we find similar examples of girls discovering ways to experience what they want without having to show that they want it, as well as their confusion about how society would understand their behavior. Chrissie, in the first grade, went on a hike with her class and the boys disappeared into the woods. The teacher asked her to go find the boys and bring them back.

> So I went and these boys grabbed me sort of and they said you're going to have to kiss this other boy. And I can't remember if I kissed him or anything but feeling like I was special enough to be, like, they wanted to catch me and have me kiss him. I enjoyed the drama and I enjoyed the whole sort of thing. It wasn't even as though they thought they had to coerce me, they didn't really have to do that sort of thing. . . . I know it's sick. Yeah, I want to be raped.

Something about Chrissie's narrative, as well as the narrative of others, reflects the current trend in our culture about sexuality, that it is almost al-

ways about victimization, that there are no in-betweens or ambivalences about things called "date rape" or "sexual abuse." The boys grabbed her so it's a rape.

"No is No," male college students are taught with regard to date rape. So the girl who says "no" and still sort of wants it is a "bad" girl. "Good" girls say no and mean it. What Chrissie didn't know when she said she is "sick" because she "wants to be raped," is that the rape scenario (being passive and then forced to participate) is a sexual script that all girls are taught. For some it's the only way they know they can feel pleasure. Some girls, in a dreamlike way, want to be captured and adored and admired and forced to feel pleasure. But this is not the same as wanting to be raped.

Heather, whom I spoke of at the beginning of this chapter, played out scenes from her teenage romance books with her best friend, Bess. The two would get naked under the covers and enact some of the scenes from the book, always being involved and not involved at the same time, because one would act like a director, instructing the other where to be and how to act to make the scene almost identical to the scene in the book. In retrospect, though, Heather is confused about her play, because she and her friend enjoyed enacting a rape scene. Indeed she and Bess had a deep interest in reenacting a rape scene from *Playing with Fire*.

> *I think I felt something really twisted. I didn't understand rape at the time. I didn't really understand that, you know, a woman doesn't want to have sex. I think because in this book the boy who she was on the beach with was supposed to be this really popular gorgeous guy. So I think that in my eight-year-old mindset I thought that was something really exciting. Like this was a cool thing to play at, and now that I think about it, I mean I am so against rape now, and when people say that women have rape wishes or whatever, I'm like, "What are you talking about?" But at the same time . . . it was kind of like the perfect thing for that stage of life, you know [and then Bess moved away], and then I didn't have to confront her or see her.*

Notice that Heather told me that she didn't understand at that age that "a woman doesn't want to have sex." In her eight-year-old mind, as she put it, she wanted to have sex and couldn't see anything wrong with being passionately "taken" by a boy on the beach. She didn't understand that the girl in the story's resistance might be because the girl actually didn't want to have sex that way. This points to the positive attitude toward desire that an eight-year-old can have before acculturation teaches girls about "proper" attitudes toward sexual feeling.

Looking at it from an eight-year-old's perspective, Heather seems kind of healthy, rather than, as in her own words, "twisted." It's as if she hasn't quite learned the gender relations of predator and object, and misreads the book to be about two mutually excited teenagers. On the other hand, she does understand that good girls do resist, and that there is excitement in that resistance, in playing out the ambivalence.

Chapter 8

Two Kinds of Guilty Pleasure

*"I kind of like experienced kissing a girl—I think about it now like,
'Oh, God!'"*
—Tai, Puerto Rican, 30

Being a "good girl" and resisting men's advances is especially important to
Puerto Rican girls. In spite of Ricky Martin's song of *una chica loca* (a crazy
girl) who makes him drink champagne and dance naked in the rain, such
stereotypes of aggressive Latina sexuality are not played out in childhood,
where many girls live under the "cult of the virgin" and among "macho
men." Many of these girls were so close to their mothers they slept with
them every night into their teens, avoiding childhood sexuality.

Whereas some girls can negotiate slightly (or somewhat) around
wanting it and not wanting it (like Toni, who in the last chapter was
"asleep," or Heather, who allowed herself the pleasure and excitement of
being "harassed"), some girls feel enormous guilt about this ambivalence.
Tai and Diana, both Puerto Rican women, had childhoods in which they
began to learn about their own bodies, the bodies of others, sexual pleasure, and sexual desire, but they also felt deep ambivalence and thus guilt.
Most of the other Puerto Rican women I interviewed did not share many
childhood secrets of sexual pleasure or desire. Maybe they kept these stories to themselves, the guilt too immense. Perhaps the protection from
their mothers and the worship of virginity, both strong aspects of Puerto
Rican culture, precluded development of this kind of play.

Diana and Tai, although sexual, had two very different kinds of initiations. Both experienced pleasure, both made choices to experience that pleasure, and both felt guilty afterward. Even though both felt tremendous guilt, today we would call one experience abuse, the other play; the stories show two kinds of guilty pleasure.

Diana was tough. Today, if you were to meet her as a parent at a PTA meeting, you wouldn't want to contradict her. As a child, I would imagine, she was a force to be reckoned with. Her memories of childhood included the boy whose "ass [she] kicked every day" and the day she punched a teacher who "had this thing" with her. Though she fought with her sister every day of her life, the one time she raised her hand to hit her mother, her mother "beat the shit out of [her]" and that was that. Diana never tried it again. Out of all of her family members, it was neither Diana nor her mother who was "the hitter." This distinction goes to her father, who used to beat the kids up regularly, at times losing control because he drank. She recalled:

> Once he almost killed me. I was laying down in the sofa because I was crying, and he threw me with a big figurine, a big one that we had. He threw it, and if I didn't, if I wouldn't have stood up, it would have hit me. But it was because he used to drink at that time.

Living in a household with three stepbrothers, two brothers, and a sister, Diana had learned to fight for what she wanted. Parental supervision was nearly absent. She described herself as different from the other kids: "I was meaner."

The story of Diana's sexual initiation came out gradually, with reluctance. She was a kind person to interview, and seemed to want to help me out, feeling bad when she couldn't or didn't answer a question. A large woman with a baby face, long hair, and soft cheeks, her English, which was her second language, was pretty good, but she talked to me in streetwise words. Early in the interview she told me repeatedly that her memory was gone, that she can't remember much. And when I asked about kissing games she talked about her first boyfriend, whom she became involved with at the age of ten; "just a kiss," she said. Later, the truth came out. She told of an older female cousin who taught Diana what she knew and engineered Diana's sexual initiation.

The use of the word initiation may be inappropriate, as I have argued already that children are sexual and have sexual feelings from early on. But in this case, initiation refers to a transformative experience in which a child or teen comes to see herself as a sexual being, someone with sexual feelings and desires.

Early in the interview Diana answered simple questions about sexual games by saying, "I was curious, I was curious." She was cryptic, avoiding something. Later, when I brought this question of curiosity up again, her eyes welled up with tears, and she said, "My cousin. She taught me a lot of bad things." With a sigh Diana went on:

I just want to say she [her cousin Tina] made me have sex with my own cousin when we were young. I was nine years old.

She then added:

Her brother. He's my cousin. He was maybe two years older. . . . She didn't, like, make us, but we were so by her, you know, I didn't know how it happened. All I know is she started it, you know, and we used to do it.

As the interview progressed I discovered that this had happened quite frequently over a period of two years. Diana said, "I used to like it." But when she turned eleven,

then I became, then I had my period. I never did it again. After that I never did it. And then maybe a few years after that, that's when I realized it was wrong, and I hated her. I hated her.

Diana holds simultaneously two positions: Her cousin Tina was wrong to make her do this; her cousin didn't make her do it because she enjoyed it. It was wrong; and it was pleasurable.

There are all sorts of reasons to call what Diana's cousin had her do wrong. First, there's Diana's age: only nine. Intercourse is rarely the first thing that nine-year-olds come up with as a way to experiment with their bodies and their sexuality. In addition, it is rare that a girl would come to this male-oriented pleasure on her own.

The elements of voyeurism and coercion also make this exploitation. This older girl had power over the two younger children, the power to teach them about a lot of things because they were "by her," as Diana put it, so frequently. This older cousin should have had the knowledge that would indicate to her that Diana might grow up to regret this early sex, as well she did.

More important, there is an element of "wrongfulness" particular to the Puerto Rican community that affects Diana greatly: She lost her virginity there. Years later her husband and her father still argue about it. Her husband, whom Diana married in her teens, often reminds her father that he "didn't take her as a virgin," as if to apologize to the father for having married Diana so young. When Diana finally told her father the whole story, her father wanted to "kick his ass"—the ass of the now thirty-year-old man who as an eleven-year-old boy had taken his daughter's virginity, and not that of the female cousin who had arranged it.

The conversation between Diana's husband and her father has little to do with Diana's experience, her guilt or her pleasure. It has to do only with the disrespect a man shows another man by "taking" the daughter's virginity. Before this experience, she was prized as a virgin; after, she was ruined as a sexual girl. Diana knows this. Still, her own regret today may have less to do with when she was "taken" and more to do with her agreeing to participate, her pleasure, and the fact that the boy was her cousin, part of the family.

Diana's regret is indeed immense.

All my life is—my mind is stupid for making all those mistakes. . . . I should have known better than that . . . maybe that's what destroyed my career in school. . . . I used to always think about that. Maybe that has fucked up my whole life.

Her story shows the capacity for children to enjoy sex, but also the great shame and preoccupation that having sex too early can bring. Who knows if it actually took her away from her schoolwork, especially considering her six siblings, her alcoholic father, and a way of life that kept her in the streets day and night. There was other interference.

Today social services would label these early sexual encounters as abuse, qualified as abuse either of a child by a child or by a teen perpetrated on two children. It would be presumed that Tina, her cousin, probably had been sexually abused herself and that is why she made these children do what she wanted them to do. Victims of sexual abuse sometimes act out their trauma on other children. Diana would be a victim in this scenario. And I have to agree that this cousin, Tina, did something that hurt Diana and her cousin.

But while Diana's remorse and guilt over her part in it should not be denied, she also carries the memory of the pleasure it gave her. Is that part so wrong? Can we hold in one hand her enjoyment of the "game," while in the other feel awful about the abuse? That would be to say that the pleasure in and of itself is not wrong.

Experts in child sexual abuse would say that Diana became oversexualized because of this early experience. Hypersexualization is indeed the one symptom that over and over again differentiates the symptomatology of sexually abused children from those who have been physically abused or neglected. These same experts would say that she became preoccupied in a way that interfered with normal friendships and school pleasures. Having problems in school is on the list of the many symptoms sexually abused children develop. But she was curious. She was curious.

The real shame here is not Diana's sexual curiosity; it is that her interest was not allowed to develop on its own. Her cousin's manipulations introduced into Diana's life elements of adult heterosexuality that she would not have encountered in our culture until later. Though the impulse might be to mourn her lost youth or her lost agency, it's important to remember the pleasure she experienced. Would that that pleasure had come about from her own choices. And would that it all had occurred in a context where girls were given the opportunity to learn about sex and to experiment with their bodies to find out what is truly pleasing to them. This would be a context free from the male guardians of virginity or from the older cousins who frame girls' sexuality in terms of intercourse with men.

Growing up in a similar neighborhood and with similar restrictions on good girls, as well as with the cult of virginity for Puerto Rican girls, Tai found a way to experience sexual pleasure, however guilty it made her feel. Her experience might serve to contrast with Diana's in these ways: She chose to do what she did totally and fully; she experimented with what felt good and found it; it did not preoccupy her but instead possibly even enhanced her childhood. On the other hand, she, like Diana, still feels guilty about what she did and didn't know what to make of the fact that she had been aroused as a child, with another little girl.

While Tai grew up in a neighborhood similar to Diana's in New York City, she led a much more sheltered life. She remembered the heat of the neighborhood, and people lining up to buy drugs down her street. But her parents were religious, and her time with her four brothers was often spent in church activities.

Tai's major sexual experience as a child came out of a friendship with a girl in her mother's best friend's family. There were five children in this family, and although she was friends with all the children, and even played kissing games with the boys, it was with the girl in this family that Tai experimented with sexual pleasure:

> *Oh boy, this is a secret, and nobody knows about this. [Laughs] Okay. This is a major secret. Well, I don't remember how that was. I know I was young, and one of the girls, it must have been the youngest one, and she kind of brought this on. But when she would spend time in the house and there was no one else, it was just me and her. So we used to play house, and of course one of us had to be the husband and one had to be the wife, because that time it was always a husband and a wife, you know, not like nowadays . . . and the dolls were the babies, or whatever, and I kinda like experienced kissing a girl, which was like—I think about it now like, Oh God!! But then . . . I was growing up. I was like, oh gosh, this is like a major secret. No one can know about this, and even when I see her it never came up. . . . Actually, ummm, body contact. Both. 'Cause some girls, you know, we used to shower together, take a bath together and everything, and yeah, there was touching involved.*

Tai took a long time to describe what she and this girl did together, punctuating her narrative several times with exclamations of how big a secret she was about to tell me. In her story, the part of her experience that she expressed the most shame over was the idea that there was "body contact." And she added the word "both." Did she mean both were doing the touching? Both were involved? Neither girl was the passive recipient? I wondered here, because of her brevity, whether I was even getting the whole story. She found it so hard to say what she wanted to say that I didn't feel comfortable pursuing her or asking her to speak more graphically. I would have had to introduce words that she wasn't using, and it is so difficult to describe these experiences without using words that evoke feelings of being dirty and ashamed or the medical and clinical side of sex. What words could I have used? I let the words "body contact" suffice.

I wondered too why this experience was so enormously hard to talk about. She had never talked about this with anyone before. Why was this her biggest secret? Because it was with another girl? Guessing at what might explain her guilt, I asked, "Was it pleasurable at the time?"

> *I would say, yeah. You know, because it was something we were just, we were experiencing, like I had never experienced with anyone else be-*

sides the kissing. . . . So it was like we were exploring and, umm, yeah, so there was some pleasure there . . . I did get aroused, you know, during that time when there was the body contact and the touching and stuff.

At the time Tai didn't feel guilty about it, though both girls kept it a secret. Only later did guilt enter into the equation. She later labeled the experience a lesbian one and, as a heterosexual adult, this same-sex encounter made her (and continues to make her) feel guilty and wrong:

Nowadays being a lesbian is like so free. You know? Or like being gay men. Yeah, back then it was taboo, like you know you can't do this. Everyone was like very secret about it. But at that age I didn't know about lesbianism or anything like that. . . . Then after, when I was growing up, I was like, oh, they do that? You know?

Even though Tai was eleven and the other girl was eight, Tai sees the other girl as the instigator.

Because she was the type like, she was in control. She was the one who would come up with the "Okay, we're going to play this today." And I would go along with it, and I didn't feel bad about letting her be in control.

With Tai, it is the arousal, the illicit pleasure, and the fact that it was with another girl that makes this experience her "biggest secret." She mentioned that she and her girlfriends, as adults, once discussed whether or not they would or could have a lesbian relationship; during the interview, she confessed to me, "I didn't tell them about this."

But why shouldn't this experience be classified as lesbian? On the one hand we can say it fits the bill. Two girls. Sex. On the other hand, childhood sexual play and games can't be classified in the same way as adult sex. It's not a choice, not a lifestyle, not an orientation—yet. It's childhood. To call this experience *only* experimentation, though, takes something away from the idea that this pleasure in childhood is something real.

Diana and Tai both had sexual experiences in childhood that today they look back on seriously. Both of these experiences meant something to them in terms of how they defined themselves sexually. Neither could quite accept the sexual pleasure they felt as something positive. Because of their Puerto Rican upbringing, the loss of virginity is disruptive for Diana.

But also the fact that intercourse is not the best way for a girl to learn about herself and her sexual feelings, especially not under the command of an older cousin, Diana feels permanently damaged. Tai, on the other hand, had a more gentle introduction to sexual pleasure, from another girl, a younger girl. And although her experience brought with it some confusion and guilt, there was also some delight. Perhaps her delight was more unspoken, something that I as an interviewer had to intuit in her laughter and expressions of exuberant exclamations as she told her story. Perhaps it was only in contrast to Diana, the burden of whose guilt and trauma seemed constantly present in the interview, a shroud she could not throw off, as an adult, with a laugh.

Chapter 9

African-American Girls and Their Secrets

*"To name ourselves rather than be named we must first see ourselves.
. . . So long unmirrored, we may have forgotten how we look."*
—*Lorraine O'Grady, in* Olympia's Maid: Reclaiming Female Black
    Subjectivity

African-American women "have no acknowledged sexuality," according to Hortense Spillers, a scholar who writes about Black women and fiction. But Gail Wyatt, an African-American psychologist at the University of California at Los Angeles, reminds us in her book *Stolen Lives* that when there isn't a "deafening silence" there is a barrage of "negative messages and expectations" about an African-American girl's ability to control her sexuality. Researchers consistently look at African-American girls' sexual behavior in terms of "deviance" rather than "development." Ironically, the media perpetuates the stereotype of the promiscuous Black teen by disproportionately profiling Black girls who are "out of control" and at high risk for early pregnancy. They set up an assumption that all American Black girls grow up in the projects and city streets and add to that false assumption that these urban girls are loose and immoral. African-American girls and women, however, do have sexual lives in childhood similar to white girls, and experiences that are not always as difficult or as tragic as the media would have you believe.

Because of the prevalence of such stereotypes about African-American girls and women and their sexuality, and because of how these stereotypes affect these girls, I chose to write about them in a separate chapter. Their stories are also integrated in other chapters with the stories of white girls, middle-class and low-income girls, and girls from other minority groups. But because there appears to be an absence of attention to healthy development in African-American girls, it is particularly important to give these girls and women a space here where their experiences are heard together. This does not mean their experiences are so different. In fact, the only difference is that African-American girls tend to play with boys rather than other girls.

Other ethnic groups of girls aren't covered in separate chapters simply because I didn't interview enough of a variety within each group to feel comfortable making statements about them as a whole. Although I interviewed a number of Puerto Rican women who live in the States, unlike the interviews with African-American women and girls, I interviewed very few girls, and most of the women came from the same neighborhood. These interviews are intermingled in other chapters, and I hope they serve as a springboard for studying how other racial stereotypes may affect young girls' sexual development.

Some but not most of the interviews of African-American women and girls took place in a housing project, and some of these sexual stories take place in the context of very difficult childhoods, a few involving abuse; however, even the girls who grew up under these circumstances also shared happy tales of childhood exploration and healthy interest in sex.

Included also are stories about middle-class African-American girls whose similarities to other middle-class girls are immense. These girls and women share a history of oppression with other Black girls, but this oppression, given the neighborhood, the income, and the decade in which they lived, affects them to differing degrees. Altogether, the stories of Black girls and women in this chapter do not and cannot coalesce into one single story of African-American girlhood. Yet overwhelmingly, they are positive stories, and presented together will show a certain strength and honor and healthy sexual presence in African-American girls.

Toni, Josephine, O'Brishia, and Denitra grew up in the projects. Called "urban girls" today, they experienced much the same environment that Shamika, Tanisha, and Rashonda, the youngest African-American girls I interviewed, are experiencing today. Even though they all grew up or are growing up in the city, they defy stereotyping. Some of these girls were out of control and some were just observers of the scene. Some were beaten and abused, some protected or able to avoid abuse through the help of others. Some could leave their neighborhoods, some stayed, and some who had left returned and ended up being brought down. Some girls had sex early and seemed not to respect their parents or teachers; others stayed far away from boys and did their homework. African-American girls are as different from one another as white girls.

There are Robin and Marissa, both college girls at a good school. Both had warm, upper-middle-class upbringings with loving parents who kept a close watch on them. Their experiences are not much different from the white girls who grew up in the suburbs and whose parents were professionals. And yet they remain African-American women, carrying additional burdens because of racial prejudice and special talents because of racial heritage.

Lillian, Cora, and Betty grew up in the 1940s and '50s in urban areas, but with a lot of the South in their families and personalities. They knew the "switch" as a rightly deserved punishment, and laughed about it looking back, but they also got undeserved beatings, some that left lifelong scars. They had sex with boys or older men fairly early, getting pregnant and marrying in their teens like many of their peers. Despite such "sophistication," that didn't mean they didn't play chase and kiss, post office, or house!

Valerie, Lynn, Felicia, Charise—they grew up in the fifties, sixties, and seventies in a city neighborhood. They grew up in an African-American working-class neighborhood, usually with fathers around, extended families, and church playing a big part of their lives. They didn't suffer the abuse that Betty, Cora, and Lillian did. But like those three, they too played around and experimented with boys in a way that shows interest and self-esteem.

While their games show a resistance to good girl mythology, a particularly white mythology, as well as a healthy, if secret, attitude toward sexual play and games, they differed from white girls in one respect: most African-American women do not remember playing sexual games with other *girls*. While the white women I interviewed had played games with either boys or girls, African-American women played primarily with boys. The same sense of experimentation and pleasure is present, only it occurs mostly in games with boys. The ones who played with other girls are the middle-class African-American girls; for them, there was a lot more freedom to experiment and play before teenage sexuality grabbed them. Teenage sexuality gets pushed on the urban girls a bit sooner, leaving less room for girl-to-girl sexual play.

Cora, a fifty-seven-year-old woman who grew up in the South and then moved to the city projects, remembered her little games with the boys with great pleasure.

> Y'know, we would be out in the yard. Y'know, we always would be in the open, not in no little closed part . . . this was our little thing and this was the life that we wanted to live. We were seven, eight, nine, ten . . . so it was just the typical little stuff that we used to do. . . . We want to get married and have children. . . . I know my mother would say, Oh, y'know, you don't have no business playing like that . . . and we just never told them. We knew we not supposed to do that. Okay, after I got my period where she always tell me to keep your dress down.

One thing that may have prevented more exploration in Cora's childhood was the threat of beatings. Her father would abuse her brutally, sometimes to bleeding; she still bears the scars. The possibility of a beating kept her and children like her scared.

> One time, me and my girlfriend and the brother they always, they want to show private parts, and I say, "Oh no, no, we can't do that, 'cuz Mom" and y'know they call their grandmother, Moe, they call her Moe and my mother we called Mama, and so we say, "No, no, we can't." I said we couldn't go that route. . . . Yeah, and so I felt a little guilty. We were scared if one told it everybody gonna get in trouble.

In contrast, Lillian had a lot more gumption. She was one of those girls who played quite a few sexual games, remembered them fondly, and never worried about whether she was "normal" or not.

Lillian, now sixty-three years old, played a funny little game with the boys in her neighborhood when she was a preteen.

> We played "pinch and grow." The girls would stand in the closet or in the corner of a dark room, and you never knew who was comin' at you, but it would be a guy, and he would run in and the fellows always felt that if you'd pinch the girls' boobs they'd grow. . . . I loved it! I thought it was the greatest thing! 'Cuz pinch and grow worked two ways. The guys would be in the room and the girls would have to go in there and would pinch a little lower . . . the girls would call it grab and hang. . . . I liked the idea of doing that because I felt it was something I could get away with doing and nobody knew who did it.

She also talked about the old-fashioned game of Post Office:

> *Post Office was different. . . . You didn't know who the guy was that*
> *came in, but you'd have to go to the post office to mail a letter or to buy*
> *a stamp or whatever, and you knew that there was a guy in there. But*
> *no one on the other side knew what was going on. So you could go in*
> *there and do darn near anything depending on how fresh the fellow was*
> *or how fresh the girls was. . . . It wasn't until I was much older that I*
> *did things that I felt that I was really way in over my head and didn't*
> *know how to get out of it. . . . It was still play. It was a lot of fun.*

And there was a game in which she and her friends would run into the al-
leys to meet a boy, kiss in a doorway, and plan to meet in secret later at
night.

> *Mmmmm. There was a lot of things that we did. I guess you might con-*
> *sider them games, but then again they're not games. We'd write notes*
> *back and forth and tell each other what we're gonna do, and then we'd*
> *try to make that come true. . . . And I used to tell him I'd meet him in*
> *the basement, and I guess that's where I learned a lot about sex, because*
> *we called it playing the game. They'd play hide-and-seek outside and I'd*
> *be in the basement, and I'd open the door, and that was when the one*
> *twin would come in to hide. The other twin happened to notice that this*
> *one was going there and they could never find him. . . . One day both of*
> *them came in. Well, there was nothing goin' on that day, and then my*
> *mom heard about my back door being open down there. So that was*
> *over.*

Despite a variety of hardships that Lillian had suffered before she turned
thirteen—the threat of beatings by her grandmother, a chaotic home
life—she still played several of these games that involved sexual feelings
and sexual fun. Like ball games with boys:

> *If you could hit him you had to go up in the back with him to soothe his*
> *ache. We didn't have a name for that, but all the girls would try to hit*
> *him in the testicles, because wherever you hit him with the ball you had*
> *to rub that spot.*

She also played a game where the kids would sit in a circle and pass around
a cigarette: "We never smoked, but whoever dropped an ash would have to

take off a piece of clothing." She even encouraged her friends' sexuality, explicitly instructing, "C'mon Mary, you'll like it. You know, it ain't bad. Let him put his finger over there. You'll be surprised what'll happen." Then Mary would say, "*Oh, my God, you're dirty!!!*" Lillian would say right back, "It's not dirty. That's life."

There's a lot of power and pleasure in Lillian's childhood explorations with boys and sex. She invited it. She taught other girls about it. Maybe she even talked about pleasure: "You'll be surprised what'll happen." She went on to tell her best friend, in a healthy way, that sex is not dirty, it's "life." Despite this seeming maturity, Lillian knew nothing about contraception. In addition, she maybe trusted men too much.

At thirteen, Lillian got pregnant because of a deception. Lillian got pregnant from a twenty-eight-year-old man whom she had sex with willingly. He said he loved her. He said he would protect her. He said he would wear a condom, and he did. But when she got pregnant, he told her that he had purposely put a hole in the condom before having sex with her. Nevertheless, she married him. Not unexpectedly, he was not a good husband; he beat her, just as she had been beaten by her grandmother at home. After enduring beatings at home for such a long time, a girl will sometimes take the first chance she gets to get out of her house, even if she ends up in a similar situation elsewhere. But how was she to know at thirteen?

Lillian's sex education until the age of thirteen was a sex education in which she felt like a full participant, not a victim, not a passive object. That's a good way to feel as a child. So where did things go wrong? The problem may not have been in the sexual games but in the partner whom she trusted, the man who lied to her. Raised by a grandmother who beat her, unprotected by parents, her decision to hang around a twenty-eight-year-old man came from lack of supervision rather than a self-destructive impulse.

Many of the other stories of African-American girls, including the more recent ones, have better endings, and they have been told in previous chapters where they fit, unseparated from their sisters. In chapters on "chase and kiss" or "practice kissing," African-American girls' stories show Charise, for example, who played "catch a girl, kiss a girl" (at least that's what the boys called it), where the girls would eventually go off to kiss the boy who caught them in the alley. And there is Yvonne, who kissed boys in truth-or-dare games. Jeanine practice-kissed a boy in a closet from about the age of six until it "really" mattered, around age twelve.

Nevertheless, few of the African-American women worried about whether what they had done was normal or not. It is possible that because I was white, they didn't want to be in the position of asking a white woman to judge them on issues of normality. Perhaps they thought that my normal couldn't possibly be theirs. But none of the African-American women that my assistant Bev Colston interviewed asked her this question either, and she is Black. None seemed as concerned as the white girls we interviewed to ask of their experiences, "Is this typical?" or "Am I normal?"

It could be that African-American women gave up a long time ago trying to understand normal, which meant to them trying to measure up to white society's version of what a "good" or "normal" girl was. There is a long history of white people calling African-American people abnormal or crazy because they are different. Perhaps, as Lillian said, even without sex education, they simply grew up knowing that sex was a part of life. Yet these guesses do not fully answer the question.

Perhaps the lack of girl-to-girl games explains why African-American women, looking back, had fewer concerns about whether they were normal. In the few girl-to-girl sexual games that African-American women remembered, they described them as being about curiosity and experimentation, rather than desire. Lynn played one such game with another little girl, her best friend Billie.

> *They were games like mostly close examination games. Yes, very close examination games. It wasn't a game, but it was really like intense curiosity and like just having to see absolutely everything. So I remember that clearly. . . . So it was something with having to do with health and investigation—pure science and health, and so all the rules would follow from that. We would come up with things that we thought might be wrong and that had to be checked out. And everything was always okay after a thorough checkup . . . maybe we assured ourselves too that everything was okay and normal.*

Arlene had a very protective mother who was concerned that she not get in trouble with boys. Like the middle-class white mothers, she tried to protect her daughter from them. For example, she would not allow Arlene to have boys in the clubhouse, although Arlene would sneak them in. She moved the family when Arlene was twelve, to get her out of this "fast" neighborhood where kids started having sex early. Arlene remembered all-girl sleepovers at this age and earlier, where the girls "getting dressed would show each other stuff." It didn't feel sexual, she recalled, "it felt curious." Like other African-American women interviewed, she drew a boundary there. She did not identify play as sexual if it was with other girls.

Valerie also described a girl-to-girl experience that is similar to Arlene's; it is about curiosity rather than sexual feeling. She showed her growing breasts to other girls, and they showed her theirs, everyone comparing to see if everything was all right. Valerie's mother, like Arlene's, was "very strict, very straight with everything." With this straightness at home, curiosity games may have been the limit to what they permitted themselves.

Strictness and straightness in African-American families who have close ties with their church may be one reason sexual play between girls didn't go very far. But the concern was probably for a different kind of straightness: that is to say, the taboo against homosexuality in African-American culture. Often noted in relation to African-American men who feel the need to prove their masculinity and power to a world that tries to beat them down, this taboo is well documented. But what about for girls? Does the fear of homosexuality extend to them? It would seem so.

Thirteen-year-old Kalinda wouldn't play truth-or-dare games because it was too close to kissing girls.

> But I mean, like I won't kiss somebody because we could be like five girls and like two boys playing. And every girl has this dare to kiss both of the boys, and then when it's your turn to kiss 'em, like everybody has already kissed him. It's like kissing all the other girls and I don't like that.
> . . . If you want to kiss the boy that just kissed five other girls, why don't you kiss the five girls, because it seems like it's the same thing.

What kinds of risks do girls who play sexual games with boys take? Rarely does a girl-to-girl game become abusive. In girl-to-boy games girls have to set boundaries more clearly. LaShauna, a twelve-year-old, described this in her idyllic treehouse setup with Julio.

> I mean, like, I wouldn't necessarily lay on top of him, but I'd like hug him and stuff. And then I wasn't too into reading, but when I did have a chance to read I would read to him and stuff. . . . And I knew that as long as he didn't go over this line, like there was a boundary, as long as he didn't cross over it, that it was okay.

LaShauna knows the boundary. But the risk for other girls may be abuse or getting too sexual too soon and orienting their own sensuality and sexuality toward boys' pleasures rather than giving themselves space and time to discover their own bodies.

Playing sexual games with other girls can help girls understand themselves before seeing themselves so totally from a male perspective, as adolescent girls often do. Through this kind of play they begin to experiment with adult images and versions of sexuality before being forced to face a male-defined adult world of sex, a world that requires boundary-setting from girls and an assertiveness they may not yet have developed. The transition to real-life heterosexual sexual relationships can be a dangerous one for girls, both in terms of the expectations regarding romance and the amount of violence and devastation that can take place in the high school years. Girl-girl play may be a safe haven before the storm, but African-American girls look upon such play with suspicion.

From another perspective, African-American girls' play with boys may be helpful to them in different ways. While it may put them at risk of exposure to more male-related definitions of their own sexuality before they have a chance to understand it themselves, it may also help them to grow up to be more comfortable around boys. They may be more able than girls who play with other girls to envision themselves later as sexual partners to men, rather than objects, prey, or victims. They may also develop a special empathy for boys and men as being just as vulnerable as they are underneath that veneer of hypersexualized masculinity that many boys are encouraged to develop in adolescence. Still, it wasn't only a preference for girl-boy sexual play that many African-American girls showed, but sometimes a fear of girl-girl play.

Marissa, from an upper-middle-class African-American family on the West Coast, also balked at girl-to-girl sexual games. In one instance, she had gone to a predominantly white summer camp where the girls decided to have a "naked party." All the girls took their clothes off and ran around the campground; Marissa was the only one to keep them on. To her, the whole experience was "really scary."

As the home-schooled daughter of a family that prayed together every morning, Marissa's feelings could have been due to her strict upbringing. The whole idea of girls playing this way was most likely foreign and shocking to her. Marissa was also the girl who felt terribly guilty about the time she sat naked in the dark with a younger girl, not touching, but feeling the thrill of just being naked. Strictness in families may have more bearing on the way children make sense of sexual play and games than on whether or not they play them.

The strictness in African-American families can be a source of pride. There is often also humor in the older African-American women's memories of their mothers or fathers getting out a switch, "a peach tree limb that was about two miles long," to beat them with when they were bad. This strictness sometimes can seem too violently enacted or, ironically, to go hand in hand with a lack of supervision over the children. Still, it reflects a respect for family rules and parents' authority.

While the strictness around sexuality that white girls described was more about being a good girl and not a slut, the strictness that the African-American girls described as present in their families seemed to be either about respect or about protection. Respecting one's elders by not talking back, making trouble, or creating more work for them meant children were forced to obey parents more exactly. When the strictness came in the form of protection, these girls had fewer opportunities to play sexual games.

The strictness may also have come out of a fear that their daughters would be judged as "typically oversexual black women." Aware of the conventional assumptions and the particular vulnerabilities to being stereotyped as loose and immoral, black families may have created a protected space around their daughters. Unfortunately, this protection may have had its costs in terms of freedom even within the family.

More than white girls, African-American and Puerto Rican girls orient their sexuality toward boys and men. This may be because they play more with boys or because the gender relations of adulthood, where men are dominant, play out in their childhood games. Though this extra gender contact makes them more comfortable with boys, it could make them vulnerable to engaging earlier in sex. In a later chapter called "Too Sexual Too Soon," I give examples of girls' vulnerability to defining their sexuality in terms of pleasing boys and men.

Feminist author and cultural critic bell hooks, speaking for African-American women, writes: "We lose sight of the way in which the ability to experience and know pleasure is an essential ingredient of wellness." A challenge for African-American women that is different from white women is to find a comfortable sexuality that works with their culture and yet won't substantiate white myths of looseness and lack of control in the African-American community.

Janie Ward, educator and author of *The Skin We're In*, a book for African-American parents today, writes of the temptation among African-American adolescents to invest in clothing and appearance as a means of distinguishing themselves in a frequently dismissive society. Feeling unseen and invisible in the larger culture, it may be similarly tempting to girls to become an object to someone, to be admired and felt and seen and desired.

African-American girls take a risk in losing themselves to the white myth of the loose African-American woman when they acknowledge their own sexual desire. While the image of the sexual Black woman might serve to make white women feel more pure or good in a world that tries to put down all women by calling them sluts when they simply express desire, that same image can make an African-American girl feel wrong and stereotyped. Furthermore, it can make her feel less deserving of the respect and consideration granted to white girls and women.

Is there a place for a girl and her sexuality in this world if she is African American? Elijah Anderson's street sociology of an African-American urban community presented in *Streetwise* shows maybe not. He reduces their experience thus: "[G]irls have a dream, the boys a desire." On the surface, the African-American girls and women may look like they want a man and a baby and a house, but they want to feel sexual desire too. They want to feel pleasure without being labeled a whore. If even this African-American sociologist denies this part of women, seeing girls' desires as merely tricks to get men to be with them, then we see how large the problem is. We must all recognize and support the healthy sexual development of the African-American girl without degrading her.

Chapter 10

Periods, Pubic Hair, Boobies, and Bodily Torture

"God didn't want—he wanted some land of perfect, dry, carcasslike beings that had no leaky parts, emotions, water, blood."
—May, white, 33

Girls develop sexual feelings before they "develop," so to speak. If they get any sex education in the schools, it's not until fifth or sixth grade, sometimes long after they have begun to experience sexual feelings and play sexual games, but near the time they reach puberty. Society and schools believe that children aren't and shouldn't be interested in sex until then.

Despite common reservations about introducing sex education at such a young age, there are all sorts of anxieties that it could address before puberty. The most burning question girls have, but don't ask, is simply "Am I normal?" Girls are anxious about sexual feelings, masturbating, and about what it means to be "sexy." They are impatient to know "what's down there" and what people call it. Later, girls worry about getting their periods and about how their body is developing. The more opportunities girls have to discuss these changes, even comparing bodies with a close friend, the better they feel about themselves and their changes.

Most children around the world do not get their sex education from their parents. In fact, anthropologists have found that they get it from their peers. This has been true and is still true here in the United States. Plus, research shows that African-American and Puerto Rican girls get even less than Caucasian girls, although I suspect that the research reflects socioeconomic class rather than racial differences.

Back in the thirties, forties, and fifties, there wasn't any sex education in the schools. In less educated, lower socioeconomic areas, the sex education consisted of merely a mysterious warning about staying away from boys once a girl got her period.

Cora's mother, who raised Cora in the forties' South, may have been typical.

> *Okay, after I got my period, where she always tell me, keep your dress down. She never talk to me about that. No nothing about it. Everything I know I eavesdropped it from my older sister and a cousin. And so that's how I found out everything. First thing my mother say, "Well, you better keep your dress down." And I said, Well, I got to go to the bathroom, but that's all she said.*

Like Cora, another African-American woman, Yvonne, grew up in the forties and fifties in the South. She told me that when she went to ask her mother about sex, "Where do babies come from?" her mother pushed her away and scolded her, saying, "Don't get fresh with me!"

This attitude pervaded into the fifties when, Elenora, a thirty-eight-year-old Puerto Rican woman from Manhattan, told me, her mother would not allow anyone to talk about sex in the house.

Patty, who grew up in this era but in a white Irish and Polish Catholic neighborhood of Massachusetts, got a similar brush-off from her mother.

> *I remember my mother handed me a booklet she must have gotten from, you know, Modess or Tampax, and that was how she explained my period. That was it. She didn't talk to me about it, and sex was never a discussion.*

By contrast, Miranda, an eleven-year-old girl, said she can talk about everything with her mother, including sex: "I can go and say, 'I want a bra mommy.' Actually, I did that just today."

Even though we might think that Americans have become modern and liberal about sex education (compared to our parents and grandparents, perhaps we are), most sex education courses still don't offer enough to girls. If parents take a proactive stance in the home, their daughters might learn a lot. But if they leave it to the school, the sheer absence of discussion of desire and play allows girls to remain ignorant or forces them to rely on other—often unreliable—sources of information.

Sex ed's primary purpose these days is to teach girls about menstruation and abstinence. In fact, in some states it is illegal to teach anything in a sex education program except abstinence and parts of the body. In 1969, in my junior high's sex education course, we were given a slide show with close-up images of penises infected with gonorrhea and syphilis in its later stages. Accurate about the diseases, yes, but should this be a young girl's first impression of male genitalia? The sex education I remember from that year had very little to do with the little Kotex booklet my mother gave me, which was entitled, "Very Personally Yours." It had more to do with the punches I received from Scott Hansen, the boy who had a crush on me, and the admiration I felt when I saw the beautiful Mrs. Lang, my language arts teacher, at her second job, waiting tables in tight pants and a halter top.

Sex education, at its best, teaches girls about sexual pleasure and about relationships (in addition to biology, contraception, abstinence, and disease). Girls want to know about intercourse. How to do it. Will it hurt? Girls focus on the details of intercourse because both the movies they see and the boys around them define sex this way. Unfortunately, sex education becomes male-oriented in that it usually focuses on prevention of intercourse for girls. This focus on intercourse is also problematic for boys, as they grow up to have a very limited view of what brings them sexual pleasure.

Sex education needs to teach girls that sex is more than intercourse. Sex is about sexual pleasure as well as reproduction, about relationships and mutuality, about knowing one's body.

Current arguments against sex are based on the fear that if girls are taught about pleasure, they will want sex more. Under scrutiny, the fear appears to be of girls becoming more like boys, or our stereotypes of boys in their insatiable sexual hunger, that girls will not be girls anymore.

Both feminist author Sharon Thompson, in Going All the Way, and feminist professor of education Michelle Fine, in "The Missing Discourse of Desire," suggest that if girls understood more about sexual pleasure they would be less likely to be hurt by the expectation of great love and romance, less likely to be swept away (without birth control), more likely to think of themselves and be a little more selfish in sexual encounters, more free to bring out birth control, and more likely, I think, to avoid intercourse at an early age. What would be so bad about that?

Masturbation

Author Karin Flaake wrote these wise words in her essay "A Body of One's Own," speculating about how a mother might talk to her young daughter about masturbation:

> *Your body, like mine, is female, it is good and valuable, and you can experience physical enjoyment and sexuality with your own body independent of me . . .*

She goes on to say:

> *The girl can experience her own femininity as an autonomous source of enjoyment and creativity, and with this fundamental self-confidence, she is no longer exclusively dependent on the opposite sex for the acknowledgment of her femininity.*

Many adult women, though no girls I spoke to (understandably), told me about their first masturbation experience. Masturbation challenges the idea that children are sexual innocents. Even so, I didn't feel comfortable enough to ask most of them explicitly. May, however, asked me, "Aren't you going to ask about masturbation?" Her generous offer to talk about masturbation helped me to listen better to the women I interviewed after her to look for an opening in the conversation when I might ask specifically about masturbation.

As a girl, May was ashamed of masturbating. Ironically, her mother was a nurse and genuinely approved of it; she taught May all about the human body as she was growing up. But May still felt guilty. She would come downstairs after masturbating and tell her mother she had done it, and her mother would say, "That's fine."

> *Of all the people, my mother is the most open, so that's why I find it tragic that a young girl can think it's bad, even when their primary caretaker is telling them it's okay. It's all right. One time, my father came in while I was in the midst of masturbating. Oh my God! And I remember that stern look—you did not do that!*

Patty, who grew up in the sixties, a decade before May, also remembered masturbating. In a household where no one discussed sex at all, she seemed to have found bodily pleasure.

I do remember sort of playing with myself and my mother coming in and saying, "Girls, don't do that!" You know, I'd be in bed at night, and just kind of, yeah, "What are you doing? Don't do that." . . . So yeah, that was a sexual feeling. It just felt good, whatever it was.

A decade earlier, in the fifties, Linda used to rub against a hassock. She still remembered the sexual pleasure she got from it.

I think I accidentally discovered sexual feelings while rolling around on a hassock, and discovered masturbation. And she [her mother] was very, very upset with me. . . . I just remember her being very stern and telling me that good girls didn't do this. . . . I thought I had done something terribly wrong.

Linda also drew pictures of naked women with breasts and pubic hair: "I was curious, just curious, I guess."

Clearly masturbation was not something that good girls did, or do. Although by that time experts were telling parents that masturbation didn't lead to blindness or mental retardation, it was still something ladies or good girls didn't do.

Parents probably saw it as their obligation to teach their girls appropriate behavior. They probably would have stopped a son from masturbating too, for that matter. It is partially parents' embarrassment that makes them act the way they do. They honestly don't know what to do, thinking that they are not supposed to *see* sexual pleasure in a child as much as thinking that a child shouldn't find sexual pleasure. They would prefer it if that was something very private, something they didn't have to deal with. To be generous to these parents, I think that many were saying something more akin to "Cover up; it's embarrassing and unladylike" rather than that it is morally wrong.

Even so, the message to girls is still that masturbation is unacceptable and wrong. More important, since it is rarely discussed, especially among young girls, it remains unknown and, to a certain extent, taboo. The parts can't be named. The feelings have no place. The pleasure has no words.

Body Changes

Sexual education about pleasure should also address the changes in girls' bodies. Girls are fascinated by naked bodies from early on. Quite a few people I interviewed remembered drawing pictures of naked and voluptuous women. Robin, an African-American college student, even remembered standing on a toilet in a stall to spy on her teacher going to the bathroom.

But there's anxiety as well as interest. The transition from girls to women, through breast development and menstruation, requires that girls negotiate the forces of adult femininity. Breast development teaches them about being "sexy" and being looked at. Menstruation teaches something about subordination and dark secrets. Researcher Janet Lee, in her study of forty women's narratives of menarche, writes that menstruation made many of the women in her study feel dirty. They talked about hiding the evidence, the stains, the bulges. Many talked about a sense of bodily alienation. Even in the joking among kids you can see this sense of body alienation. There is a loss of control.

The young girls I spoke to joked and giggled about busty women. Eleven-year-old Miranda and her friend play a game that expresses both wonderment and embarrassment about how breasts are sexual. In the bathtub they put squishy things in their bathing suits and pretend to bite each other on their breasts, saying, "Oh, I love you," and then they crack up.

When a girl can share this anxiety, fear, or pride with another girl, positive things happen. Valerie, an African-American woman in her forties now, recalls that she and her friends started developing breasts around age eleven. She remembered that she and her girlfriend showed each other their first bras and later, with their friends, everyone showed each other their breasts. This kind of sharing brings relief to kids who can't get that kind of reassurance from even the most liberal of parents. It reminds them that they are not alone and reintroduces a sense of wonderment in the process.

Some of the anxiety about bodily changes manifests itself in troubling ways. As May puts it,

> Good meant being nonsexual. God didn't want—he wanted some land of perfect, dry, carcasslike beings that had no leaky parts, emotions, water, blood. . . . To this day I have this sense of God as a stern, white,

marble male who is looking down, and just things about me which were
like sensual or, you know, from the body, the leaking of the body . . . it
was just a nightmare.

Because of these "leaky parts," it was embarrassing to be a woman.

Daria and her friends, who used to tie up their Barbie dolls and pretend to pluck the pubic hairs out of them one by one, captured this embarrassment about bodily changes. (Barbie already wordlessly shows ambivalence about the teenage body because she comes with no hair anywhere except on her head.) My friend Debbie told me a long time ago, when we exchanged secrets, that she and some other girls who were seven or eight at the time went into the forest and rubbed dried leaves on their vaginas. Whether exciting or not, the symbolism of this is pretty clear. Dirty leaves on a dirty spot—the leaves look like the pubic hair that would grow there soon.

When I was in the sixth grade, my friend Candy and I did something weird (yes, I call it weird, knowing that we all say that about our stories!). We left art class with red paint and secretly painted red streaks on the bathroom Kotex machines. Neither of us had gotten our periods yet, and we thought this was great fun. It was as if someone who was dripping blood from getting her period was desperate for a Kotex.

Connie, who, as I did, grew up in the sixties when there was sex education in the fifth grade, remembered teasing another girl mercilessly about getting her period. She and her friends would go on and on about how "bloody" she got. The girl would be totally embarrassed.

Sometimes being with a friend helps a girl to feel less anxious, comparing how much pubic hair she has or how her breasts are developing. Joining together fights off humiliation and provides support and comfort around shared worries. As psychiatrist Harry Stack Sullivan wrote, having a chum is a way to see yourself reflected in another and to know that you are totally acceptable the way you are.

Sexy Rather Than Sexual

Admiring my language arts teacher, Mrs. Lang, as a seventh-grader, I knew the importance of having a sexy body. Somehow all the changes of puberty are supposed to result in just that, a sexy rather than a sexual body, a body to be looked at but not one which expresses one's own desire. It is the unusual girl who grows up with such a connection between her spirit and her body that she feels her body to be an expression of all parts of herself. Anne Stirling Hastings, in *Body and Soul,* writes about how children learn to cut off awareness of important information about their bodies from an early age. She says that we are not taught about what it means to "live in one's body." She points out that "all women are shamed for having a body that isn't sexy at some time or another." The idea that how one looks comprises one's sexuality, that sexuality is conferred on a girl from the looks she gets from others, is true in part, and also dangerous to girls. When they are taught to deny their sexual feelings as coming from within, they become dependent on others for pleasure. And they feel tremendous guilt.

There's a lot that goes on today to try to teach girls about not succumbing to media pressures to judge themselves by appearance alone. The alternative given to girls is to take pride in their accomplishments, in school, in sports. But this alternative supports a different notion of the good girl, a notion that can be oppressive itself. Can we have an alternative that tells girls that *anyone* can be sexual, even if they don't look sexy? Yes. By teaching them that sexy is not only being desirable, but being being desirous; by affirming their sexual feelings and wants as their own, and all right.

We can offer girls a way to be sexual and not just sexy, to feel in themselves sexual energy and erotic pleasure, through a more comprehensive program of sex education. What a joy to them such an education could be.

Chapter 11

Guilty Minds and Sexual Obsessions

Asexual boy is considered a normal boy, but a sexual girl is seen as a problem that has to be solved. We are used to the idea of girls being innocent of sexual thoughts and desires. But if a girl has them, we automatically assume that she has had a seductive parent who introduced these ideas too early or that she has been abused and is trying to master her trauma.

The following three stories push the boundaries of normal, at least for the women who reside in them. These women look back with tremendous guilt over sexual feelings, thoughts, and acts. They see themselves as either obsessed with sex, evil, or terribly strange. Each came to the interview as one would a confessional. And because I did not think that their sexual stories were so shocking or particularly abnormal, each of them seemed to come away from the interview a little more lighthearted.

The first girl, Chrissie, called herself weird and deviant: "obsessed with sex." She is a college student from an upper-middle-class white family in New England. Her guilt comes in part from her father, who is a "committed Christian" with his own anxieties about sex. Her "obsession" with sex, and her guilt about it, enacts a conflict in her parents' marriage.

The second girl, Olivia, called herself a weirdo. She, like Chrissie, is also a college student, but she comes from a Latino family that had some financial struggles, and she grew up in the Southwest. Olivia's childhood sexual life is full: she got to know her body and bodily pleasure early; she experimented, played, and found pleasure through sexual activities with other children; and she was also coerced, harassed, and bugged sexually by boys and also even girls. She took it all in; she worked it through; and she emerges as someone who feels quite able to cope with sexuality and make healthy choices as an adult.

Dorothy Jean also saw herself as strange, so different and deviant that she insisted we do the interview in her own home, where no one could hear or see us, and also while her husband was not home, lest he overhear. Still, even before I stepped foot in her house, just the idea of a book on the secret lives of girls led her to revisit some of her early experiences and reevaluate them. If these experiences could be talked about, maybe they weren't so bad. She wondered whether she could risk talking to me? She hoped that I would be able to tell her that she was not deviant.

These are not stories filled with giggles and the sexual delight of mutual, hidden girlhood games, although there was pleasure. Other women who played one or two little childhood games were well able to other them (someone else made them do it) or dismiss them (because it was a single incident, it wasn't really them). But women who played many games or played a game that went on for years became convinced that they were doing something terribly wrong. Their guilt is exceptional for its persistence.

Kissy Killer Chrissie: The Sins of the Father are Visited on the Daughter

Chrissie loved to chase the boys on the playground and kiss them. She even remembered making a deal with one boy that if she played the game he wanted to play, then he would have to play "kissy killers" with her. "I would get into it," she confessed. She liked the "active" part of the game, she said, and she also liked that in the game she was allowed to "get violent,"

> like I liked the struggling, like not letting them kiss you, but having an excuse almost maybe to even fight. . . . It's like, if they caught me I could kick and scream because I was allowed to do that . . . and I was supposed to be resisting.

Chrissie clearly knew that the role she must play is the resister, the one who doesn't really want to be kissed. Yet ironically, she played that role with relish, allowing herself to be violent, to feel powerful and sexual in the struggle.

Chrissie was thrilled by the game, the risk, and the thought that she was dangerous. She enjoyed the "victim" role as well, enacting the struggle, enjoying the resistance. But she also carried the name of Kissy Killer Chrissie, confirming that in the eyes of her peers her own sexual desires were dangerous.

Chrissie's background in part explains her feelings of guilt. She grew up in a well-to-do family, attended public schools, and did very well: she was a "good girl" and never liked to disobey a teacher or receive a disapproving glare. Her father was a very religious man, and Chrissie knew the story of her parents' romance from a very early age. When her parents met, her father was struggling to remain a virgin until marriage because of the teachings of the church. But he didn't, resulting in pregnancy and then marriage. Her father felt tremendous guilt over his premarital sexuality, and told Chrissie, "You know, your mom seduced me and I couldn't control myself." To Chrissie, her mother was always the "naughty parent," the one who was rebellious, who would drink at parties and had a sexual past. Her father was the virtuous one.

She described herself as preoccupied with sex in childhood, noting the plans she made to invite a little boy, Drew, to her house after school in order to "model" for him a sexy nightgown her mother had given to her for dress-ups. Calling herself "very bizarre," she wanted to appear before him, as if to say "Look. I'm so sexy." Although she was young, six, seven, or so, she knew at the time that this was a weird thing to want. She knew, or thought she knew, that other girls did not think like this, did not like to pose in sexy lingerie.

She remembered how she was drawn to the magazine section in bookstores to look at the photographs of scantily clad women on the covers of men's magazines. At home she and a neighbor girl would draw naked people with genitals showing, never embarrassed to show them to her mother, who would be "very accepting." Her father "would have gotten mad or he would have thought they were really dirty."

Her father's doubts framed the way she viewed her many sexual experiences. Her mother, for example, had gotten her sister and her *Where Did I Come From?*, a sex education book for children with cartoons and silly pictures. She and her sister were looking through it and giggling and her father came in and "got all mad because it was supposed to be something that was informative." It wasn't supposed "to be like pornography."

Chrissie defined her "weirdness," her deviance, almost totally in terms of interest, not acts. For example, Chrissie was at a cousin's house and they discovered a hard-core pornography tape among the videos under the family room VCR. She remembered feeling obsessed:

> Like I really wanted to watch the whole thing. It wasn't like, That's disgusting, let's turn it off. It was like, That's disgusting, let's keep watching it.

But we should remember here that she watched it with other children. In many of her stories she is not alone. So certain is she, however, that she is the deviant one, that she dismisses this fact.

Chrissie's deviance means something more to her than an interest in sex. It means that she's not like a real girl, but more like a boy. Girls aren't supposed to be interested in sex, she realized at an early age, and if they are, they are wicked.

> I was a girl and I shouldn't want that. . . . It might not be so much either that I was a girl, but my dad wanted to raise good, healthy children that didn't want to watch pornography, so I was like, "Why do I want to?"

Again, Chrissie criticized herself for being too sexual:

> I just feel that I have this list of all these sorts of things that I feel like are deviant or bizarre or violent. Why do I want to do that? I often find myself trying to figure out, What is the source of it? Why do I seem to have this much stronger desire for that than other people?

There is one incident that unfortunately confirmed to Chrissie that she was different from other girls. Like many other girls, she initiated a sexual game. But unlike most of the other stories about girl-to-girl sexual play and games, she was rejected. She asked a friend of hers whether they could play a game where they take off all of their clothes and pretend to be having sex.

> I didn't know exactly how we'd do that. Maybe just wiggle around or whatever. I said, "I'll be the boy if you want or whatever."

Her friend said no, leading Chrissie to feel bad that she was the desiring one, the deviant one. Here Chrissie, like so many girls, equates desire with deviance. If her friend had said yes (and we know from many other girls' stories that sometimes they do), she would have had a "partner in crime," a buddy, a chum.

The psychiatrist Harry Stack Sullivan, in *The Interpersonal Theory of Psychiatry*, now a classic, wrote about how important a "chum" is to correct the self-images children develop about how weird and strange they are. With a chum who does everything with them, they never feel alone or isolated. Their chum reflects back to them that who they are, what they do, is thoroughly acceptable. In the following exchange, with a different girl, Chrissie began to feel better about herself, as if she were not alone or unusual.

The one time her great burden of guilt was lifted was in conversation with a friend who said she had found some porn magazines in a cabin in the woods. The friend asked Chrissie if she knew what the word "come" meant. Her friend seemed "obsessed" with that word—"come." Since Chrissie didn't know what it meant, the friend explained it to her. Then Chrissie confessed that she had once seen a movie and had seen "come" in this movie, although she hadn't known the name for it at the time.

> *It was really a freeing feeling to admit that, to know that I'd seen a porno magazine and that I could say that I'd seen a movie and I wasn't some sort of freak because of that.*

Aside from that moment, Chrissie saw herself as a freak.

Not surprisingly, Chrissie asked me at the end of the interview whether or not she was deviant. I told her that there is a range of how sexual people are and how sexual they feel. That boys and girls both exist on the continuum. The problem is that we tend to think that girls are very low on this continuum and boys are very high. But men and women differ so much more in personality characteristics and temperament than they do by gender-stereotyped characteristics. There are some women and girls with a lot of sexual interest and drive and a lot of men with just a little. But when women have a lot, they think of themselves as deviant, especially the girls who are high on the continuum. They think of themselves as more malelike, more crazy, and more strange. They do not fit the mold of the asexual good girl in our culture. Chrissie seemed relieved after this explanation.

When women are sexual, men become afraid. Societies become afraid. It's as if the girl is usurping some essential form of male power. The sexual woman is seen as sucking out the vitality of the man, his prowess, his dignity. That's why history has called sexual women temptresses and witches. In addition, that's why some cultures have formed practices such as cli-toridectomy that ensure that women do not have sexual feelings.

Sex is power, and in a culture that doesn't explicitly take away a woman's sexual feelings, the backup strategy is to have the woman or girl learn to take them away herself, through guilt. I wouldn't want to say that Chrissie's guilt is as debilitating as a clitoridectomy, but it is certainly a presence that disempowers her and makes her less than she feels, less than she is.

Olivia: Weird Pleasures

Olivia, like Chrissie, thought she was a "weirdo" in childhood. Growing up in a rural, Rocky Mountain town, with only about thirty other children in the area, someone would have to be excluded. Olivia described herself as the only "ethnic" kid in the school, smart, musical, but also the "chubby girl who was black and stuff (actually of Hispanic/Native American her-itage) and kind of sweaty and hairy."

Olivia said straight out: "Younger children do find things sensual. They do have a sex life." She has masturbated since the age of six, and more than anything else she did as a child, this made her feel the most guilty. It was pleasurable and, from an early age, she remembered she could even have orgasms. Once her mother walked in on her masturbating in front of the television. Her mother pretended that she didn't see what Olivia was doing, but for the next few days she wouldn't let Olivia watch TV. Olivia tried to talk to her mother about masturbating and what her mother saw that day. "Mom, I'm sorry for that," she said. But her mother claimed she hadn't seen anything. Olivia's mother taught her about shame in numerous ways; in Olivia's words, "she had a big history of being ashamed of your body."

Some would explain the sexual stories to come as resulting from sev-eral features in her environment: her mother was an alcoholic and ne-glected her after Olivia's sister died from cancer; her father encouraged her interest through dirty jokes and porn photos in his garage. Like Chrissie, Olivia may have been acting out a hidden conflict between one sexual par-ent and another, repressed and guilt-ridden. Children do pick up on the anxieties within marital relationships. But then again, they do have an in-terest in sexuality all their own.

Aside from her early experiences of masturbation, Olivia's first sexual or sexualized experience occurred at a baby-sitter's house where she stayed after school, the year she was nine. The baby-sitter's youngest son loved to dress up in girls' clothing. Day after day the two would play dress-ups. The husband of the baby-sitter, who was the boy's father, home all day, would observe them, railing against his son for liking girls' clothes, but never stopping them. The two children would prance around in girls' dresses, feeling pretty and sexy, until once her friend asked to borrow her underpants. Though it upset her at first, she went with the flow of the game and began to try to help him by thinking up magic potions to turn him into a girl. The two friends were also curious about genitals and would arrange to play in a way that satisfied that curiosity. For example, they would put on dresses with big fluffy slips, and then do somersaults for each other without their underwear on, so that each could see the other's private parts. Only looking, no touching.

While Olivia was enjoying her sexual play with the boy her own age, his older brother would sometimes attack her. He would jump on her, wrestle her to the floor, and rub himself against her. This taught Olivia a different story about sex, a story that "wasn't fun." She doesn't remember feeling scared so much as "this is not right. . . . He had an advantage, and most of the time he was on top of me."

Older boys tend to teach different lessons and are more prone to exploit younger children. That is why, in advocating for a more relaxed atmosphere around childhood sexual play and games, it is important for parents to encourage same-sex play. In a small community such as Olivia's, she was exposed to older boys quite often. Riding the bus in first grade, for example, she would endure shouts from the high school boys such as, "What would you do if I made you suck my cock?" Never the shy one, she yelled back at them and said, "Yucccchhhh," and the bus driver yelled at them all to keep quiet. Though Olivia still felt this was abnormal, it didn't upset her and she didn't feel stigmatized, unlike her experiences with the older brother at the baby-sitter's.

Olivia had another friendship with a girl who she thought was kind of bizarre. This girl came from an athletic family, and so "they weren't big on keeping your body hidden or anything." One of her friend's favorite games was to get "totally naked" and play a pretend game of a policeman finding a naked person on the street:

The person who was supposed to be a police officer would catch the naked person and then start stripping himself.

She described the game as stimulating, but reassured me that she is hetero-sexual. Her assumption was that this kind of game with another girl de-fined her in some way as gay because she had sexual feelings during it.

She had another sexualized friendship at an earlier age, from about age six through seven, with a boy. When she would stay overnight at his house, their parents would let them sleep in the same bed. They would undress completely, and there was

> *a lot of feeling and groping and stuff like that . . . there was no gig-gling . . . and the next morning we'd wake up, and I remember one time we said, 'Oh, we were a little wild the other night." It was so weird. It was bizarre, because we were six years old, and we were thinking all these thoughts, and we were like waking up the next morning looking at each other, going, I don't know if I can look at you.*

What is interesting about this incident is the seriousness. If the children are serious, is it still play? Is it experimentation or real? For children it is both. Sometimes it is for adults as well. Sex and play have a lot in common.

When we read these examples from Olivia's childhood sex life, she be-gins to look like a fairly sexual creature. However, in this town of only thirty children, she certainly had numerous "partners in crime," boys and girls. Despite, like Chrissie, knowing other kids were doing the same things, Olivia still felt that she was odd.

As an adult today she compares herself to her roommate and sees her-self as well adjusted. Her roommate, for example, who led a very sheltered life as a child and teen, is "going crazy" with the freedom of college, sleep-ing with a lot of guys, doing stripteases for college boys at parties.

> *I think all of the stuff being when you're younger actually helps you to be more well adjusted when you get older. . . . If anything comes up now [meaning if she gets physically excited by someone], you know that this is basically a biological response; it's no big deal.*

Dorothy Jean: Murphy Beds and Femme Fatales

Dorothy Jean was the woman who needed to talk to me in her own home, who told me in advance that she had secrets to tell that nobody had heard previously. She wanted to find a time when her husband would be out. She wanted a space that would be private. And, I think, she wanted me to see who she was and who she had been for the whole of her life before I heard the small, shameful parts that still loomed large in her mind.

While she was growing up, sex was all around Dorothy, although she didn't see it that way. She grew up in the 1940s in the Midwest in a three-flat (three apartments, one on top of the other); her aunt Mary, uncle Danny, and cousin Jim lived below her, and her grandparents lived above her. Her grandparents' apartment had a Murphy bed in the dining room that the children would pull down and play on. A Murphy bed is a bed that is stored upright, hidden in a cupboard. Open the cupboard, pull the bed down, and a room that you use for other functions during the day becomes a bedroom at night.

Dorothy remembered the day her grandmother and she were watching the streetcars go by in the rain, the sparks still igniting on the tracks, when they saw a woman holding an accordion faint, right at the stop in front of their house. Dorothy's grandmother ran out to the woman and brought her in, drenched and weak. She gave her a home, and the mysterious woman ended up sleeping in the Murphy bed the children loved to play on.

> *She was an accordion player and a singer and she was brilliant. And what we didn't know at the time . . . at night, she ended up working for my dad in his trio, and they would be, like, um, um, "hugging" in the Murphy bed, in grandma's dining room . . . he ultimately married her. Mom and Dad split up when I was nine. At nine, everything changed, just like that. Mom and Dad split up, we moved to an apartment on the other side of town, grandma died of a heart attack, Dad committed his life to this woman, and my whole life changed.*

Her German grandfather played an important role in her life as she grew up; he kept detective magazines around the house, magazines with fictionalized true-crime stories, famous now for their covers. About the size of a *Reader's Digest*, these magazines had lurid drawings on their covers of beautiful women, scantily clothed, lying in a pool of blood or with a revolver near their limp hands. The women's dresses would pull against their bulging breasts; a bra strap or part of a slip would be exposed. Murdered and abandoned, they were both gruesome and sexual images.

And then there were the cousins. These cousins featured strongly in the sexual play that made Dorothy feel so guilty. Her grandfather had a weekend farm where he would raise the chickens they ate. Relatives, whom Dorothy calls her "white trash cousins," lived at this farm. This is the family from which she learned the most about sex.

> *They were like a Jerry Springer show. You know, it was always like they were throwing and hitting, but very emotional and loving too, and very preoccupied with sex. I grew to look forward to these visits, and then I grew to mistrust them. The mother in this family was a leathery, very handsome, very charismatic, and very volatile sort of mountain woman.*

Finally, in the world of Dorothy's childhood, there were the doctor's appointments. Dorothy had something "wrong" with her vaginal area. There was something in her "private area" that meant she regularly had to visit the doctor until puberty to have a growth that would continue to re-grow cut away. This was never quite explained to her. While in the doctor's office someone would have to pull apart her labia while he would use a razor blade to cut off the growth. Dorothy used to fight them tooth and nail, but they would hold her down until the procedure was over. It hurt. And it was deeply shaming and embarrassing to Dorothy to have to do this: "If I see a man who resembles that doctor . . . that's something I never talk about."

In this context, Dorothy's sexual life began. And it began with her love of Wonder Woman. Transforming her abusive medical experiences into stories of power and agency, she would play at being Wonder Woman. Wonder Woman was tied up and tortured, and she needed to break away! She would pull and twist herself against the imaginary ropes that bound her until she could break free. Dorothy, all by herself, with a towel over her shoulders, imagined herself with a big chest and a tiny waist and long black hair, feeling totally sexual and powerful, fighting off her torturers with bravado.

At other times her anger over her medical appointments was enacted under a table she called her "zombie chamber." Here she would put Vase-line on her dolls' pubic areas and torture them.

The secret game, "Playing Dead," was different. She was not alone but played with her wild cousins a game they all called "Playing Dead." Two or three of the girl cousins from the country would come to their grandpar-ents' apartment to visit, and in the Murphy bed, or in the back room of her grandparents' apartment, they would "play dead" just like the ladies on the covers of the detective magazines. To begin the game, one of the cousins usually would say, "Do you want to play dead?" And then

> *one of us would tie up the other one, you know, in a provocative pose, and in various stages of undress. And then the other kids would go out of the room, and then the kid tied up would play dead, and then the other kids would come back in the room, and they'd say, "Oh, she's so beautiful." "Oh, look at her! She's so gorgeous!" "She's so beautiful." And you'd get this real sexual rush. It was very sexual. . . . I was posed very provocatively. . . . It was really titillating and fun, and it was a feeling because I was so physical.*

And there it was. The secret game that she hadn't told anyone about all the forty-seven or forty-eight years since she had played it. A game that festered in shame within. But why? It may have been in response to the sexual pleasure she felt. Perhaps it was because she played with other girls. Maybe the fact that she was tied up made her feel as if she was deriving pleasure from something that was especially sexually decadent or deviant.

There are other games of "playing dead" that girls played together that other women I interviewed told me about. Dorothy was not the first. These kinds of games express girls' ambivalence about their sexuality. To feel anything sexual, they needed to be dead, or pretend to be dead. But with another's gaze, girls became the beautiful object of desire: sexual, untouchable, and at the same time both sexy and pure. Doesn't death, in fact, purify? Pretended death purifies the girl by transforming her from a sexual agent (one who desires) to a sexual object (one who is desired). It makes the wicked seductress into the sad, tragic beauty.

What is also interesting is that the words in the game created a sexual thrill in the child: "You hear someone's voice and your body tingles. It was great, actually, but not—it was naughty." Sexual pleasure, then, was learned through imitation, by being a beautiful, pornographic object. Sexual feelings arose from being admired.

This was the secret that Dorothy had kept from her husband, the one she didn't want anyone to hear. As she told it to me, the old pleasure came up again. She smiled when she told me how wonderful it felt to be admired, the shame evaporating for the moment. Reflecting on the times, the early fifties, Dorothy said to me, "Y'know, you don't have Oprah to say, 'This is normal; this is natural.' At the time, this was something shaming to me, and I was losing, at the time, everything I had."

Once she had a sleepover at about the age of ten with a girlfriend, so Dorothy taught her how to play this game. Then the girl's mother walked in and asked, "What are you doing?" Dorothy had no answer. It was bedtime, but the mother told Dorothy to get dressed, that she was taking her home. Dorothy's friend kept crying to her mother, "She won't be bad again. Let her stay. She won't be bad again, Mom."

As observers we are forced then to rethink what these games really are. Doesn't it depend on how the child feels it at the time? Does the child feel it as just a game? Rarely. Children never see themselves as "just children," excusing their actions by way of immaturity or childishness. They see themselves as full human beings who make choices, have feelings, and experience things heart and soul. So why should we expect anything different? At the time, Dorothy was sexually excited by playing with her female cousins. She turned out to live a heterosexual life, but that doesn't mean that her early impulse wasn't "real" or really her.

After she told me about her secret game, the power it held over her was gone. There's power and control in secrets. And if anyone believes that children should be left alone in their secret worlds to figure it all out, they should learn from Dorothy Jean:

> Until I said it out loud, and I have never addressed it, ever . . . so I think, and here it gets a little complicated. I think that part of me allowed that game to have a power and allowed a part of me to continue to be shamed, and I could work that way. Now I have no excuse. It was a secret that now I don't have . . . so I have to love it, and bless it, and let it go. I am who I am, and I'm unique, and there's no one to punish and there's no one to blame. So I have to let it go.
>
> So I'm normal, huh? I don't feel so bad.

Chapter 12

Too Sexual Too Soon

"I see no reason not to believe that soon a substantial number of youths will be having intercourse in the middle-school years. . . . It's already happening."
—Dr. Richard Gallagher, April, 2, 2000, *as quoted in the* New York Times, *"Sunday Styles" section*

Some girls have sex before their teens. And while sexual exploration at an early age is fine, I see many problems with early sexual intercourse. Rather than contributing to a girl's understanding of herself as a sexual being in her own right, it orients her sexual development toward what she believes a man wants. It cuts off her own process of development and redirects her to another's. Aside from issues of pregnancy and emotional maturity, which are important issues in and of themselves, another consideration is that girls simply do not develop to be sexually secure when they have sex at an early age. Mothers and fathers are smart to try to shield their daughters from early sex, but in urging their daughters away from sexuality and sup-porting their dreams of romantic love, they inadvertently push them to-ward younger, male-oriented sex.

Early intercourse is a cultural practice that benefits boys more than it does girls. One minor reason is that most girls do not enjoy first sex. Many regret it, although boys obtain a higher status among peers from early sex. A more important reason is that girls do not learn to know their bodies better through first sex, nor do they experiment with their own feelings through intercourse. It is often simply about pleasing their boyfriends. Look at the new trends for oral sex in junior high school. When journalists have investigated this trend they overwhelmingly refer to girls performing oral sex on boys rather than boys performing oral sex on girls. Sex research informs us that oral sex for women is one of the most pleasurable female sexual experiences. If early sex is not a male-centered experience, if it were being demanded by girls, wouldn't it have more to do with female sexual pleasure? Instead, it has more to do with the conferring of adult woman status on a girl by a man or boy through intercourse. In the *New York Times* article on the subject, boys say that oral sex is "fun" and they do it out of "curiosity." Girls are curiously silent on the subject.

The media panics about children having sex too early, yet constructs the idea of "too early" on experts' knowledge about child development, when a child should be doing what they are doing. Experts in the United States surprisingly seem to agree on what's "natural," even though what's natural certainly depends on what country and culture you are referring to. There is general understanding among therapists who see children that sex confuses a child and makes them vulnerable to powerful feelings they will have no control over or that will be too intense for them to sort out.

Psychologists who have worked with adolescents also believe that early sex is tied to exploitation. I certainly agree with this belief, particularly in the case of girls who, when they tend to have sex early, frequently are convinced to do it by older boys and men. This does leave them open to exploitation. Recent worries about girls reaching puberty early is more about the way they seem to attract older boys and men instead of the repercussions on health: "We already see how men look at Clara," one mother said to *Time* magazine about her daughter, who was eight when she began developing breasts.

The most important sanction against early sex is probably the fact that it isn't "play." When children play with children their own age there is a mutuality and equality that blesses the experience and which, if they take this into adulthood, would serve them well. But preteen sex rarely occurs in a play or exploratory context. For a girl it is often about being popular, submitting to an older boy, not losing a boyfriend, feeling wanted, or just about thinking one is becoming an adult woman. It is rarely about one's own body, feeling pleasure, or one's own sexual growth.

Until recently researchers believed that African-American girls are more likely to have sexual intercourse at an early age than white girls or Latinas. However, the increase over the past decade in early sex for white girls is much greater than that of African-American girls. Furthermore, urban girls and white rural girls in general have sex earlier than suburban girls of any race. Deb Tolman, director of the Adolescent Sexuality Project at the Center for Research on Women at Wellesley College, writes that when race and class are not confounded, differences between whites and Blacks almost disappear.

Yet there are differences. African-American girls' early sexuality is presented in the media as a threat to society—teen pregnancy, poverty, welfare mothers—and rarely as a risk to them. The early sex that has been reported of late in white middle-class junior high schools, however, is presented as a risk to the girls themselves. Here is yet another instance where we strive to protect white girlhood and condemn African-American girls.

It is clear that environment makes a difference for urban girls and poor girls from rural settings, where early sexual intercourse represents a lack of a protected space of girlhood. No one appears to be looking out for these girls' futures. Although the protected space sometimes makes problems for middle-class white girls in terms of the expectations to be a little lady or a real girl, in the case of preventing early sexual intercourse, it also has its rewards.

In *Streetwise*, the sociologist Elijah Anderson writes about the game young African-American teen and preteen boys play in which they feign love and caring or ambivalently express love and caring to a girl in order to get her to have intercourse. Anderson writes that the more a boy seems to exploit the girl he is after, the higher is his regard within his peer group because it shows others that he is in control. He takes pride in making a fool of the girl, while the girl underestimates peer group influences and hopes that he will stay true to her and remain by her side when she gets pregnant. She has bought into the notion of romantic love.

It has long been known that children (of any race) in homes with only one biological parent are more likely to engage in intercourse earlier than kids from homes with two biological parents. Anderson explains that girls in homes without a father are seen as coming from an "unprotected nest." They have no father that the boys are prepared to respect.

I don't mean to portray adolescent boys only as predators and teen girls as merely victims. But the lack of a protected space of girlhood for them, among so many other kinds of lacks, throws them into a game that has dire consequences and for which they have little preparation.

O'Brishia is one of those girls emblematic of the statistic that urban African-American girls have sex early. When I interviewed her, O'Brishia had just moved into the housing project where my assistant, Bev Colston, and I did many of our interviews. She had come to this new city because her mother in New York City could no longer handle her, and because recently, while skipping school and hanging around with some boys, she was shot accidentally.

Her city neighborhood was rough. Even in the chase-and-kiss games of her Manhattan schoolyard, it wasn't just chase and kiss, it was chase and grab or chase and molest. The boys would try to grab as much of a girl's chest or butt as possible and squeeze as hard as they could. When O'Brishia talked about Juan, her first sexual partner, she said that she wished she had saved herself for her present boyfriend, Marvin. Even though she had been just eleven when she had sex with Juan, she had started menstruating already and was at risk for becoming pregnant. She said she had loved Juan, and that they used no protection, even though her mother had spoken to her about things like contraception.

It's not all that uncommon in O'Brishia's peer group to have intercourse at a young age. The truth-or-dare games we think of as being a regular part of middle-class girls' slumber parties take a different twist in this unprotected place of childhood. On O'Brishia's streets, truth-or-dare games can involve having sex with someone. I don't think she was putting me on. When I asked her if she played truth or dare and she said, "No. I did not want to kiss nobody or have sex with nobody or nothing." She wouldn't play because she "would never know what the person might say" for a dare. O'Brishia suggested that for some girls this could be the way they had their first experience with sex, through a dare: "They go in another room, but there had to be a witness." When I asked her if she thought this game was as much fun for the girls as for the boys, she said:

> No, 'cause times when I made somebody do it and I had to watch it, I didn't know what they were doing and they didn't know what they were doing. The boys enjoyed it . . . sometimes the girls, friends of mine, would enjoy it, because I guess they knew what they was doing. But the boys, they swore they knew what they was doin'. Some girls didn't like it.

At first she answered by thinking about herself and how it wasn't fun for her having to watch the children she had forced to have sex through a dare. Then she considered some of the other girls and realized that for some of them, this initiation must have been confusing: "They didn't know what they were doing." These truth-or-dare games occurred in a space where adults either were not permitted or dared not go.

O'Brishia's mother is a single, working mother who has taken many steps to put O'Brishia on the right track. Although O'Brishia was mad at her mother, I am more sympathetic. Trying to protect O'Brishia, she read her diary and found out she was having sex with her boyfriend. Then she started the process of getting O'Brishia out of New York.

> She's like, "You already had sex! Yeah, you ain't goin to school, you havin' sex." I'm like, "What are you talking about?" She like ripped the page out [from her diary], "Here we go! Right here." I'm like, "How do you know to read that?" and I just never kept one ever since.

O'Brishia's only regret about having sex so early was that she has a new boyfriend and wishes he were the first.

Is it possible in O'Brishia's case to acknowledge sexual agency and give her permission for her experimentation while at the same time acknowledging that she is at risk and being exploited when she has sex as an eleven-year-old with her sixteen-year-old boyfriend? Because she is eleven, is what she is doing play? Is it adult sex? Is it being abused? Any of these responses is in part correct, but not the whole story. She is playing at being an adult; she is being taken advantage of by an older boy who has more power; but she is more likely to be seen by others as having adult sex rather than playing or being abused, because she is in fact a girl from the projects of New York City.

When girls play they begin to project themselves into the future, envisioning themselves as teenagers and adult women, and it is then that they start to imagine a sexual life embedded in a romance. Before any boy has come along to join them in their exploration or exploit them for their own needs, girls connect adult sex with heterosexual dreams of romance. O'Brishia believes in her play that she is in love with Juan. As Sharon Thompson writes in *Going All the Way*, the association of sex with love may be girls' biggest vulnerability.

O'Brishia is also vulnerable because she lacks close supervision, due to the poverty in which she is growing up. Poverty hurts girls in specific ways, and Black girls have a legacy of being treated poorly in those conditions.

We Americans think we've come a long way from the days of slavery, where there was a sharp distinction made between the southern belle and the slave girl. The southern white girl was training to become a lady, and ladies were seen as delicate and genteel. She was sheltered and protected from the war, from male society, from all things brutal or unseemly. Slave girls were used to do heavy fieldwork; they weren't spared from the whip of the master simply because they were small, or girls, or frail, or young. They were not "allowed to be girls."

There is no space for an Alice in Wonderland girlhood of tea parties and secret gardens in the housing projects I visited, not for the African-American girls, for the Puerto Rican girls, or for the white girls living there. Here the cramped quarters reflect the little psychological space available. After reviewing the lives of the middle-class girls and comparing them to their impoverished sisters, black, Latina, and white, I think it is the poverty that keeps certain girls out of that necessary protected space where little girls are cherished.

When girls have sex with a man or teenage boy early, the game they are playing is a boy's game, and sometimes even a man's game. It's not that middle-class white girls don't also play a man's game. It is true that the patriarchal overseeing gaze of the white man enters into the middle-class white girls' play and games through the girls' joyful enactment of being an object, stripteasers or sexy dates for men. They are playing out male fantasies in the hopes of becoming good objects for men. But they are playing out these fantasies in a space that permits trial and error without risk, and that incorporates their own enjoyment of looking at themselves.

Poor girls who grow up in the city also need this period of experimentation and play. Their mothers rarely talk to them about sex. The TV doesn't show many images of middle-class African-American, Latina, let alone poor Black, Latina, and white women being sexual in a positive way. A significant number of them have been touched or exploited sexually at young ages. With regard to African-American girls in particular, African-American feminist author bell hooks warns that white feminists have ignored the impact of abuse on the lives of African-American women and girls. What a period of play and experimentation provides abused girls is the chance to relive and redo their own sexuality in a more positive way.

Streetwise author Anderson writes, "The ignorance of inner-city girls about their bodies astonishes the middle-class observer. Many have only a vague notion of where babies come from. . . . Parents in this culture are extremely reticent about discussing sex and birth control with their children."

Lee Rainwater, the sociologist who wrote the classic book *And the Poor Get Children*, explaining that middle-class people cherish a fantasy of the lower classes as impulsive and self-indulgent, not hemmed in by prudery and constriction. However, the girls I listened to are much more prudish in a deeper sense of the word. Uneducated by their mothers about sex, they yield control rather than take control over their sexuality to men whom they see as initiators and educators, and allow boys to define their own pleasures. While girls in mother-only households have intercourse earlier, girls whose fathers disapprove of early intercourse have intercourse later. Fathers, in their absence, play an enormous role in sending girls to other men for so-called sexual training.

Many girls who grow up in impoverished conditions conform to the status quo by believing that sex = intercourse. Meanwhile, the boys and men who instruct them take pride in the number of women they get, how often they get it, and the freedom from responsibility they establish in their relationships. Each bestows on men a certain kind of power. But it doesn't have to be that way. Imagine for a moment if women made up the rules of sex. What would people picture in their minds when they heard the word sex? What would be the essential component? What would "going all the way" mean? If it was based on women's pleasure, intercourse might be some side issue. Oral sex might be central: "going all the way" might mean something erotic that had to do with the whole body. It's hard to know, because we've all been living in a male-oriented sexual world. In spite of the limits to the collective imagination, a French feminist, Luce Irigaray, wrote about a powerful form of women's sexuality that celebrates its womanliness, a sexuality that doesn't define itself by intercourse or the single orgasm. She writes about multiple bodily places of pleasure and the capacity of women to find a deep sensuality and sexuality in these places rather than focusing on the vaginal hole, the site of intercourse or penetration.

When a girl introduces another little girl to sex, there is a possibility that they might grow up to have a different view of what sex is, a different view of what might bring them pleasure. Many of the adult women I interviewed who had masturbated as a child or had played sexual games said that when they grew up they were less curious and less rebellious, making better choices because of that experience. They weren't overwhelmed by the sexual feelings they felt.

By contrast, girls who grew up in the projects or in poor urban communities didn't play with other girls very often and were more vulnerable to prevailing societal and male views of sex and girls' role in it. We know so much about the negative outcomes of early pregnancy, but will anyone look at the question a different way? What happens, as bell hooks asks, to the girl who does not integrate her sexuality into a positive view of herself? Ask many dissatisfied adult women and they will answer: she becomes us.

Chapter 13

Unwelcome Intrusions: Sexual Coercion in the Lives of Girls

"Those were my little secrets I kept for years and years and years."
—Roxanne, African American, 38

Karen grew up in rural Vermont and likes to tell how she and her best friend would run up and down the beach, the wind in their faces, pretending to be Amazon women who could fight, run, do whatever they want. Would that all girls had such joyous freedom. There's a depressing reality of abuse and coercion that knocks the wind out of girls. Even though we want to acknowledge all the power and sexuality and assertiveness of girls growing up in the United States, this book would not be complete without also acknowledging the pain of abuse.

We live in an era during which it is easier for women to tell each other about their sexual victimization than their sexual delights. Way too many girls are sexually abused or harassed during their grade school years. For some, the abuse is so traumatic or long-lasting that it precludes any experience of sexual play and games in childhood. For a few girls, abuse and mutual sexual play existed side by side, and they knew the difference.

Dealing with Boys' Entitlement

Some incidents in elementary and junior high school knock the wind out of girls. When I was in the fifth grade, I was pushed down by a group of boys and held down on my back in the snow while another group of boys pushed Jeffrey Omar on top of me and made him kiss me. The girls in the class who were my friends just watched as I fought and yelled, "Get off of me." I went in to school that day crying and angry. I guess that's why I expected, as an adult, to hear that chase-and-kiss games were games of harassment, showing boys' entitlement. I was surprised to find that they weren't games of harassment to most kids; the majority enjoyed the game.

Even though it does not occur frequently in the chase-and-kiss games of childhood, boys' entitlement is present early. Research documents boys taking over the use of science equipment in coed classes. It records mothers of preschoolers making their little girls share toys with others more often than they make their little boys share. In this climate, boys develop early an attitude of entitlement toward girls and sex. This is not exactly the "rapist mentality" that feminists have shown "normal" men to exhibit through their belief in rape myths; it is an imitation of it at a lower frequency. For example, one boy in a junior high in Ohio chased Gina and told her he would kill her if she wouldn't go steady with him. "So I did," she said.

Elenora, who grew up in New York City with her mother, an emigrant of Puerto Rico, was chased every day by a little boy who "scared the hell out of" her, yelling, "I'm going to get you." After her mother talked to authorities at the school, Elenora learned, "It turned out that he liked me and that was his way of showing he wanted attention." Amazingly, this behavior became more acceptable when the adults heard why he was doing it. It was as if the adults no longer could look at the experience from Elenora's perspective after they were given the perspective of the boy: he "did it out of love."

Laura was sexually harassed in the second grade. There was a boy in her class who she said was "very sexual" and, like the little boy in Elenora's story, he decided he liked Laura.

> And he would like say he wanted to fuck me and he wanted to hump me and he would chase me around and tell people he wanted to [do that to me]. And I got really upset.

Her mother called this boy's mother, who said, "Oh, he's very precocious." The mothers left it at that.

Danielle, an African-American teenager I spoke to, talked about a boy who continually pressured her to sleep over with his sister so that he could get to her at night in his own home.

He was my brother's friend—he liked me a lot. . . . We moved there when they [my brother and he] were in the third grade and we [his sister and I] were in fourth, and he used to cuss me all the time, and I was wondering why. . . . Boys just don't understand some things. . . . And that's why I wouldn't spend the night at her house, because he'd always want me to, but I'm, like, "No."

To grown-ups these incidents are often cute. In the minds of many grown-ups, they already see boys as the chasers and girls as the unwilling victims, but they also find it adorable when kids act out these roles. Adults seem to be especially proud of their boys. To girls, this harassment is annoying and sometimes upsetting. Robin, the girl who spied on her teacher going to the bathroom, recalled that in the fourth grade a boy pulled up her skirt so that the whole class saw her underwear.

I was really mad about that and started crying. And I didn't really know what to do. And he just laughed, and I think I told the teacher.

Felicia also suffered from the liberties boys would take with their sexually charged behavior. Left in the care of her popular sister, Felicia would go with her to the shopping center, where the clusters of boys she and her sister passed intimidated her. She dreaded this.

And they'd say little things or they'd try to touch me the way they would touch my sister. I'd find myself having to fight and run, and I just hated it. It was not something I ever wanted.

Like Felicia, May recalled being frightened by boys. A white woman in her thirties, she told a terrifying story of a group of boys ganging up on her and her friends when she was in fourth grade. Asked if she remembered a time when kids forced her to do anything she didn't want to do or when she felt uncomfortable about a sexual experience, she answered:

[Some boys] took us off, and they wanted us to take our clothes off, and this is a friend of my brother's, who I actually sort of had a crush on. It was his neighborhood friends, and they took us off into the woods, and I remember being very upset by that. . . . I was about nine . . . and it was such a yucky feeling of being forced, you know, to take off your— and we went off in the woods together under some other pretense, and they were like, "Okay, now you have to take down your pants." And I

*remember crying. And they said, "You have to take down your pants."
. . . And I just remember I did that.*

Overwhelmingly, the women and girls I interviewed said that when they entered junior high school the harassment continued. During a game of Choo Choo with the boys, the boys would keep trying to "hold your butt," Valerie said, and the girls would have to fight them off.

In Becca's junior high, the girls never wore white T-shirts, because after lunch the boys would throw water on the girls to have their bras or chest show through their shirts. Unfortunately, this kind of thing, like much recess harassment, was tolerated by the school.

Today, sexual harassment, defined unfortunately broadly as anything sexual said or done that makes the other feel uncomfortable, is regulated to prevent this kind of play in the school. Nevertheless, the idea that boys chase the girls and girls chase the boys so all is well is used sometimes to dismiss the scarier kinds of attacks that boys make on girls. While not technically sexual abuse, these incidents not only threaten girls, but also make sexuality dangerous. They are upsetting, angering, and humiliating for girls, yet somehow boys feel entitled to chase, push, grab, insult, and pressure the girls in their classes and schools.

Child-to-Child Abuse: It Happens

A whole new variety of sexual abuses have been discovered in which children are the perpetrators. Sometimes children who themselves have been abused act out and force other kids to experience the hardships they had to. Freud explained such a repetition of past trauma as attempts to master what happened to them by modeling themselves after the aggressor. Many experts who work with sexually abused kids label these children as "sexualized," as if to imply that normal children are not. Vermont, among other states, has instituted a special group therapy (the STEP program) for kids who have been caught abusing other kids. Despite my preconceptions, when I heard stories of these kids who are sent to group therapy for sexualized behavior, I wondered whether what the kids have been caught doing should really be called abuse.

It's hard to decide what is abuse when sex occurs between kids unless one of the children is coerced or upset. That doesn't mean that sexual abuse by kids on kids doesn't occur; it does. But in my interviews I heard about several incidents which defied simple categorization.

Vicky, one of the few Asian-American women I interviewed, told me of an incident at her baby-sitter's house, when she was forced to take a bath with the baby-sitter's granddaughter, who was a bit older than her:

> [The other girl] would ask me, you know, "Do you have this?" And she would show me hers, and the first time it wasn't, you know, but then, be-cause we were there everyday. . . . One day we took a bath to-gether, and I guess she was just showing me hers, and I felt really weird, but then of course I was naked too, so she saw me too and, like, she touched me there. And it was just, you know, it felt weird. That it wasn't right.

Vicky felt "very ashamed afterwards, like I was always happy to get out of that place." When I asked if the girl made her do things she wasn't comfortable with, she replied, "No, it wasn't that she forced me, but I felt, I don't know, I felt like I had to or something. I felt like I had to. And I felt really dirty, very ashamed."

In many ways this story bears similarity to the many stories I heard about showing and touching that were pleasurable. The only difference was that Vicky didn't really want to do it and felt in some way compelled to. Perhaps this is a story without a perpetrator, because one child simply was ignorant of the other's discomfort while she tried to indulge her own sexual curiosity. Nevertheless, Vicky still sounds like a victim. She recalled that she felt "dirty" and "ashamed." She didn't really want to do those things after the first time, but she felt that she had to. Furthermore, she was "always happy to get out of that place." It was the only example of possible girl-to-girl abuse that I heard in all of my discussions.

In another interview, Charise talked about an experience with a male cousin that was abusive, though her description presents her as having some control. Professionals today would categorize this as abuse, and by making Charise only a victim, they would focus on her feelings of discomfort and ignore her remembered feeling of agency.

> I remember this same cousin who was related to my grandfather, he had me going in the backyard, and pulled my panties down, and I was standing in front of him. He was standing behind me. And I guess he was just grinding on me, but it was something that I didn't really want to do, but I think I did it to make him happy or something. He was one of my favorite cousins. . . . I knew it wasn't right but it was just something that he wanted to do.

Like Charise, Maura was involved in a situation that most professionals would call abuse, but she seems to have come out of it particularly
healthy and unscathed. She grew up in a loving family in the suburbs of
Los Angeles, a great neighborhood with lots of kids around. Among them
was a boy who lived nearby, who was fifteen when she was ten. Maura recalled that

> my parents trusted him, and he was our baby-sitter, and he was very
> free. He taught us a lot of things. He was kind of the older boy that
> everyone looked up to, and we would put our things out in the backyard
> during the summer and all sleep out there, and that summer he started
> coming, messing around a little bit . . . and it was all very innocent.

At first they would "smooch and stuff" and later on they would start "going
to the bodies a little more." Though this relationship lasted nearly two
years, they never did

> any big stuff. You know, we never had intercourse, but we just messed
> around with each other's bodies, and we looked at each other and
> touched each other. And he knew more than I did. So, I mean, he taught
> me some things that I think I was much too young to know.

Professionals would say that her youthfulness is the crux of why it was abusive. As the older, much admired boy in the neighborhood, he not only
knew much more but also had a certain amount of power over Maura. In
the interview, Maura claimed, "I don't think it damaged my psyche that
much . . . but it definitely changed how I looked at the world." She had
mixed feelings: "I did feel some shame about it, because I knew that it
wasn't, that my parents would not be happy about it, but at the same time
I was so intrigued and excited about it."

Although this was a potentially harmful situation, there can be abuse
with no harm. It may be that there is some hidden harm that she doesn't
acknowledge or which has yet to emerge. However, girls can make use of
such experiences, reframing them in useful ways. Comparing the gentle
two-year-long exploratory introduction to sex to the sometimes rough introduction to sex some girls get on their first date with a "bad" kid in high
school, suggests that Maura, though abused, was not as bad off as some. Despite the way the relationship may have interfered with Maura's other
childhood activities, and despite the assumption that the fifteen-year-old

should not have done this, in her mind Maura's first experience with sex was still a relatively positive one.

Looking back, Maura clearly differentiated this experience from another experience she had with a boy when she was thirteen. In it, she was briefly trapped by another boy in her neighborhood: "He chased me around, but I got out of it. I escaped. He wanted to have sexual contact with me, but I got away from him. That was an experience!"

The above examples should not give reason to believe that child-to-child abuse is usually an innocent mistake easily gotten over by its victims. Nor does it mean that all women or girls will recognize the abuse either as it is happening or in retrospect. In fact, several children had intercourse at ages that, no matter how mutual, create more psychological questions and worries than they answer.

Roxanne, who was nine the first time she had sex, remembered:

Oh yeah, my brothers had the cousins come over and stuff, and they used to abuse me. . . . I was eight or nine and they actually had intercourse [with me]. Those were my little secrets I kept for years and years and years.

Bev, who interviewed Roxanne, was shocked when she heard about it. She asked, "Did they force you? Did you know what was going on?"

Oh, it was attention. It was attention, so I knew that they liked me. You know? As far as I knew, they were my special friends. . . . I didn't like myself very much because of the things I would do. . . . I knew it was wrong, but it was a way to . . . [then her voice trailed off]

Though she described her cousins as her "special friends," Roxanne also described the harmful repercussions of these encounters: "But it did so much damage, though. It did. It really did a lot of damage as far as relationships with men. No respect for them. Not no respect but, I treat them now like they treat women. That's how I treat them."

Despite the remarkable catalog researchers have collected both on children and on sexuality, we know too little about the combination of the two to know who would come out of such an experience "damaged" and who would come out fine. Girls certainly are at risk. Studies show that girls who have higher rates of intercourse at twelve have higher emotional distress; the same is not true of boys.

Robin, the African-American college student from an upper-middle-class home in the Washington, D.C., area, had a strange experience with the brother of a friend that most professionals would conclude was abusive.

> *I remember one time, I was eight and he was thirteen. Emma left the room and he was, Robin, can you get my keys out of my pocket of my jeans? And, like I went in and he had a hole in his pocket, so like I really felt, really, really weird. . . . So, I mean, he sounds like a big pervert. And I can't really think of any other time when he was like perverted to me. . . . And at the time I did it, and then I was, like, oh, what is that? . . . But then I realized, and then I felt like really weird and bad, and then I never like talked, like I never was comfortable around him.*

Psychologists who work with sexual abuse victims easily see this as an abusive experience, tricked as she was to feel this boy's penis. The betrayal and shock are more salient than what might be called the prankishness of the incident. Robin's shock and discomfort make it easier to label this relatively minor incident abuse, and yet more difficult to clearly define abusive those experiences of sex that other girls had that were not traumatic. For example, Toni, who pretended to be asleep when her cousin entered her room to have sex with her, or Maura, who spent all that time with the fifteen-year-old baby-sitter, although abused, appear less like stereotypical victims because of their understanding and agency at the time of the sexual acts.

Those clinicians who work with sexual abuse victims might say I am blaming the victim. But I think I am just recognizing that in some cases of abuse, girls feel as if they had some choice. It's not as if these experiences are not abuse, but they are something else too. The bottom line is choice. The white, middle-class girl who explored her sexuality with her fifteen-year-old friend—even though he was much older than she—felt she had choice, control, and a degree of mutuality in the situation. It was at her speed, if a little advanced. Roxanne, with her problematic family and her desperation for affection, made a choice too, but it was a more coerced choice than Maura's. Instead of participating equally, she allowed the older cousins to abuse her because she felt it was her only option. She still feels the aftershocks of those days.

Valerie, the African-American woman who was six when her fifteen-year-old cousin started touching her, said:

> *I was young, but he used to come over and I used to sit on his lap, and you know how you wiggle and play, stuff like that. You don't know much about it, and I remember one time he touched my vagina and we just kept playing and I didn't think that much of it. But then he'd always give me money and stuff like that. But I felt he was so nice at the time that I always let it go. Then, maybe like a month or so later, he would come over and the same type of thing would go on, and he did it again. . . . I'd say about four or five times that may have happened, but there was always money and stuff involved. It happened really quickly.*

Once, when she was playing with all the boys and sitting spread-legged on the top of a bunk bed, he came right over and

> *put his hand in, and he stuck it in my vagina, and I remember so clearly saying to him, "Don't do that. That hurts! You shouldn't be doing that," and I remember my brother Jay and somebody, they said, "What are you talking about?" And then as quickly as he said that my cousin kind of said, "You know, here, you want some money?" . . . And we went on playing.*

When she got older, she realized these incidents were abusive, but she never brought it up with her cousin, whom she still sees.

Despite the abusive nature of Valerie's interactions with her cousin, she doesn't feel particularly harmed by that part of her past. In retrospect, she especially dislikes the money aspect of it, though it explains to her why she didn't mind so much at the time. In addition, she was able to stick up for herself one of the times, setting a boundary for her cousin.

The matter of choice and control means as much to girls as it does to women. It was certainly coercive when a neighborhood teenager asked Caroline at the age of eight or nine to give him her panties or let him feel her chest (a choiceless choice). But to her mind, she was "curious," and so she let him. Now, as a woman in her forties, she thinks she was abused, but she didn't experience it as abuse at the time because, as she puts it, "I had a choice."

It is very clear that when there is no choice, and when control is taken away from a girl, the abuse is more terrifying and the trauma more long-lasting. Vicky was pushed into a broom closet in the seventh grade by a boy at school who felt her up:

I like started to cry, and it was just so, but the weird thing was—I couldn't scream! I couldn't scream, I couldn't do anything.

She was frozen by terror and still feels bad about this incident.

Julia, molested by a group of boys in an alley who ripped her clothes off and felt her up and down until she escaped, wasn't frozen, but she was still traumatized by that event. She continued to see her perpetrators on the street afterward, but she never told anyone. Brenda, another Puerto Rican woman, had to fight to escape a boy trying to undress her in her own house when she was a girl.

The girls who got to play games of mutual delight and exploration with girls seemed to have been the lucky ones. Girls who hung out with boys were in riskier situations. Sometimes these girls could play games of mutual interest, but boys frequently chased, humiliated, abused, and hurt them. While there is much to be admired in the sexual assertion and fun that girls have behind closed doors in childhood, we also shouldn't forget the harassment and abuse that many, over a quarter of the women and girls I interviewed, also experienced.

They aren't all victims. Girls learn about sex in many ways, from the choices they make and from the abuse or harassment they encounter. Some come away fine and happy; the ones who fared the worst were the ones abused by adults. These experiences were in many cases more confusing or frightening for the children, and continue to make me so much more angry on behalf of all the girls it happened to.

Sexual Abuse of Girls

Clearly, an adult should not have sex with a child. Even if a child is willing. When a child is confused, when she feels complicit because she has sexual feelings, the shame and trauma sometimes are greater. Some of the girls or women I interviewed were abused by grown men: Cora by her uncle, Denitra by her mother's boyfriend, Jennifer by her grandmother's boyfriend, Annette by her grandfather, Lucy and Yolanda by men living in their apartment buildings. There was June, the oldest woman interviewed, who bent over to pick something up in an alley, when a man came over and tickled her bottom. She turned around and scolded him, "That's not very nice!" and that was that.

About 15 to 20 percent of the women and girls I interviewed talked about some kind of sexual harassment or abuse. Unfortunately, this kind of experience for girls is not uncommon. Research shows that, for at least half of them, they will continue to suffer long-lasting effects, such as depression, anxiety, problems in relationships, low self-esteem, eating disorders, drug addiction, and more. On the bright side, girls do not always fit the typical victim mode: sometimes they freeze and are silent and never tell; other times they tell people, avoid their perpetrators, and even yell at them, "That hurts!" or "That's not very nice!"

But just because abuse and harassment are so prevalent in the lives of girls does not mean that our protection of them needs to keep them away from all things sexual or from boys. If parents can emphasize mutuality and respect as well as the notion of play, girls may be less vulnerable to adult male predators. Raising girls to understand sexuality and to understand their bodies, to make their own choices and to feel their own power, will serve them well in this sometimes dangerous world, and help them to preserve a small area in which they can develop and feel their own sexual potential.

Chapter 14

Raising Sexual Girls: A Few Words to Parents

"all other passions pale into insignificance."
—From "What Every Girl Should Know," a series of articles for The Call,
    written by early feminist Margaret H. Sanger in 1912, but confiscated by
    postal officials on grounds of obscenity

*"We may have to learn to let our sexual feelings come without our
judgment or control and accept them as part of ourselves."*
—Boston Women's Health Collective, Our Bodies, Ourselves, 1971

"Sex is people communicating with their bodies. . . . Sex is play."
—Deal With It!, 1999

Few women are satisfied with the sex education they received, either in school or in relationships. Although these experiences are something that adult women laugh about today, few take the next step of envisioning a different process for their daughters. This passivity could mean that we as adults are comfortable leaving girls' sex education to TV, adolescent boys, booklets distributed by Kotex, or websites that advocate a wild, male-oriented sexuality that in the end could leave them feeling vulnerable and ashamed. But most parents would disagree. The problem is that even adults are not sure what constitutes a good sex education. But if we begin to think this through together, I believe we would agree that we want girls to know their bodies, to understand pleasure, to gradually grow in their development so that puberty does not attack them with a vengeance, and to love themselves as sexual beings.

To this end, adults need to let girls explore the range of human potential even when it means letting them play sexually. I see nothing wrong with two eight-year-olds closing the door to the bedroom, stripping down, and playing "puppet-talk" with the lips of their vaginas (true story!). Nor do I see anything wrong with a group of ten-year-old girls pretending to make out with each other, taking turns going into a closet. Nor is there something wrong with a game of house that incorporates a little humping. This is practice, this is experimentation, and it is also "real" sex—real to the children who play it.

For those girls who have been given that wonderful, protected space of play, this kind of play is happening already—there's really no need to advocate for it, only a need to help them to not feel so guilty. While sex isn't and shouldn't be the main focus of childhood, it is part of life, and as a part of life it will enter into the games many children play. Adults only need to watch out for feelings of shame and guilt and bullying and coercion.

As in any activity in childhood, coercion, bullying, forcing, and teasing is wrong in sexual play. Just as it would be questionable for a child to actively and compulsively pursue playing sex games with all the children in the neighborhood, it would be wrong for a child to force another child in any way to participate in any of these kinds of games. Still, just because there are problem versions of sexual play and games doesn't mean that all sexual play is harmful to children.

Parents may wonder how to know when enough is enough or when it is okay to simply close the bedroom door and walk away. Closing the door does not mean dropping the subject. A parent might close the door that afternoon and, in the evening, ask her daughter about the game: "Was it okay with you? Are you having fun? Are you enjoying yourself?" or, as one mother yelled in to her daughter, "Don't do anything you'll be ashamed of!"

If a parent knows her daughter is easily led, passive, and desperate for friends, she might have a right to worry and wonder whether her daughter enters such games mutually. If her daughter is playing with an older child, a mother has a right to worry whether the older child is taking an interest in her daughter for the wrong reasons and introducing her daughter to concepts she herself would not readily be interested in at that age. This kind of monitoring goes on for all sorts of play, not just sexual, and a parent who is on the ball monitoring her or his daughter's play in other areas will be well prepared to ask the right questions with sexual play.

These are just a few of the ways adults can help girls feel good about their sexual interests and feelings:

- Accept her as a sexual being, from birth through the grade school years, and, of course, thereafter.
- Rather than taking a moralistic approach to a sexuality of do's and don'ts, parents should explicitly assert that sex is normal and a natural part of life; the same for sexual feelings.
- Take a moral approach and emphasize that any relationship, sexual or otherwise, is one built on fairness, respect, and caring for the other.
- Create an atmosphere in which sex can be discussed, not only in the sense of gathering information, but in the sense that it is a part of life.
- Respond frequently to sexual messages on TV in front of your child if your child sees them. Kids observe people joking about sex on TV, adults joking about wanting it and getting it and holding out. It's a limited and unimaginative way to be exposed to sexuality, quite devoid of sensuality, and shouldn't be left undiscussed. Talk to children about what's missing in all the joking about sex. Talk to daughters especially about the portrayal of romantic sex on television and in the movies. For instance, a mother can say about a made-for-TV movie, "They make it seem like a girl wants to be treated roughly, but I would think most girls want to be treated tenderly and asked if everything is okay." Or she might say about a prime-time drama, "They make it seem like she's wild with passion, but most girls when they first meet someone are unsure and want to take things slowly."
- Be proactive about the sex education programs in your community schools. Ask for curricula that talk about sexual feelings, pleasure, interpersonal relationships.
- Let them play. Ask about their play. Ask about their comfort level when they play with certain kids. Be sensitive to their relationships with other kids. If she is generally able to have mutually satisfying play that's nonsexual, then she is probably all right with sexual play.
- Always teach your child about coercion and bullying and how to stand up to it. Teach her to recognize when someone is interested in her for herself and when it's something else they want.

The erotic is a "resource within each of us that lies in a deeply female and spiritual plane," wrote the poet Audré Lorde. These days, Americans often confuse it with the pornographic or the superficially sexual. But children need to move through and work through these competing images to come to some satisfying knowledge of their own place in this lively world.

Secrets and sexual secrets are not all bad. The best secrets of childhood are the ones a child keeps while knowing that in some sense her parents already know, to some extent, what's going on. Shameful secrets corrodes a girl's love of life, her longing to be a part of things, and her spirit of adventure. While I don't know all the answers about how sex and sexuality can be a part of girls' lives, I do know that it already is for many girls, and we would do well to acknowledge that fact and lend our support to the healthy development of sexuality they seek.

Part II

Aggression, Destruction,
and Being Mean

Chapter 15

Aggression in Girls

"I don't want to be sweet and nice."
—*Naomi Campbell, Black supermodel of the nineties, in an interview with Barbara Walters on 20/20, a newsmagazine television show*

Discovered at fifteen, Naomi Campbell was the first Black model on the cover of the French *Vogue*. Widely known for being a "bitch," she's even been to rehab clinics to deal with her anger. Her trips to the clinic came after she was brought up on assault charges by a former assistant in 1998. Though Naomi claims she threw a phone at her assistant, her assistant insists that Naomi also grabbed her by the throat. When asked by Barbara Walters why she acted "this way"—Walters demurring from using the b-word—Naomi said, "If I don't, they're going to walk all over me."

This belief, that if you're not tough people will walk all over you, is absolutely the fear of many girls and women who are aggressive and act aggressive openly. They are the girls who, like Campbell, grew up in tough neighborhoods filled with gangs, drugs, and disrespect, places where girls are more vulnerable to harm because they are on the streets and where no one has time to watch over these girls. Girls who grow up in such environments wear their aggression with pride, while in a different context they still may refer to themselves as "good girls" and brag that they please the teacher and do their homework. Whether they are good or bad, aggression is a part of their life, but not just theirs—everyone's.

In middle-class neighborhoods, however, white, Black, and Latina girls consider aggression wrong and bad. They see it as making them more male and less female. When they are aggressive they have deep, long-lasting feelings of guilt about even their smallest acts of meanness.

In the chapters to come I spell out the differences in girls' lives that lead to different relationships to their own aggression. The potential for acting aggressively is latent in all of us, in girls as well as boys. Though both should use acts of force with restraint, it is important that girls as well as boys understand their own impulses toward aggression as something that is a part of life, even normal, and not something to fear.

Today aggression is permitted among those girls in our society for whom we don't care much, whose development and futures are of little concern. But adults rein in middle-class girls' lives so that the smallest slip of aggression tends to haunt them into adulthood. Society ignores and accepts the aggression in girls from low-income neighborhoods because their images don't matter. In fact, because Americans deem aggression in women inappropriate, this expectation keeps low-income women down, in impoverished neighborhoods where it is both acceptable and necessary. If Naomi Campbell were not a supermodel, no one would be concerned enough about her aggression and her anger to help her enroll in a rehab clinic; her friends and family might see this anger as appropriate and even natural. Some of it would indeed be appropriate, a kind of righteous anger about what other kids have. Only when aggression takes place in a middle-class setting does it become a cause of concern.

Our culture does a disservice to both kinds of girls: to the girls who need to hide their aggressive impulses, who rein them in so tightly that they find release in the unexpected, strangely hostile act that they claim came totally out of nowhere; and to the girls who are left to fight it out alone on the streets, to survive the pecking order of who is the toughest. Neither can survive well in these two opposing environments.

For middle-class girls, the message that aggression is inappropriate shackles them with feelings of guilt for acts that if performed by male children would be dismissed with a simple "boys will be boys." Research shows that mothers increasingly punish girls between the ages of four and six for aggression and decreasingly punish boys. American culture further indicts girls for their so-called sneaky aggression, the way they use social exclusion, gossip, and cattiness to punish and hurt. It is often said that "girls can be much meaner than boys" because they manipulate their social groups in aggressive ways. Few remark that girls are not permitted a physical expression of anger that might allow them to confront the other person with whom they are mad in a different way.

Girls' aggression comes out in other forms when it is reined in physically, but not just through purported cattiness. Girls turn it against themselves: through eating disorders, self-mutilation, hypercriticism about their talents and bodies, and depression. Girls aggress against themselves. Society's recent attention to these self-destructive acts seeks to empower girls by addressing them through self-esteem exercises and encouraging self-understanding, but smart psychotherapists know that the girl who can acknowledge her anger and feelings of aggression toward others is on the right track to health. Girls who own their aggression—even feel entitled to it—have a source of energy and creativity that will do them well in the lives ahead of them.

The world can be a tough place for poorer as well as middle-class girls. Teaching both to fight, and to fight aggressively, may not be first choice in coping mechanisms. But if girls learn to accept their anger and their feelings of aggression, they can tap into this potential and transform it, sometimes in creative and positive ways. The ways an urban girl chooses to be aggressive aren't so much wrong as they are ineffectual; she doesn't usually have the means to turn the aggression into a socially important act such as standing up against injustice or expressing such rage through writing or art. The middle-class girl also can learn to tap into those feelings to fight injustice or contribute to society through the arts. Both can use such aggression to fight their way to the top in our competitive society and withstand the prejudice they might encounter when they try to enter mostly male businesses or professions.

This is not to say that empathy is not an important quality in girls as well as boys. Caring and concern are aspects of being human that help to tame raw aggression. Parents and society have done so well at socializing the middle-class girl in empathy that they most likely fear that a girl who gets fighting mad will no longer care or be empathic toward her victims. But it's not a zero sum equation. Being a full human being means having the capacity for both compassion and anger and frustration. Along with the former comes the ability to care; with the latter the ability to act aggressively and be angry.

We supposedly teach children that it's okay to feel angry but it's not okay to act aggressively when one feels that way. Much research has shown, however, that for middle-class girls it is not okay to feel angry and that adults teach girls from a very young age to mask their anger so that, after time, it is even unrecognizable to themselves.

Anger in adult women is also made problematic by American culture. An angry woman is someone who needs help, who is sick. But, as Carol Tavris said in her book *Anger: The Misunderstood Emotion*, a woman's anger is only a problem because she is likely to be in a position subordinate to the person she is angry at.

Physical expressions of aggression are even more problematic than expressions of anger in girls. In this culture adults closely identify aggression with masculinity and believe that it is a biological imperative. Many Americans assume that men are more violent than women because they have more testosterone and because of an evolutionary history as hunters. According to this biological model, it is only acceptable for women to be aggressive when it comes to their children, when they become like fierce mother bears protecting their cubs. By decontextualizing a hodgepodge of biological and anthropological guesses about the past, we simply reinforce notions of acceptable feminine behavior, of "woman's place."

Whether biologically based or not, many today think that there is nothing good to be said about aggression. Indeed, the prevailing dialogue about youth culture suggests that children are exposed to TV and computer game violence too early, and that in some cases such exposure leads to school shootings like the ones in Littleton, Colorado, and Jonesboro, Arkansas. But when the media talks about exposure to violence they are primarily talking about boys. The increase in youth violence that the media cites is also typically based on boys' behavior, not that of girls. Certainly boys, more often than girls, get encouragement, support, and training in acts of violence that generally aim at desensitizing them to human suffering and lure them to the excitement of gore and guns. But just because boys may be too attracted to aggression, developing fewer alternative skills for negotiating interpersonal relationships, does it mean that girls will do the same?

Anthropologist Victoria Burbank argues that in some circumstances "aggression can be a positive, enhancing act." She adds that when we deny women "aggressive possibilities, we potentially diminish their being." Her claims come from years of work in an Australian Aboriginal community where anger and aggression are almost one and the same and where fighting stories are common among men and women. One of the ways women in this community use aggression is as a showy display that safeguards them from more private, hostile aggression that might occur one-on-one. These women believe that Western women have made themselves more vulnerable to aggression from men because they neither fight nor make displays of their aggressive potential. In a similar way, psychologist and author Janice Haaken collaborated with West African women to envision a battered women's shelter quite unlike the secret, hidden sanctuaries of the United States. There, burly women with Uzis would guard the periphery, making a display of strength rather than hiding in supposed weakness.

One of the only venues in which we support aggression in girls in our culture is in sports. Those who coach women's sports praise the girl who can be aggressive on the soccer field or on the tennis court. They see the usefulness of aggression and aggressive displays in terms of showing a team's or an individual's strengths. Still, many argue that the tacit acceptance, even encouragement, of girls' aggression comes not from any real progress in American culture but because sports have been a male domain for decades.

Others suggest girls' aggression in sports is simply "borrowed" or influenced by male/male aggression. Feminists of the seventies and eighties saw aggression as a patriarchal power tool and claimed that women's use of aggression was a sign of how much they had been influenced by patriarchal forms of interaction. Each of these responses to female aggression categorizes it as a tool of domination, in which case the ultimate source of aggression must be male. But is aggression only a tool of domination? Perhaps it has other uses.

Dana Jack, in her book *Behind the Mask,* argues that anger and aggression in women and girls are fundamentally about connection and loss of connection, and not about domination. Burbank acknowledges that much of women's aggression occurs in relationships, but she prefers to call it a form of communication. While I agree that aggression can be about connection and preserving relationships, it is also about power and respect. By allowing female aggression to be about more than connecting or protecting, we can see more clearly the sometimes complex ways that it plays out in girls' and women's lives. Their aggression can be used to connect or to destroy, to hold on to or to push away; it's not just about mama bear and her beleaguered cubs.

In the chapters that follow I take a closer look at both anger and aggression in girls. These are the secret stories that rarely get heard in the public discourse. By necessity, I interpret them in the context of the culture in which aggression erupts, and look at it in terms of the different expectations that each community (racial, ethnic, religious, and class) has for its children. To set the stage, I examine the girls' ideas of what a good girl is, as well as their perceptions of their communities' expectations of them. What follows are stories of aggression and a discussion of how parents might approach their daughters' aggressive potential—when they have cause for worry and when they can even encourage it as their little girls grow up.

Chapter 16

A Good Girl Doesn't Do That

"I used to pray every night that God would show me the difference between right and wrong because I always wanted to be with the 'good girls.' "
—Arlene, African American, 56

There is no question that girls, women, men, and parents today in the United States understand girls to be more caring and sensitive than boys. But this notion of girls as caring and sensitive in contrast to boys also creates a burden on girls that plays into a larger myth that "girls are good." The "tyranny of the nice and kind," a phrase coined by Lyn Mikel Brown and Carol Gilligan, forces girls to express in public those aspects of girlhood that people expect. Because this vision of girlhood targets white middle-class girls in particular, it serves to exclude and handicap entire groups of girls who don't meet the standard.

Nevertheless, most girls measure themselves against this ideal of the good girl, though ultimately it hurts them. Because ideals of goodness often are confused with real or possible behavior, living, breathing girls cannot live up to the image and find themselves demoralized from trying. Not only does the ideal shut out girls from low-income neighborhoods whose lives don't match up, it rejects middle-class girls who know in their hearts that they are not as good as they should be. Girls know that their claims to goodness are never secure. On some level, she still feels she is phony, that deep down she is indeed lustful, angry, and rebellious. The very women researchers and psychologists who have done so much to bring attention to girls and their problems have also, in some ways, played into a myth that keeps girls from developing in a more complex and profound way, acknowledging all these aspects of being human.

Thus, in this age of "girl power" and "girls rule," it is important to re-examine good girl ideals to see how much leeway they leave for "real girls." During the course of my study, I asked girls what they think of when I say the words "good girl," who they imagine, and whether they think there is such a thing as a good girl. As one might expect, girls talked about being nice and caring—not mean. But one theme that recurred in many of the middle-class girls' descriptions of what a good girl is was perfection. In the following examples, girls describe goodness in absolutes, using words like "perfect" and "never." This ideal of perfection creates a burden and makes them feel both overwhelmed by the expectations and resentful.

> I'm never *like really bad*. I never *call my mom names and stuff*. I never *really did anything like breaking something on purpose*. I never *really got mad at her on purpose*. (Serena, white, 8)

In Serena's comments, you hear not only the striving for perfection but the idea that good girls never get angry. Nora, age eleven, said: "A goody-two-shoes *never* does anything really bad or like wrong, *never* is mean to anyone."

Miranda, age eleven also, said: "There is like this good girl who is *perfect* to all the teachers and all, yeah, yeah, yeah."

You can hear the resentment in Miranda's voice while she mimics the good girl for being a "yes" girl. Kelly, a ten-year-old Asian-American girl, said that being called a good girl "means nothing. They just say 'Oh you're a good girl, good girl.' But they don't really know you."

When I asked her what a good girl might be like, Kelly answered:

> *She would go to a private school, wear glasses, braces, ugly little clothes, braids in her hair. She would act* perfectly. *She would raise her hand and say please and thank you.*

Others confirmed her assessment:

> *Someone who is nice to mostly everyone; doesn't hate anyone and makes that clear.* (Maya, 11)

> Never *does anything bad;* always *really, really good.* (Kiely, 10)

Chrystal, a white teenager growing up in the projects, addressed her sensible response to the idea of perfection:

I believe every girl has somewhere a fault. They may try to hide it as much as they can but somewhere there is a fault.

This perfection was not something that most of the low-income white, African-American, and Latina girls and teens seemed to aspire to. Bev, my assistant, and I noted, after our interviews, that these girls seemed to have more trouble answering the question "What is a good girl?" than others, and even appeared resentful that we were using words such as "good girl." Several felt they had to teach us that there was no such thing:

My mama might consider myself a good girl, but she knows that I'm not exactly good. She knows I'm not an angel.

When pushed to come up with something, their responses pointed to things other than perfection. Tanisha focused on happiness and care: "Happy all the time; caring and loving."

Rashonda, age eight, even said a girl didn't have to be perfect; she gave the good girl a lot of elbow room: "She don't pick on *that* many people."

Kezia, who is eleven, self-assured, and chatty, defined a good girl, and then told me how she both is and isn't one:

She doesn't do bad things; she has a good education; she's nice and caring. Gentle and just wonderful—I'm nice and caring. I have a good education, a full scholarship! . . . I'm bad too. I yell at people and I'm pushy. I push and I'm very bossy.

Rather than suggesting she doesn't fit the mold, LaShauna also exuded self-confidence:

I'd describe me. A person who loves doing the things that she do from like day till night. A person who thinks of others before she thinks of herself . . . a person who is all about education, a person who is all about people.

The African-American girls from low-income neighborhoods were particularly confident in their answers as well as in offering themselves as prime examples of goodness. Researchers over the past decade have wondered why African-American adolescents seem to succumb much less frequently to anorexia and bulimia. Some have proposed that because the mainstream ideals of beauty are not attainable or relevant to them, they are immune to the media's deleterious influence.

The African-American girls I spoke to seemed to be not as burdened by the idea of perfection in their judgments of what makes a good girl. In contrast, middle-class girls resent girls they imagine as good or perfect, and to achieve the ideal they hide parts of themselves from others and even from themselves. Furthermore, in describing their aggressive behaviors, they significantly othered it. They described their behavior as something coming from outside of themselves, not truly a part of them. Dana Jack, author of *Behind the Mask,* observes that all kinds of women, when they get angry or aggressive, often describe themselves as being in "unfamiliar territory" or say that their anger took them totally by surprise as if it "came out of nowhere." Jack also remarks that both girls and women are taught to disguise their anger so that they often "act nice and feel mean."

While girls and women are critical of themselves for the duplicitous nature of their anger, they shouldn't take all the blame. The culture at large supports the suppression and masking of anger. We don't want to see it in little girls, so much so that we're blind to it. Despite my own interest in this phenomenon, I missed it in Veronica, who projected the ever elusive ideal of the perfect good girl.

Behind her Mask

Perhaps since I don't have a daughter, I fell in love with Veronica during the interview we had in her bedroom, both of us under the canopy of her big bed in a suburb of Philadelphia. Her face was so open, her eyes wide, and even her voice seemed eager to tell everything to help me with my book. Most of all, I was touched by the way her eyes teared up when I asked about her relationship with her mother.

> *She is like my number one best friend in the whole world. She is really there every time, and if you knew her I'm sure you'd really like her . . . and I think that's so special to just live with someone that is so special like her.*

To understand what made her mother so great, I asked Veronica to elaborate.

> She's just her! You know, she does—she's kind in the morning; she gets
> you up and says, "Did you have a nice sleep?" And she says all these
> kind things, and it's just—she's so nice! . . . If I could have anybody in
> the world for a mother, I'd just want her. She's just perfect.

Perfect! She saw her mother as perfect. To me, Veronica seemed to be
the essential good girl. The kind whom teachers admire and parents are
thankful for. She is above all appreciative. She is easy to talk to and open
with her feelings. She is reasonable and adultlike, despite a childlike innocence, resembling Alice in Wonderland with her long blonde hair and her
wide blue eyes. She does well in school. She listens to her mother. She understands others who might be having a hard time and offers them help. Of
all the girls I interviewed, she seemed closest to the much ballyhooed ideal
that girls often strive for.

But after my interview marathon of girls in this upper-middle-class
neighborhood of Philadelphia, I reviewed the day with my dear friend who
arranged the interviews. I was exhausted, so we drank some tea and chatted. Then she asked me whether I had enjoyed the interview with the girl
who was having so much trouble in school. I said I wasn't quite sure who
she meant; I thought all the girls I had interviewed seemed to be doing
quite well. She then described how one of the girls I had interviewed had
been writing obscene graffiti on the bathroom walls and toilet stalls. This
girl would excuse herself from class and write, in my friend's words, the
"filthiest, vilest things," mostly "fucking this or fuck that." She said that
even the girls' friends were concerned about her. Though they had caught
her in the act and she had admitted it to school professionals, her friends
still didn't know what to say to her about it. Nobody knew what to do
about it. This girl, of course, was Veronica.

If a boy had written this graffiti all over the walls we would probably characterize him as a bad kid, or someone who needed more discipline. But it was strange to everyone involved that Veronica—so good
and loving in her presentation—would act in such an unexpected way.
Because the girl and the graffiti didn't seem to fit the image Veronica
projected, many of us wondered whether there was something seriously
wrong with her. When girls act bad or angry, and they don't seem to us to

be bad girls or fresh-mouthed or bored and angry, we wonder about their sanity.

Was there some sign of this earlier in the interview that I had missed? During the interview, Veronica had struggled with her description of goodness.

> *I know that nobody is* perfect. *That nobody can go through all their life just being* perfect, *but I think about people at my school and how they are all different from me. . . . One girl, Caitlyn, she's* perfect, perfect teeth, *perfect* friends, *perfect* everything. *I always think of the bad things I do, like maybe doing something wrong.*

Not only does Veronica already invest in the absolutisms of goodness, in the following story she goes on to invest Caitlyn, a friend, with all the attributes of the ideal.

> *Like one time—this is a secret—one time me and my brother—oh, it's not really a secret to my mom, but we were sitting, we have a big driveway and the road is right there. We were sitting playing marbles, and one of them went out into the road, and it was across the road, so I went to go get it, and a car came by when I was on the other side, and I went to go walk across and my foot hit a rock and the rock went flinging up and hit the car, and it made a huge dent and I just looked, Oh, my God! And I thought, Caitlyn would never have done something horrible as that.*

When I asked Veronica why, if it was an accident, it is such a huge secret, she whispered that

> *I think I feel so guilty, and it's kind of embarrassing, you know? I mean just, you know? . . . I really, I really don't think I did that, but I feel really guilty. I definitely didn't touch it with my hand. But my foot had hit it and it went flying up . . . (but) I don't think that it's possible to kick it and make such a big dent. I mean, you have to be throwing it really hard.*

She is in agony over this small act. She may actually have thrown the rock, but knowing that she had done that would be so absolutely horrible, she could never admit it, not even to herself.

The interview gave me pause about interviewing girls and the secrets they keep. The restrictions around being a good girl made it difficult for most of them to tell me the things they felt most guilty about. Luckily I had many adult women to reflect back and share, to look from a distance. These women could confess their secrets with less fear of rejection.

Still, I wasn't sure about how I should interpret Veronica's presentation to me. Perhaps I was bamboozled and she presented a persona, not her "true self"; however, I doubt that Veronica's experience of being interviewed was one of feeling as if she had made herself up for my benefit. I don't think she felt at the time that she was lying when she claimed she did nothing bad ever, nothing aggressive or sneaky, or when she told me that she didn't like to swear. She certainly was leaving things out. But I'm not sure that she knew at the time that she was lying.

Instead, she was constructing herself, as girls do daily, leaving things out, aspects of the self that are unacceptable to the culture at large—aggressive parts, sexual thoughts, vicious feelings, angry words, erotic imagery. And, I wondered, what happens to the curse word denied one day? It may appear on the bathroom wall the next.

And I had fallen in love with such a creation. This was hard to admit. I had played a part, as we all do, in creating the good girl, in forcing the real girl to conform to our expectations of what is good. Even I, the interviewer who came to celebrate the secret lives of girls, re-created a situation conducive to the big lie about girls. I fault myself for falling in love with the vision rather than the real girl, whoever she may be. But I fault the culture for making it so hard that even within an interview that is especially designed to give all sorts of signs that aggressive behavior is understandable at times, it is so hard to see these secret parts of girls' lives. My interview and interviewing skills were not enough to always overcome the implicit rules that keep girls reined in: Keep your anger under wraps, your curse words hidden. These rules tell them that if it should slip out, deny it, distance yourself from it, throw it away, but don't ever accept it as part of yourself. My experience with Veronica serves as a warning to parents about how hard it is to undo these restrictions about being a good girl, even when we want to see beyond them.

No wonder that with so little help from adults, girls experience enormous guilt for letting aggression show. Boys in our culture have greater freedom to engage in transgressive activities. Within certain limits they are free to explore, rage, and experiment; they are free to be sexual, ravenous, outrageous, and plain mean. They're restricted in other ways that are most likely equally damaging, yet they are allowed their anger, their aggression. The guilt that girls feel when they do these perfectly human acts is so powerful that it forces them to construct themselves in a way that leaves out crucial parts of their experience. They as much as boys need to break the rules sometimes, get rowdy, throw their weight around, and feel their sensuality—none of these are antithetical to goodness, and we should make a point in telling girls so.

Zeroing In On: Tomboys

I know I'm a girl, but I would act like a boy, and I thought that was bad in a way. I thought I was a bad girl because I wouldn't do girly things. (Aidee, Puerto Rican, 17)

American culture has an outlet for girls who refuse to conform to the stereotypical ways in which girls are supposed to behave: It's called being a "tomboy." The fact that almost half of all adult women remember themselves as tomboys speaks to how important such an outlet is. I call it an outlet, or an "out," because it's a term that's used to allow girls the freedom that boys have without the condemnation girls normally get for such behaviors. Tomboys are allowed to be aggressive, to play rough, to hang with the boys, to explore the neighborhood more thoroughly, and to get dirty. They can swear without fear of punishment. They can squabble and run and throw. And they quite consciously see what they are doing as a form of resistance to being a "girly" girl.

Being a tomboy, as opposed to being a sissy boy, has a positive slant to it. It's not only that male activities are more valued in our culture, but tomboyishness is associated with fun, adventure, and courage. It's interesting, is it not, that to have fun, adventure, and courage a girl has to come to see herself as identified with a boy? Still, while being a tomboy is generally accepted in our culture, almost all the girls who were tomboys, whether middle class or low income, white, black, or Latina, were pressured at some time to be more like a girl. This was true of the women that C. Lynn Carr, a sociologist at Rutgers University, interviewed in her study of tomboys. All these women had rather positive memories to share, but almost all had been pressured to conform to more stereotypical images of girlhood as they approached adolescence.

Sometimes being a tomboy means not only taking on more boyish activities but actively rejecting "girly" things. It's interesting that even in the eighties and nineties, long after Title IX had its effect in bringing girls into sports, girls still associate being involved in sports as a male activity. Jody, for example, called herself a tomboy because she played all kinds of sports. She also "always related better to guys; girls were kind of stupid." She devalues girls and girls' activities as if she were a boy.

It's interesting how having a brother sometimes gave girls permission to do the more male activities they craved. Jessie saw herself as a "goody-two-shoes" who "liked the dangerous stuff." With her older brother she set fires, "blew stuff up," shot ants out of caps and then took notes, like a scientist, on how many of their legs had fallen off in the trauma. She also sat there for hours burning bugs and thinking, "Cool." Jessie had an older sister who she said was a "nice lady, but she tried to curl my hair and buy really girly things for me"; still, she craved the activities her older brother led her into.

The freedom and bravery of tomboys stands out in Julia, a Puerto Rican, who used to "run with the boys" on the streets of New York. There is pride in her voice as she describes herself playing "forest hunters." She would sneak out in the middle of the night and be back home before her mother woke up. One would think that that kind of fun would be dangerous for a girl. But the fun she was having as a tomboy wasn't dangerous; in fact, simply being a girl and walking down the street to do an errand was. A gang of teenage boys attacked her when she was ten and tore her clothes off. She fought them off and escaped before she was raped.

Although we usually think of tomboys as spirited and wonderfully adventurous, there is a defensive nature to it also. We don't know if Julia was a tomboy before this attack or in response to it, as a sort of protection. This doesn't mean it was effective protection, but girls who are abused or treated as sexual objects early can sometimes defend against this by constructing a boyish, hostile, or withdrawn exterior that says "stay away from me."

Denitra, who had been abused by her mother's boyfriend from the age of nine, was one such tomboy. She had no friends, no family member she could trust. Alone she would fight with the teachers, act aggressively toward her peers, and dress like a boy. This was true until she was eighteen and met a man who was interested in her. He started telling her to dress like a woman, would take her out and buy her things, even bought her her first dress. But was this encouragement for her or for him? Denitra said, "So I grew into dressing more girly and acting more girly, and then when I got pregnant [by this man], I just grew up." Her story is complicated because there was not much joy in her acting like a boy; rather, it was a form of protection so that no one would see her vulnerability. But dressing like a girl did not bring her pleasure either—first it brought her attention, and then a pregnancy from a man who left her.

Aidee used her tomboyishness as a form of protection also. She excused herself from kissing and other preteen activities by saying out loud that she couldn't kiss a boy because she was a tomboy. As a tomboy she was able to resist doing some of the chores she associated with being a girl. Playing and running around outside with the boys, she avoided the washing and cleaning her mother demanded of her when she was inside the house. Nevertheless, Aidee was not entirely happy as a tomboy. Although she had wild adventures (like the time the boys dared her to pull the tail of a wild pig), her mother thought of her as a "devil child." Aidee said she was "really confused about how I should act."

Being a tomboy, in Carr's study, afforded some girls the opportunity to be closer to distant dads. Maura called herself a tomboy. Her dad flew planes, and she was his "flying buddy." She had "lots of freedom," played baseball, football, army, and boxing. She remembered wrestling with her brother, pinning him, letting a spitball slide out of her mouth to almost touch him, and then suck it up. But she also was the one who began a sexual relationship with a fifteen-year-old when she was ten. On the other hand, Maura saw herself as an equal partner in this relationship, never the victim. Was her adventuresome tomboy spirit the thing that led her into this early mutually exploratory relationship? Or did boys have easier access to her because she was a tomboy?

Why do so many adult women claim that they were tomboys when they were younger? It's a way of valuing their childhood in terms of what the culture values: independence, freedom, and authority. But it's also a way of reconfirming the stereotypes of what a girl was supposed to do and what a boy was supposed to do. Looking back, women remember fondly their mischief and adventures, and because these adventures don't fit with a cultural image of the good girl who stays home with her dolls, they call what they did tomboy behavior. But if so many girls do these kinds of things, maybe we should instead start talking about the wild adventures of "girly girls" and claim a little space for this activity in their own gender. When someone asks, "What kind of little girl were you?" they can answer, "I was a free, wild, independent, mischievous, hard-playing little girl," and not, "I was a tomboy."

Eighty percent of female executives of Fortune 500 companies self-identify as having been tomboys. Do girls who run with the boys have a better chance at working with the boys later, of dealing with the issues of competition and hierarchy because of early training? Yes.

Chapter 17

Dear Diary, I Hate Her!
Secret Anger in Girls

"anger is a molten pond at the core of me, my most fiercely guarded secret."
—Audré Lorde

Abbie sat at her desk quietly, as little girls often do, looking like the perfect girl student, attentive to the teacher, keeping her hands to herself, and getting her work done. But while she posed as a good girl for the classroom, she used to imagine that her toes were guns and that she could shoot people with them. Little boys around her had "permission" to turn their fingers into .45s, point, and shoot at whomever whenever, but hers was a secret pleasure.

Because middle-class girls in our culture are not permitted to be angry, they go to great pains to deny, suppress, mask, or hide it. Patricia Pearson, author of *When She Was Bad*, writes that girls are masters of indirection when it comes to anger. Psychologist and educator Dana Jack writes that among women and girls "attempts to hurt, to oppose, or to express anger go underground to reach others through hidden channels, while surface behaviors mask the intent."

This masking behavior seems to come from socialization practices. Researchers show that at an early age, girls more than boys learn to mask anger in their facial expressions. In experiments where researchers disappoint children, preschool girls contain themselves more in the presence of an adult. Researchers who study communication and language acquisition have shown that mothers avoid talking about anger with their daughters, while they do not avoid subjects like fear and sadness. The reverse is true of mothers speaking to their sons.

When girls do not deny or mask anger, it emerges in ways that elicit strong cultural disapproval. Pearson calls it social manipulation on the playground. Researchers Crick and Grotpeter show that girls' "relational aggression" includes gossiping, excluding, and withdrawal. These are usually indirect forms of expressing anger and earn girls the culturewide label of being "catty" or even "meaner" than boys. Teachers who spend a great deal of time with grade-school girls often claim that they think that girls are "even meaner" than boys, because they've witnessed the cruelty of a malicious rumor or cold shoulder.

But are girls really meaner? Or is it just more surprising because we expect girls not to get angry and not to express it when they do? Dana Jack argues that the culture cannot accept female anger. She suggests that this is because women are supposed to be the nurturers; in a profound way it is upsetting when mothers, and mother figures, show their capacity for anger. When women are angry, normal hierarchies with men in control are overthrown, threatening the status quo and men's easier access to advantage and power.

So women feel there is something wrong with them if they are angry. This feeling does not come out of thin air. Deborah Cox, Sally Stabb, and Karin Bruckner interviewed girls and women about their anger for their book, Women's Anger, and found that the girls were treated badly by those around them when they were angry. Some research that looks at emotions has found that parents show greater acceptance of anger in boys and greater acceptance of fear in girls, and girls show more fear, boys more anger.

Acceptance of anger in women varies by ethnicity too. Within Latina cultures, stereotypes of marianisma (acting like the Virgin Mary) require martyrdom and quiet suffering rather than anger. However, in immigrant communities being able to stand up for oneself is also a source of pride. The middle-class white and stereotyped view of Latina women's anger is that it is acceptable because "Spanish" women are supposed to be "hot-blooded." African-American women, on the other hand, are not given such leeway but are seen by whites as "uppity" or dangerous when they get angry. African-American women's assertiveness is often labeled as anger by whites because of this stereotype.

Within psychiatry, women's anger in general gets converted into diagnoses that are seen as "women's diagnoses." For example, Dana Becker, in her book *Through the Looking Glass* points out that disorders such as borderline personality disorder have emerged and been constructed around the image of the angry, demanding woman gone to extremes. Becker has shown why women more frequently than men are diagnosed with BPD; there is a bias in mental health professionals to call women "borderline" instead of describing them as having post-traumatic stress disorder. Given the same symptomatology, clinicians will describe men as experiencing PTSD and women as being BPD.

When anger is suppressed, it either comes out through other channels, as in gossip or social manipulation, or it is suppressed, so that the women or girls experiencing it can still conform to social expectations. It can even become self-destructive, as in the case of girls who cut themselves purposely or get stuck in a cycle of bingeing and purging instead of expressing their anger. Cox, Stabb, and Bruckner write that anger for a woman is "a feeling she cannot readily embrace or give voice to in herself." Because of this, it changes "from an instrument for self-clarification to a weapon of self-destruction."

The problems with suppressing anger are many. Girls know themselves less. They run the risk of heavy social disapproval for slippages. People generally come to see women as more manipulative and cunning, less trustworthy. Women have less of a chance to work out problems directly when something angers them and less of an opportunity to use anger constructively.

Many of the girls and women I spoke to told me of secret anger. Diaries are the place where girls can write their secrets and, after writing about crushes, the number one use of diaries was to write about people who they hated. With bold pens and several exclamation marks, girls write over and over again phrases like "Mary is such a bitch" and "I hate Lisa!" It may be good that girls are "getting their feelings out" in this safe way; at least they are recognizing their hate. However, there is a pleasure in claiming one's feelings as one's own and not secreting them away that girls who write in diaries are not experiencing. Remember, they are writing this in their diaries, not telling their parents, not telling their best friends, not confronting the girls who wronged or slighted them. They reserve their strongest feelings for a secret place. While it may be resourceful and self-protective of them to write about their anger rather than express it, these girls also are missing the opportunity to practice using their anger in a constructive way to bring about change.

Most frequently their secret anger is aimed toward their mothers. The mother-daughter relationship is particularly charged because mothers teach their daughters to suppress anger and because they themselves have been taught to suppress anger. Nevertheless, mothers are the major disciplinarians in most households and so take the brunt of girls' anger.

Whether toward their mothers or toward girls at school, girls suffer from enormous guilt about these strong feelings. One girl wrote at the top of the first page of her diary, on January 1, year after year, the New Year's resolution: "Be nicer!"

Carol Tavris, in *Anger: The Misunderstood Emotion*, suggests that it is women's subordinate position that makes them mask their anger. Emotion theorists remind us that people with more authority more often receive permission to feel, display, and act on anger than those with less authority, and women are less frequently in positions of authority. Perhaps if girls trusted that their anger would be accepted and could bring about change, they would express it more. Poet Audré Lorde writes that trying to train her anger to be accurate rather than to deny it has been one of the major tasks of her life.

For most girls, though, suppression of anger can be a source of pride. For example, Annie, a white middle-class college student, said, "If I was ever mean to someone, I was never mean to anyone to their face. . . . I was really nice. I just didn't like doing that."

Marissa, an African-American college student, was a very good girl. Being a pastor's child, she felt that she had to be good to set an example for others, whereas she envied her brother, who felt no such obligation. In fact, her parents told her last year that they believe they had made a mistake in raising her to believe being angry was bad. She remembered being angry at her mother, who home-schooled her, and "there were times when I would just be like so ahhhh!!!" But, Marissa added, "I don't think she even knew that there was like conflicts." Why? Because the conflicts were within her. Marissa admitted, "I would never, ever express it."

Serena, a nine-year-old white girl from Chicago, said she's never "really" mad at her mother. In her definition of what a good girl is, she said, "And I never really got mad at her really," defining a bad girl as someone who actually does get mad at her mother.

Robin, an African-American middle-class woman, remembered that when she was a child she tolerated playing with a girl she didn't like because she couldn't bear to tell her mother she didn't like the girl. The girl was her mother's best friend's daughter. So she would play with this girl but do mean little things to her, like give her the cold shoulder or change the rules of the game so that the girl would lose. She didn't want to upset her mother, but she needed to release her displeasure.

Robin also wrote about it in her diary. "Most of the time I wrote bad things about Jenny. 'God, I was so mean.' And Robin added, "It was so irrational." She thought there was no reason for her to hate this girl. She could write about how much she hated her in her diary, but she could not tell her mother.

Robin may be better off than Serena, who won't even admit to being angry. Writing it down takes the edge off the anger in more ways than one. It helps simply to express it, and it's not quite as bad if one writes it privately rather than says it out loud. It is one step removed. But wouldn't Robin have been better off had she a person to speak her frustration to?

For Serena, a bad girl is someone who "always writes notes on papers like saying, 'I hate school,' or 'My teacher is dumb, stupid.' " She can't even imagine that a girl might say something like that out loud. A girl who says this out loud must be practically evil!

Marissa wrote in her diary about how much she hated the girl across the street. This girl was prized by teachers and parents because she was excellent at a number of different activities. Marissa wrote all the mean things she might have said to her in her diary. And she hated her because she was even a better good girl than she was, very much "into" the Christian missionary girls' club Marissa's parents had made her attend.

Nicolette described herself as a wimp who never wanted to hurt anybody, but in her diary she wrote for several years about how much she hated her mother, how unfair she was, "she's such a bitch!" and more. She wrote it, but never expressed it. When asked why she never expressed it, she said, "I let her do what she wanted to do and just figured out how to make it easy for us all."

At thirty-two she is still angry at her mother, but her mother still doesn't know how much and what about. The power of her anger seems so huge that at thirty-two years old Nicolette wondered whether she should throw out her diaries "because it would be devastating if my mother ever saw [them]." Her mother lives in another state now, and the chances are much more slim today that she would come across Nicolette's diaries; but the anger is still there.

As in Nicolette's case, girls and women fear that their anger could destroy others. So what happens when anger gets so large that a girl can't handle it, when it hasn't been or can't be siphoned into petty squabbles, gossip, or cold shoulders. Typically they either find secret destructive things to do, go to their rooms and cry, or finally, for a very few, lose it.

One girl was so angry at her brother that she "lost it" and punched a door until she made a hole in it. Another, Becca, whose mother wanted her to be a ballerina, cracked the legs off the ballerina doll in her mother's doll collection to show her how much she hated ballet. "I knew it was wrong," she said. "I knew I would be found out and get in trouble," but she had to do it "because it was like a way to express I hated it." Even girls who lose it seem to still be in control.

Dorothy Jean, who grew up in the Midwest in the fifties, said, "Any time I expressed my anger I was punished, and yet I was in a household where everybody seemed to be angry." So she sprinkled garlic in her sister's hair when she got jealous, and put broken glass in the cookies she made for her father, the father who had abandoned the family. She was so mad at her mother once, she poured out the entire contents of her mother's perfume: "That seemed like a very angry act to me, and it was directed toward my mother, which leads me to believe that whatever was going on I didn't feel obliged to tell my mother, and I was angry at her for not knowing."

Penny, who is nine, white, and growing up in the projects, got angry at a girl who was being mean to her, but she couldn't say anything. So she thought, "She has puffy hair. I have scissors. I want to cut her hair." But she didn't do it.

If not destructive or imagining destruction, girls simply cry. Avery, eleven, has moved far too frequently. It clearly has made her unhappy to have to leave her friends and move across the country because of her father's job, but she doesn't tell her parents it makes her unhappy. When I interviewed her I tried to determine whether it also made her angry, but she was vague: "I think I tried to tell them," but then told me that she doesn't think that they *should* know. When asked how she copes with being angry, though, she said, "I stomp off to my room and cry."

Girls cry when they are angry. Usually this means that they have expressed or felt their anger and feel overwhelmed by it. Laura got really angry at a girl in camp: "I never had any fights in school, and I was so angry at her and we were yelling at each other and I started to cry, because when I get really angry I cry." So do grown-up women, and most of them hate this tendency, because they know it undermines their ability to express themselves when angry. Why do they cry? Because they assume from the start that they won't be heard. Because anger and hurt get all mixed together. And because they are simply overwhelmed with all kinds of emotions.

Mary Valentis and Anne Devane, in their book *Female Rage*, write that for many women rage is like a foreign language over which they have no control.

Lucy, a Puerto Rican woman, expressed this feeling of being out of control when angry: "If someone tells me something, I just get nervous and start crying. I just want to pick something up and hit them with it."

Feeling out of control causes some women to "just lose it" when it comes to holding in their anger, and many express a fear of losing it, while few discuss constructive ways of expressing it. It is as if the assumption is that one should have suppressed it. Miranda, an eleven-year-old girl from Boston, almost "loses it" whenever her aunt baby-sits. This aunt "gets on everyone's nerves" when she sings. "I literally had to string myself," she said, using a graphic if unusual word. "I don't know the words for that, but keep myself from reaching over and slapping her and telling her to shut up because she's getting so on my nerves."

Whenever we talk about anger in girls the conversation almost always turns to extreme displays of it—girls who kill, girls who explode, girls who can't control their anger. To suggest that girls be encouraged to express anger, be taught how to handle their own anger, and to show them ways in which anger can be used constructively is not to suggest that girls pick up guns and go on shooting sprees, as many fear. Jumping to this extreme conclusion plays on girls' own fears that to express anger threatens annihilation. Today girls are too afraid of their own anger and feel it as an alien force within them. The goal of parents and educators should be to cultivate it, understand it, and even deepen it for many girls before even beginning to talk about "letting it go" or confrontation. We do no less for other emotions. Our fear of hearing girls' anger, however, is too great.

Chapter 18

The Aggressive Acts of Good Girls

"And then I get so mad that I shake her to death. . . . And then I let go and look around to see if anyone saw."
—Kelly, Asian-American, ten, *referring to her sister*

Aggression in women and girls is a hot topic. Some study the cruelty on the playground, others girls in gangs. Some look to the more unusual forms of women's anger, such as women who murder or women who take on careers in the police force or army. But few have looked at what I call "normal" aggression in the lives of girls. I don't want to glorify aggression; on the other hand, I am not nor should you be horrified by it. Aggression is a part of girls' as well as boys' makeup, and there is variation in the lives of girls just as there is in the lives of boys (from kids who are slightly aggressive to kids who are highly aggressive). When it occurs in the lives of middle-class girls, however, it has to be kept hidden. But hidden away, small aggressive acts bring too much guilt into girls' lives.

Good girls keep their lapses in goodness secret. Lapses are times when they do something that does not fit the image of how a girl is supposed to behave. While most girls would feel the need to keep sexual secrets, keeping aggression a secret really separates the good girl from the bad. Elenora, a Puerto Rican woman, who was, in her own words, a "goody-two-shoes," secretly sneaked into her sister's room and cut off the heads of all the dolls in her sister's paper doll collection. Another girl, Heather, and her sister would fight and punch each other, and then, crying, promise each other, "Don't tell that I hurt you, okay?"

For girls who are deeply enveloped in good girl expectations, aggressive acts seem to them to come out of nowhere. As noted earlier, Dana Jack, in *Behind the Mask,* calls this unfamiliar territory. Because the act seems not to jibe with who they think they are and who others expect them to be, these girls feel confusion and tremendous guilt.

All or none thinking, in the field of psychology, is considered problematic and dysfunctional. It is the kind of thinking that leads girls to say to themselves, "If I'm not perfect, then I'm nothing, I'm horrible, I'm really, really bad." It leads them to conclude, "If I did this bad thing, I must be really bad." It's a no-win situation, for to feel that much anger or rage, a girl must see herself as a horrible person. To not feel it, she will never own it or come to understand it in herself. She may even experience it as depression or turn it into self-hatred. While boys, it would seem, can integrate bad behaviors into a fuller image of themselves fairly easily, girls cannot without bringing into question who they really are.

Hear the extremes in Maya's thinking. Maya, an eleven-year-old white girl growing up in the suburbs, said that a good girl "never really hates someone," a bad girl "is mean to everyone." Serena, who is nine, said that a good girl "never pushes or shoves." And what happens if she does? Just once? Maybe twice? Elyse was sent to "the bench" in second grade for talking during an assembly, and in her own words, she was absolutely "appalled": "I don't think I had ever known of any *girl* being sent there. It was always like the boys in the class. . . . It was a really big deal."

There is a range of aggressive acts that girls have kept secret. The range goes from saying the "F" word or breaking a brother's toy, to even kicking a kitten. The point is, there is a range. We think of little girls as nonaggressive simply because they are *less* aggressive than boys, just like for years we thought of girls as less good at math because at the very extremes in math knowledge, boys scored higher. Despite the stereotype, there were many, many girls who were better than boys at math. By dichotomizing girls' math skills as we dichotomize their behavior (good versus bad) instead of pointing out the considerable overlap, we promote either-or thinking.

Girls don't know that there is a continuum of aggressive behavior, not a division between aggressive and not aggressive. We have worked hard to teach them not to think this way about math (good at it versus poor, with no in-between) and have had great success in helping girls to succeed in

math. But teachers and parents are loathe to teach girls this lesson with regard to aggression. The culture would prefer to have girls strive to be all
good and never aggressive, while parents approve of violent video games
for boys and take their sons hunting.

Out of Nowhere

So, if a girl is good, all good, she is nonaggressive and has no way to explain
it when she isn't. Natalie, an eleven-year-old from the suburbs, noted that
she doesn't like to swear but, "like I said like a swear once, but it like
popped out. I didn't like mean it." How does a curse word "pop out"? She
also remembered that once she "whipped a girl's naked butt" with a towel
and made the girl cry: "I felt really bad," said Natalie, "because I didn't
mean to." If she had meant the swear word or meant to hurt the other girl,
she would have difficulty explaining to herself why. For Natalie and other
girls, there are too few paradigms of women's aggression through which to
understand themselves.

When good girls do bad things, they don't understand it. It seems inexplicable. Instead of saying, I must be more angry than I thought I was,
they think, What just happened? Was it me? It doesn't make sense. This is
a way of othering the act, seeing it as coming from outside oneself.

Chrissie, for example, did something mean that, to many of us, might
seem inexplicable. Her "bizarre memory" (her words) when she was in second grade is about

> being over at a girlfriend's house, and she had this younger brother. I
> don't know if he was sleeping or just sitting there or whatever, but she
> walked out of the room and I just had this urge to pinch him or hit him. I
> can't remember what I did exactly, but I wanted to hurt him. I don't
> know. He was just smaller, sort of vulnerable . . . it was this cute little
> boy, but for some reason, I wanted to hurt him. So I did. He started cry-
> ing, and I just walked out of the room and acted like I hadn't done any-
> thing, like I didn't know why he was crying.

She asked herself, "Why [did] I want to do that?" and said, "I often find myself trying to figure out what is the source of it? Why do I seem to have this
much stronger desire for that than other people?" While we as adults might
be able to see the pinch as an expression of being overwhelmed by jeal-

ousy—"he was so cute"—or some deeper anger about growing older and no longer being allowed her own vulnerability, Chrissie, even now, cannot own this anger: "It wasn't an act of anger or anything like that." She called it "an inexplicable urge" and today she feels deeply "ashamed" and "definitely amazed."

Like Chrissie, who pinched her friend's little brother, Jackie kicked a kitten, and she also has no idea why: "I don't know what the kitten did or whatever, but I kicked it . . . and I felt so bad."

Dolores, a "good girl" from a very strict Puerto Rican family, also experienced her aggression as inexplicable. But it clearly is explicable. Dolores was, in her words, a "loner" who never did well in school because of a learning disability. She had few friends because her mother didn't allow her daughters to play at other children's houses or out in the streets of New York City. Generally well-behaved in school, Dolores remembered once hitting a teacher.

> I guess she wanted to talk to me, and she pulled me, and I got so upset I smacked her. . . . I was like, "My God! I hit a grown-up!" You know? . . . It's just that she took me by surprise when she pulled me . . . and I just turned around and smacked her.

It seems likely that school was very stressful, that Dolores was constantly on her guard because of criticism and her lack of success, and angry about what she couldn't achieve, even angry at the teachers for pushing her. And this anger stayed until the small tug on her arm became the last straw in a building anger. But Dolores didn't say she was angry; she understands it simply as a crazy mistake.

Connie was part of a gang of girls who teased another boy every day at school. She "loved the feeling" and really "got into it," until one day she got a little carried away and spit on him too. The other girls thought that she had gone too far and became quiet; Connie also thought that she had gone too far. She said to herself, "Oh, my God," and had no idea where she had found that kind of aggression. But there were many reasons for her to be angry. Her father had died recently, and her mother was less available; there was more competition among the three kids in the family for her mother's attention. These kinds of events make a girl sad, we know, but why not also angry?

I Must Be Really Bad

Some of the aggression expressed by girls is, like Connie's, in a gang or group of girls. But that doesn't mean the guilt is not felt individually. Abbie, for example, "did something very bad when [she] was a little kid, like five or six years old." She was following around a group of older boys and one of them started throwing rocks at the windows of a set of summer cottages. Abbie said,

> And then at a certain point I just started doing it, and it was really fun. We were throwing rocks. We broke every window in every single cottage and were just this band of little children. And I was tremendously guilty about it. I lost sleep about that for years. Every time I saw a policeman I was afraid. I would have these fantasies of sirens and police coming to the door, and they would trace it to me and my fingerprint was found on these rocks, or someone had seen us. That preoccupied me for a long time.

Although Abbie was only five or six, she was disturbed by this act "until I was about fourteen." She explained, "You have to realize that I was considered the perfect little girl and I had done this thing, probably a felony." She is right. It was a horrible thing to do and it was a crime. But she was five years old, and had she been able to tell someone about it, the eight years of fear and guilt may not have followed. Rather, she may have been asked to make reparations. Because her act was so out of character, it had to be kept secret, and eight years of guilt is the sentence when a girl who is supposed to be perfect commits a secret act of aggression.

Devin also felt "guilty for life" about a sudden act of aggression she committed. At about twelve years old, she was sitting on the couch doing her homework and getting into a fight with her little brother.

> I just happened to be holding a pencil and thinking irrationally. Even now this is the worst thing that I've ever done and the thing I feel most guilty about. I stabbed him in the knee on the side. He still has a little piece of graphite in his knee that he likes to taunt me with. . . . It was the kind of action that you do and regret immensely afterwards.

So immensely that it has followed her into her college years. While we may admire her for feeling bad about this act, there is still something exaggerated in her description. She said she hurt her brother "in such an evil, painful way . . . in such a horrible way." Like other girls and women she finds the act inexplicable, and said about the pencil, "It just lunged out by itself." But she takes responsibility for the lapse in goodness, too much perhaps, saying that afterward she felt horrible: "I wanted to die . . . I was just sick, feeling I had done this, and I think I started crying, because I couldn't believe what I had done. I remember George wasn't even that hurt." The key to understanding this incident is the fact that her brother "wasn't even that hurt" so she was not horrified by the harm that she had done, she was not crying in sympathy with her brother; instead, she was horrified by the act that she committed, horrified at herself.

It's interesting that it was mostly the adult women looking back, not the little girls I interviewed, who told me about an aggressive act they feel guilty about. Are girls today so much more likely to accept their own aggression? This may be true about aggression in sports (see Chapter 20). But I don't think this is why I didn't hear much about guilty aggression in these interviews. I think that for these girls, the really "bad" acts are still a secret, still so horrible, that they are too ashamed to talk about them. Although many adult women still felt guilty about these acts, the edge has been taken off, allowing them to spill the beans. They didn't feel quite the same visceral shame that they had when they were children.

May, for example, remembered hitting her mother:

That was a big deal for me, because it was, like, wow! That was real, lots of anger there. And it just . . . I remember again feeling very ashamed of that, and I think one thing that I, one thing that I found very mean is, I could tell when my mother's blood pressure could go up, like when I would push her to a limit, like her patience or something. And I could tell, she'd get very red, and even sometimes there were blotchy red patches, and there was a sense of hating myself for doing that and yet not being able to control the fact that, you know, I would say, I don't want to do that. And I would watch her physically change and that was scary, and yet, it's like there was a sense of I couldn't control it.

The guilt of "good girls" is very long-lasting and detrimental to their understanding of themselves and human relationships. Chrissie recently apologized to a friend of hers: "I think I have a real worry that I've done something really horrible that she can't completely tell me about or that I can't remember or whatever."

Isn't Guilt Good?

It is true that guilt is indeed a sign of morality. Some would say that such guilt shows that many of these girls are thinking along ethical lines, that it is a sign that these girls truly are good human beings. Guilt indeed serves to keep people in line, help them from further incidents of inexplicable aggression and nasty intent. For those girls like Jeri, now forty-nine, who remembered being very young, seeing a nest of baby mice, and killing them one by one, her guilt over this act is entirely appropriate and probably helped her to become the gentle psychologist she is today. Nobody knew, and she never told anyone until she told me, but she has felt tremendously guilty about this act that she still finds inexplicable.

In our culture, where there is constant concern about violence in the lives of our children and the development of aggression in boys, we would wish that boys would more frequently experience the guilt that girls feel. But girls take on too heavy a burden. I would rather a girl felt sorry for what she did, be able to discuss the incident with an adult, make reparations, and then use it to understand herself better than to feel as guilty as some of these "good girls" did—for life. If girls restrain themselves because of the deep shame and fear of what happens when they are aggressive and *how they will be seen by others*, this is a rather superficial morality. It is a morality based on restraint. But a morality based on values, reasoning, and integration of emotions will take to heart the anger or frustration that caused the aggression and address it in a way that will transform behavior. When these acts can be discussed, there are more chances for girls to turn their bad acts into acts of reparation. Guilt and shame might help girls to restrain themselves, but not to understand themselves. And without understanding, restraint can work only so well.

Zeroing In On: Pranks, Mischief, and Little Meannesses

Nora, a white eleven-year-old from suburban Boston, told me that a bad girl is "daredevilish." But how devilish is too devilish? Doing a prank or a little mischief is usually at the expense of someone else, and we don't like to picture girls not caring about another person. They are supposed to be good at caring, not at carousing. Some girls experience delight when they allow themselves to be just a little mean. Depending on how identified they are with being a good girl, guilt overwhelms them. Or they read their behavior as being boylike.

Pranks, mischief, and the other kinds of little meannesses girls commit have multiple meanings. Some of these reflect the more expected and traditional ways girls express anger and aggression, such as gossip, rumors, and playground exclusions. These so-called catty and underhanded expressions of anger and aggression are, for some girls, the *only* way they permit themselves to be open about these kinds of feelings. Some of girls' pranks reflect a resistance to being a "girly girl." They carouse just like the boys, getting pleasure from being a part of a group, a wild one at that. Plus, group dynamics allows them to let down their overactive monitoring of good behavior.

Another way of thinking about pranks, mischief, and meanness is that they express a kind of pleasure that girls have in being a little nasty. That makes many of us uncomfortable: We don't like meanness, and we don't like to see girls act that way.

Mean pranks often are aimed at authority figures. Fun pranks are usually done in groups or in pairs and to an anonymous victim, like when girls together make prank phone calls. When the victim is not anonymous and shows hurt feelings, girls often feel guilty. Girls also are mean to each other at slumber parties, showing great delight at making fun of bodily changes and differences in girls' physical development. Generally, when girls give themselves the freedom to carouse with others, do a little mischief, and experience the thrill of being afraid of getting caught, they speak proudly and excitedly about these times.

Because authority figures are often the ones who rein girls in the most, expecting them to be good in school, in church or synagogue, or at home, girls find particular pleasure in small vengeances toward these adults. In the lives of children there is very little other opportunity to express one's anger at teachers, at fathers. Interestingly enough, though, no pranks are aimed at mothers usually, perhaps because she is someone to whom girls are allowed to express anger. Or she is too savvy to pull one over on.

A very common prank in city schools is to put a thumbtack on a seat before the teacher sits down. Looking back to their school years, adult women remember doing this "because everybody else did" or because the other children encouraged her to do so. Toni sharpened a pencil and stuck it right under the teacher when she sat down, and her teacher was so shocked she let down her guard and called Toni a "bad nigger." The reaction stunned this little girl. "I was really bad," says Toni, "but it really shocked me [that the teacher would say that] and I hated Miss Pine ever since." Toni thought the joke was funny at the time, but today it seems "that was a cruel thing to do." After that prank, Toni knew what Miss Pine "had in her heart," so she just did more mischief, wreaking her own style of vengeance—making the eraser disappear, hiding the chalk. She did these things more than other children because of what Miss Pine had said, and because the teachers "said I was dumb," and because "I was the one that had the courage." Toni grew up and, with the help of a neighborhood activist-tutor, attended an Ivy League college, but the anger she felt through her grade school years was clearly expressed in small meannesses toward the teachers. Lyn Mikel Brown, in her book *Raising Their Voices*, suggests working-class girls' anger is a form of resistance. Here Toni resists adults seeing her as dumb, one-upping them all.

But urban girls are not the only ones who make trouble for teachers. With her best friend Frank in the fourth grade in the suburbs of California, Jody put push pins in the physical education teacher's car tires. She doesn't remember feeling hostile nor bad: "If somebody would have gotten hurt and harmed, I would have felt really bad . . . because I wasn't intending that, . . . but they asked Frank to leave the school 'cause he was a big troublemaker in general. . . . No one really understood why I was hanging out with him, because he always caused problems." The way psychologists understand such duos is that good girls tag along with bad boys to feel the excitement vicariously, and to allow themselves to be convinced to do the things that they are not supposed to do. They get the thrill without the full blame. But we might also ask whether "good girls," even when they do initiate "bad acts," do not get blamed because society does not want to acknowledge their ability to hate, disrupt, or disturb even those closest to them.

Like teachers, absent or mean stepfathers suffered from pranks, perhaps unknowingly. Julia and her brother didn't like their alcoholic stepfather, who was, in her words, mean. Once when they knew he would be home for lunch, they stuck a cockroach in his salad: "It was so funny, because he kept saying this salad was delicious, and we were just like cracking up!" Dorothy Jean's father left home for another woman, and once when she and her sister were baking cookies for him a glass broke, and they stuck a piece of broken glass in the cookie dough. Without permission to talk back, act out, or show their frustration at the powerlessness of being children hurt by their parents' mistakes, these girls found less noticeable ways of vengeance.

Adults are not the only targets. Groups of girls express their anxiety over changes in their bodies by picking on each other as well. Many adult women remember freezing the bra of the first girl who falls asleep at slumber parties. Jody remembered calling up plumbers and screaming into the receiver, "There's a pubic hair stuck in my drain." Mia, an eleven-year-old white suburban soccer player, says her friends like to put ketchup on a girl's pajamas at a sleepover if the girl falls asleep before the others. The hilarity is that when she wakes up she might think she got her period! These pranks might be mean to the odd girl out, but they serve the function of addressing the anxiety of bodily changes, and even a little self-hatred, without necessarily having to admit to these feelings.

When these pranks have a victim, when they show clear harm to another child (not usually to an adult), girls generally feel bad. For example, Leah and her friends covered a hole in the ground so that the odd boy in her class who was "kind of a dork" wouldn't see it and would fall into it.

And he tripped, and like Jess and I thought it was the funniest thing ever, . . . but he was really nice, and I was like seeing him like holding back tears after this happened, and then it just always like denigrated me.

Chanelle, who is sixteen and African American, remembered stuffing a girl's coat in a different locker. The girl cried about her missing coat, but the other girls left it there for a couple of days. She remembered this incident because it made her feel "weird." Miranda, only eleven, feels very bad that she teased a boy about his "rat tail" hair-do, calling him "Rat Tail Roy." She said, "I really regret this" about a time when she pranced around one of her best friends, Sally, and tortured her by singing over and over "Little Sally Saucer, Sitting in the Water." She "kept doing that and doing that and it was terrible . . . and we were all crying and mad at each other," but "it was so mean. It was terrible."

Kalinda, a twelve-year-old African-American girl, remembered playing a prank with a bunch of girls, writing a boy a mysterious love letter that said, "I really want to go out with you. I want to kiss you." They signed it, "Your secret admirer." The boy was so thrilled that he went around telling everyone he had a secret admirer, and she felt guilty because it wasn't true, and that they had done this prank to make a fool out of him. She ended up explaining the prank to him: "So I said I'm sorry, and it felt good in the end."

These girls feel appropriate guilt for humiliating or otherwise hurting a friend. Guilt is not a bad feeling, especially when felt for one's lack of concern for others rather than for not living up to a stereotype. But guilt is not the only feeling. Girls also get pleasure from mischief.

Mischief and Pleasure:

Researchers tell us that boys like to play in groups and girls like to play one-on-one. But really? It may be that girls simply stick to what is expected of them, conforming to the familiar, allowing their play to be shaped by the grown-ups who prefer, for safety or other reasons, to keep their play inside. While we more often picture boys roaming around in groups making trouble, girls too love the pranks they commit with others. But we would rarely expect to see a gang of girls derailing a train by placing a rock on the tracks, even though this indeed was a story told to me. Especially fun for girls are the prank phone calls where they order pizza to a neighbor's house, send a *Playboy* magazine to the woman across the street, even lowering their voices to scare someone with a threat such as "I'm going to kill you." Not fun to be on the receiving end of these, but girls enjoy these acts that seem to have anonymous victims.

Stealing, flooding someone's backyard, peeing outside, skipping school. These are all pleasurable and outrageous to girls who do them. When not feeling guilty, they associate these acts with courage. They love the thrill of almost being caught. Not one girl who described a prank recalled feeling horrible during the act; only, but still occasionally, afterward. Shamika, a nine-year-old African-American girl from the housing project I visited, said she shoots rocks at cars with other kids. Today she feels terribly guilty about it, but "at the time I was enjoying it."

How many opportunities are there for a girl to show courage? Advocates of boys' development and inherent differences between boys and girls sometimes label courage as a virtue we should promote in boys. But when we think about girls and courage we do not usually think of daredevilish acts but of moral courage, the courage to restrain oneself in the face of peer pressure or to point out a bad deed when she sees it. This is courage indeed; however, girls also seek out ways to challenge themselves, work on fears, and master them.

One thing we cannot deny, though, is that girls feel an exhilaration when they break the rules and act out. Where does this pleasure come from? It's a mixture of fear of getting caught as well as being one up on or superior to the person they're putting down. While these are qualities we don't want to promote generally, we don't want to condemn them totally either. We can point out the harm to others while still supporting the daredevil inside the good girl.

Chapter 19

Feeling the Power

"It's a great thing to be powerful. I've been striving for it all my life."
—Madonna

There are many forms of "girl power," some that draw from traditional ideas of power *over* someone, and some that draw on more feminist notions of feeling powerful within. In the past, women were able to obtain a kind of power by attempting to live up to the image of the ideal woman or wife. That may seem retro, but girls today still look for power through obedience. If they are good, they will be rewarded. Compared to the ones labeled bad girls, the ones who fight (literally and figuratively) against this image are indeed granted a sort of social power that allows them greater access to economic and academic resources than their bad peers. On the one hand, they speak the lingo of personal empowerment ("girl power"; "feel the power"); on the other, they try to be good so that those who really have the power will give them more of it.

The women's movement of the sixties sometimes spoke of power very generally as a bad thing: Men want power; women want cooperation. Power, to these early feminists, meant domination and oppression of others. They believed that when women were in charge, equality and caring would rule the day. The outcome of the women's movement of the sixties and seventies (though not intentional) was an overemphasis on our victimization rather than on our strengths. While therapy movements of the seventies and eighties encouraged women to feel angry, the "good woman" theories of the eighties and nineties encouraged women to feel "better" than men for their lack of aggression.

Today power is seen as a good thing, even among feminists, in part due to the therapeutic use of the word "empowerment" to mean feeling one's personal influence in the world, taking an active stance toward problems, and fighting against one's own oppression. So when the media uses the words "girl power" it means girls feeling good about themselves, being out there in the world, and not letting anyone, especially boys, stand in their way. But there is a darker side. Until we accept the darker side of women and girls, including our own aggression, our anger, and our urge to compete as well as dominate, we will perpetuate the myth of the good girl and the good woman that has so oppressed women for ages. Although women and girls have both found a way to use the image of the good girl to their advantage, in so doing they bury this darker aspect of the self, a part of the self that would help them in many circumstances.

"Good girls" find secret ways to dominate others, either in private or in fantasy. They not only want power, but also power over another person. The desire to have personal power, to feel one's effectiveness, strength, and even superiority, is not merely a reaction to being oppressed or powerless, but a human feeling that comes with some pleasure. Granted, it is a dangerous human feeling, because it is at the root of oppression, war, and domination, yet we deny this as a human impulse to our peril.

In gangs some girls parade around the schoolyard. In one white, middle-class junior high in Washington state, girls kick boys in their private parts, reeling in communal laughter as the boys keel over. On another playground in Chicago, a girl gang delights over a game in which they run and push down the boys. On Kezia's playground in New York, the girls beat up the boys. In some respects, such aggressive behavior is acceptable in the "battle of the sexes" on the playground. Ensconced in a rhetoric of "girls against the boys" and "girls are better than boys," girl gangs on the playground, like Matilda in the movie based on the Roald Dahl book, love to prove *Girls Rule*.

Girls also get special pleasure from the power of swearing. Adult women remembering their childhood years look back so fondly at their swearing that it's hard to believe that it was a forbidden act. Dolores and Yolanda, Puerto Rican women of different generations, both told me, "I loved cursing." Yolanda particularly loved to tell someone in Spanish to "go to hell." Rachel, who grew up in a white middle-class suburb, boasts, "It was my first language."

Thus there are ways girls get around the powerless feeling that sometimes goes along with good behavior—through cursing, through ganging up with other girls, and through beating up their siblings. These are all small ways "good girls" can express a desire to feel the power, whether it stems from the pleasure of competition, shocking others, or the desire to dominate.

Power and the Life of the Mind

Grace, who considers herself to have been "a very obedient child," fed her desire for power through fantasy. It began as a storytelling game she shared with her twin sister late at night as they lay in bed. The two created an ongoing story of twin sisters and a friend, Sarah, who had adventures. Soon after, they introduced a character called "Jarreth" who became the king around which all adventures revolved. He was a character who did "extremely evil, manipulative things." Every night for years the twins continued their story. After a period of playing this game, Grace said, "The three girls found it difficult to have any sort of time travel adventure or anything if [Jareth] wasn't around. And I guess you could say that the game grew very gendered at that point, because it shifted from a focus with female characters that were exactly my sister's and my age, too, to an older male who developed very much in terms of personality."

Jareth's character grew into "the world's biggest ego"—no, Grace corrected herself—"the universe's biggest ego." He and his "daughters," the two twins and another girl, would go off fighting evil and always win because he had the most power. Grace relates that the game was frightening as well as exhilarating, and at some points they felt weird about how much power they gave to "Jareth" in their fantasies; they felt "unease with what we had created."

Jareth was the center of "all of the stories." Without Jareth, rather than without the twins, no adventures would happen. This switch in focus aroused my curiosity because it transformed their stories to conform to many stereotypic movies and books which imply that only boys can have adventures but that girls can't unless boys bring them along. These movies and stories celebrate boys' adventurous spirit and male power, while they keep girls at home or needing to be rescued. Even within this game of mutual delight, even though it was a male character who contained all the evil, Grace felt like she needed to restrain herself. In her own words, she became "really interested in the character of Jareth. And sometimes I wanted him to be more powerful and interesting and central than my sister wanted him to be." In the game itself Grace remembered that they would "close some doors" which meant "block off certain sections of his powers so he wouldn't do horrible things without knowing it." Like so many other girls, Grace worries that she is different, less normal, even in this closed duet of her and her twin, because she sees herself as more obsessed with Jareth.

A psychoanalyst might take notice that Jareth is a kind of father figure and see the power and control these twins crave as something they crave from their father. As they fear it, they also desire it. Freud might have called this penis envy. But feminist analysts would say that what they envy really is the power. The power about which they are so ambivalent could be the power within each of them. This power within actually can be symbolized by the father, just as it is in so many religions, where we put our trust in a male god and internalize his good wishes or his commands over us. We have seen before with tomboys that when a girl wants power and sees herself as seeking it, she calls this desire male. Jareth is the power within them, a power they call male, and being male they can adore and fear it, as well as have "a real sense of unease at what we had created."

Plus, Jareth was sexual. He was first created as a representation of David Bowie in the movie *Labyrinth*, wearing tight black pants, a ruffled shirt, and high-heeled boots. Grace remembered thinking of him as both sexual and androgynous. He had long hair. And the image of him captivated the girls.

Grace, the "obedient" child, found a way to feel vicariously the pleasure of power and domination. Her power and urge for domination and even to do evil is projected onto the character of "Jareth." Perhaps this is where urges for domination should be kept, in fantasy. Wouldn't we all be better off that way? Perhaps we would. Yet the trick would be in keeping these urges in fantasy while still honoring the pleasure, vitality, and humanity inherent in such urges.

Boys go through a stage of loving superheroes, all-powerful beings. There was Superman. And then there was the Incredible Hulk. More recently it's been Pokemon, little monsters with various powers. And when they are through with imaginary creatures, they move on to men in uniform. Many little boys want to grow up to be policemen and have the power of guns as well as the law. Many dream about being a race-car driver or flying planes, with big hunks of metal at their control. And if we assume that the need for this massive power is human, and not male, that there is a part of girls that longs for this power, and not through the Barbie dream house, then we also need to ask how and where does this power get transformed.

Love of Domination

Annie, a white, middle-class girl from the suburbs of Boston, "kind of had a thing about power," she admitted to me as an adult. Looking back on her childhood, I asked her if she ever broke a rule "just for the fun of it," and she quickly responded, "I've always done that." Annie was unusual in her pure joy in recounting her tales of mischief and bad behavior. As we expect of boys, she files these acts under "fun" and "part of childhood," without perhaps realizing the differences between her own childhood and those of most of the other middle-class white girls I had spoken to.

Annie had a kind of contempt for weak girls or girls who wouldn't take chances and risks, who wouldn't "stand up for themselves." Like other "good girls" in the study, Annie proclaimed that she had never done anything mean to someone, at least not "consciously": "I never like consciously would plan something." But then see how she developed her story of a particular relationship of dominance, and even exploitation.

She introduced her story as "weird." By doing so, she othered this experience of dominance. Then she further removed herself by adding that she never would have "planned" to do anything like this. Like so many other girls, experiences of meanness, aggression, and sexuality are outside the realm of their normal girlhoods. She began this story by describing the girl whom she wanted to dominate as "stupid," needing, perhaps, to show me just why it was fine to dominate this girl.

> I remember once I had this friend who was stupid. . . . I had this weird—I don't know why—I had this weird resentment towards her for some reason. I don't know why. She was just one of those people who just always annoyed me a little bit for some reason.

In that "I don't know why" Annie is saying that this is not a part of who she is. This is the unexplainable. A girl who is never mean is mean. A girl who never plans mean things plans something mean. As she got into her story she remembered why she didn't like her friend.

Oh, this is what it was. She'd want to come play with me, but I really wouldn't want her to come over. Every day she'd ask if she could come over. I didn't really want her to all the time, so I said, I'd tell her she could only come over if she did what I told her to do. So, she said, "Fine."

A shallow interpretation would see Annie as doing the nice thing by playing with a girl she doesn't like. But such self-sacrifice takes its toll on girls. She described a relationship of dominance and pure delight because of the power she had over the friend who would do whatever she told her to do.

So we'd walk home together. We'd play. . . . We would spend a lot of time together. I remember this one time, crossing the street, I would make her. . . . There were two things. She was really easy to boss around. So I guess in that way, it was kind of neat. I really liked bossing her around, kind of like a joke. She'd play along with it as a joke. So I'd tell her to do things . . . like, I'd tell her to lie in the middle of the street until I told her to get up. . . . I'd wait until cars would come. Then I would let her get up. It was weird, but she just did it. It's really funny that she just kind of went along with it. I only did it because she'd let me do it.

Annie called what she did "weird," but also thought it was funny. Like all victimizers she blamed it on her victim for "letting her do it." While most reasonable adults would not blame the child who is being bullied, there is a sense in which Annie is correct. The victim did not say "no." She did not fight back. It is difficult to ever know if Annie wouldn't have done it if the girl had spoken up. No matter; it is clear that Annie enjoyed the power.

I thought it was funny. I thought it was really funny, because I would never go lie in the middle of the street if someone told me to. But she did. So I just kept doing it. But then there was that relationship established. So I did it this one time. We were crossing this big street near our house, and I had this weird urge to push her. Because I have this weird power relationship I think set up with her. So I was kidding around, but I had this urge to push her into the street. I would . . . I, like, touched her, and I don't remember if she was conscious of it. I think I kind of bumped her and maybe pretended I did it by accident or something . . . as soon as I touched her and almost pushed her into the street, a car went by re-

*ally quickly and I realized I really could have killed her. It was the scari-
est feeling. I don't know if she knew, but I almost killed her. I don't really know if it was that close, but it felt like it was.*

Having this power, Annie wanted to test it, to see how far this friend
would go, and more important how far Annie herself could go, thinking
that if she wanted to, she could kill her friend, actually push her into the
street when a car was coming. Having this urge, she tested it with a little
bump, a shove. The power scared her but also intrigued her. She wanted to
know its limits, and she wanted to feel the power: "It just scared me . . . I
didn't want her to die. It wasn't like I wanted her to get hurt."

The power that she wanted to feel was in the moment of the pushing.
For Annie, it wasn't about hurting the other girl; as it is for many victimizers, it was about having power over her. The other person is a pawn, a non-
person in the bully's inner struggle to prove her power to herself. Here
perhaps is an example of an abusive exercise of power. But before fully condemning this act, it is important to acknowledge that these kinds of urges
(the urge to hurt, to dominate, to diminish another person) exist in all
children, in all people—in all girls. Annie experimented with this desire
to dominate more than did other girls I interviewed. Clearly what she did
to her friend was unfair and mean. But the answer to such interpersonal
problems may not be to tone down Annie's urge for power, but to boost the
weaker girl's strength to fight back and to resist domination. It is possible to
confirm Annie's experiments in domination as part of human nature, and
even encourage her to try to acknowledge and understand this urge more
deeply, without at the same time encouraging cruelty. In the long run, this
would serve her well.

Power and Destruction

When so-called bad girls act out, it is possible to understand the power
they seek as defensive; that is, as a show of underlying vulnerability. Some
"bad girls" have gone through difficult family situations; some have so little in their lives by virtue of being poor and invisible; some feel unwanted.
These girls act out to claim their little space in the world, to show they are
a force to be reckoned with, to be noticed. But we neglect to take note of
the pleasure that they feel, that anyone would feel, when they, even for a
moment, have control, are mastering a situation.

Lillian was "a bad kid," in her own words, a "hell-raiser," but, she says now, "Oh, I loved it!" As a poor Black southern girl, powerless in and invisible to the world at large, beaten down by her own family, a fantasy life of power and domination could not be enough. Lillian grew up living with her grandmother, her aunt, and her uncle. She knew her mother and her father, but they were not around much. Her aunt treated her well, but her grandmother would beat her, and beat her regularly. Like many of the older African-American women I spoke to who had grown up in poverty, beatings were a fact of life. Some considered these beatings discipline, and only now, looking back once again, reconsidered them and found them to be abuse. Some saw their beatings as a cross to bear. Lillian was beaten weekly, but remembered the particular time in which her grandmother hit her in the ear with a high-heeled shoe and broke her eardrum. Lillian is deaf in one ear to this day because of that beating.

> She [her grandmother] would go in her bedroom with her bottle and she would start drinking, and usually by eight or so she'd come out of the room, and aunt would be fussing at me about something I'd done . . . so that's why I usually got my whipping.

Lillian claimed that at about eight years old through the age of ten she was a "fighter to the heart." When asked why she fought, she answered,

> Because I could. 'Cause I was old enough, 'cause I was big enough, I was bad enough. I used to dig a hole for 'em [in the snow] and I'd wait for 'em to come out, and they didn't see. I'd hide from 'em. They didn't see me, and they come around the corner, and I'd step out in front of 'em, and ohhhh! They'd get scared, and then I'd shove 'em down in the hole in the snow I made so I could cover 'em up in the snow and then run off and leave 'em. . . . Sometimes their parents would come to the house and they would tell, "Miss Taylor, that daughter of yours did so and so to my child and I'm getting tired of that" and I'd be hiding. "No, I ain't done nothing to that girl. Ma, I aint's done nothing to that girl" and Mom [Grandmother] would say, "Shut up," and of course when they left I got beaten, and I told them [the next day at school] you made me get a whippin'; you gonna get it today. And that's what I did to 'em. I would beat them up because they had told on me. [And] after a while nobody told any more, and then after a while I stopped fighting a lot because I think I was getting a little older, I was becoming a little more con-

scious of the fact that I was being a warlord instead of a lady. And I not
so much wanted to be a lady, but girls didn't fight a lot. I knew that.

Lillian said that her acts were not about aggression but about power. Like
Annie, she said:

> *I never hurt anybody. The things that I would do was just to let them*
> *know I was the boss. I never wanted to break the skin. I never wanted*
> *to break an arm or a leg. . . . I knew the snow wouldn't hurt them. . . .*
> *I used to run and try and push 'em, but when I pushed 'em I'd grab*
> *ahold of their clothes and snatch 'em back at me. That way they*
> *wouldn't fall down. So I was always conscious of the fact that I could*
> *hurt someone and knew I could hurt someone.*

Lillian and Annie wanted to show who's boss, who's in power. Reading
Lillian's story alone, it would be tempting to only see her story as a story of
intergenerational violence—she gets beaten, so she goes out and beats
others, possibly even growing up to beat her own children. But holding her
story side by side with Annie's, Grace's, and all the stories of sibling battles
to come, it is possible to recognize it as human, the exciting urge to rule, to
win, to conquer.

Dana Jack, in her book *Behind the Mask*, would argue that this thirst for
power as well as the need to be aggressive comes from a failure of relationship. And this might be true. She and psychologists might say that the aggression we see in each of these tales is a kind of defensive aggression, built
on the need of an insecure and weak person to make the world acknowledge that they really are strong, that they really are okay, perhaps even that
they are invulnerable.

This idea of defensive aggression may be true, but at the same time we
cannot deny the exuberance and joy that rests somewhere in these acts of
power. And while we would certainly hope that girls do not "almost kill"
their friends, nor smother them in snow to show their power, we do not
have to enforce that by taking away their *longing* for power, their *wish* to be
the boss. So maybe the question isn't so much, How do we tame these violent girls, but rather, How do we give them the experience of power and
dominance without allowing them to hurt others?

Lillian was boss because she could be. But did she feel guilty about it? I
don't think so. And this may be because Lillian *could* be out there with her
aggression. She was caught, time and time again. Girls like Annie and

Grace live with a more private, secret knowledge of their aggression. Annie's mother was never able to ask her to reflect on what she did, nor was she ever beaten because of it. Annie had a more private burden of guilt to bear—Lillian's was more public.

> And yet still my mother always said, "If you get on your knees and pray God to forgive you," but I guess it's probably why I did a lot of stuff. Because I was always praying. I'm a good prayer now. I tell you, I can say a mean prayer, and it's always, "Oh, please forgive me, because I know I have sinned today."

Private guilt and shame gnaws away; public guilt brings on beatings. Neither girl was given permission at that age to gloat over their power and dominance, but each girl found a way to do it anyway.

Power Over Siblings

Many of the girls and women who fought with their siblings did not show aggression in any other area of their lives. But they spoke about these fights with a lot of pleasure, pleasure about the physical sensation of letting it all out, of pulling no punches, of being able to show their anger.

Ethologists show play fighting as a way young bear and lion cubs and young monkeys pass the time and also train themselves to be able to protect themselves later in the wild. May and her older brothers did this kind of play fighting where they would try to hurt each other as much as possible, and then end the game when someone couldn't take it anymore. Growing up in a safe neighborhood in rural Vermont, they were not preparing themselves for life on the streets. But May felt sensual, physical pleasure at testing her limits, at allowing herself this violence.

Fighting with a sibling, the girl who is usually perfect can let it all hang out. For example, Kelly, an Asian-American ten-year-old who is generally calm, polite, academically successful, and an all-around "good girl," described what happens when her little sister bugs her.

> And then I get mad and we argue and we argue and argue, and then finally she says, "You're stupid." And then I get so mad I shake her to death. And she goes, "Mom!" and then I let go and look [gives a fake innocent look].

I asked whether she feels bad about this, and she said, "Just a little bit."

Chrissie remembered she fought her sister "tooth and nail." June, an eighty-year-old grandmother, remembered being so angry at her older brother that she threw a pewter pitcher at him. Marilyn remembered wanting to see just how far she could go with her younger sisters "as far as hitting and being violent," but her mother stopped her. Maura and her brother used to wrestle a lot, and she would get him down on the ground, pin his shoulders with her knees, "and then get a big spitball and try to torture him with letting it slide out of my mouth and sucking it back up." She even boxed with him.

Rachel, perhaps, described girls' feelings best about beating up their younger siblings:

> I would punch him, you know, because I thought he was so spoiled and everything that he wanted he got, and he was so well taken care of, and I would get so angry that he could have his own way all the time. Carte blanche. It would make me so mad I would want to punch him.

Then she would feel "great and guilty at the same split second." Rachel said, "It would feel absolutely great, and then" she would get in trouble because her brother would yell out, "Rachel hit me."

Fighting with siblings is not a problem for girls. They don't feel incredibly guilty about it. They do not have long-standing worries that they harmed their siblings. The anger doesn't spill over into other areas. And while they feel a pleasure that may make us uncomfortable, it doesn't seem to lead them into lives of violence. This is one area in which aggression has been normalized for girls and where they can act on an urge to feel superior over, to dominate another. But we often forget about these fights when we describe the essential girl or even teen. While this aggression is very much a part of many girls' lives, until recently researchers and psychologists who speak of girls' connection and caring conveniently forget about it because it doesn't fit into our versions of what a girl is like.

Fighting with siblings is about power. It's about hierarchy and asserting one's own needs over another's. Parents despair over trying to get their children to get along; however, this is the one place where a girl with a perfected public persona can let her hair down. Maybe we should let her, or at least condemn her as we condemn her brothers, no more or no less.

Chapter 20

Getting Physical: Girl Athletes

"When someone pulls my shirt, I feel like I've got to get them back, and I push them really hard. It makes me feel like, 'Don't mess with me!'"
—Mia, white, 12

Like fighting an arrogant older brother or an annoying little sister, there is perhaps one other area where "good girls" can be a little aggressive, and that is in sports. To earn this privilege of aggression, there is a difficult terrain girls have to negotiate so that they can maintain their femininity in the eyes of their peers and their teachers. This negotiation starts early.

Sports skills begin on the playground. But if a girl doesn't start playing sports before the age of ten, it is highly unlikely she will play in high school or college. She doesn't develop the skills early enough to fit in.

And many girls don't develop these skills early enough. Researchers report that boys like to play in wide open spaces, that they prefer ball games, competition, and roughness, while girls prefer to spectate, walk hand in hand around the playground, swing and hang from the bars. In a 1997 study, Lynn Jaffee and Heidi Sickler, working for the Melpomene Institute, an organization devoted to promoting health and physical activity in girls, observed over seven hundred children on the playground, but their interviews with the children afterward revealed something few previous researchers have realized. It isn't preference that keeps girls away from "boy" games on the playground; there are two other reasons: The boys exclude them, and the girls don't think they are good enough to play with the boys. While 75 percent of the boys surveyed would rather play with only boys, the majority of girls would prefer to play in mixed groups and run with the boys; but, as one interviewee said, "I can't play boy games. They don't want girls to play."

Sports is one of the few places where our culture permits aggression, even rewards it, and girls who are given that opportunity within sports may feel more powerful and know themselves and their bodies better than girls who are not given this opportunity. Maya, an eleven-year-old soccer player, described this power: "I love soccer. And my team, like they get really physical and they shove people." I asked whether she ever gets aggressive when she plays, and she replied enthusiastically, "Yeah, 'cause, I mean, if they shove me, I get to shove them back, but not like pushing, but just shoulder shoving to get the ball." She "gets to" shove them back, as if this is a special treat for a good girl.

When we think of powerful girls we almost inevitably think of girls in sports, pushing their way around a soccer field or basketball court, feeling the force, energy, and control when you have the ball and you're keeping it away from the other team. Title IX of the Education Act Amendments assured girls this opportunity in 1972, a time when girls largely had been excluded from participation. Since then there has been a huge change in the number of programs offered to girls and the number of girls participating in sports.

When girls play sports, they contradict the culture's perceptions of them as weak and frail. Susan Cahn, in her 1994 book *Coming on Strong*, about the history of women in sports, writes that in the twenties and thirties, when girls and women started participating in athletics, doctors and educators wrote of the physical and psychological dangers of physical activity for women and girls. These concerns echoed turn-of-the-century restrictions on upper-class, white, menstruating women, condemning them to bed rest during that time of the month.

Girls on the field are the antithesis of the frail beauty of yesteryear and the embodiment of power, access, and agency. They are proving that sports can be every bit a part of girls' lives as it is of boys' lives. Research points to the benefits for girls and women at the beginning levels of sports: They get better grades and they feel better about themselves; Colette Dowling calls it "physical self-esteem" in her book *The Frailty Myth*. They are less likely to get pregnant, and they have a better body image and a lower school dropout rate.

But there's another side to this celebration. No matter the greater access and participation, girls' sports still reflects society's intense management and scrutiny of the body, at least at the higher levels. Girl athletes are quite aware of how much muscle is allowed, how much weight they can gain, what kind of uniforms they can wear before they start looking too unfeminine.

And girls in sports today have to confront the cultural impression that when girls get powerful physically, they are less appealing in terms of stereotypical femininity. To do so they often tame their image by adding on femininity accessories, as do professional women athletes. Michael Messner, who has written extensively on sports and gender, points out that track star Florence Griffith-Joyner's muscular body is feminized with long nails, flowing hair, and "spectacular outfits." Female bodybuilders do their competitions in cute bikinis, make-up, and sexy hairdos. They are given points for fingernail polish, highlighted hair, and breast implants. Even when athletes don't feminize themselves, fans and the media may do it for them. Dayna Daniels, a professor of exercise science at the University of Lethbridge in Canada, argues that when women are "too" successful at sports, they not only face criticism for not being feminine, but they have to face a continuous focus on aspects of their femininity rather than on their athletic success.

Girls who participate in sports often have a double identity. While they are tough on the field or court, they may try extra hard to prove their femininity in school among the boys. High school track star Leslie Heywood writes about what it was like in high school to be marked as a good athlete. One of the best runners in the school, she also tried to be a cheerleader, but her athlete's body did not "look good" doing the dancer's steps. Because she was an assertive player and a successful athlete she was seen as "bigger than my britches" and a "bitch." She even had the nerve to demand to continue using the weight room when the coach said, "My boys need it." Over time she began to see the other girls, the cheerleaders, as "clean" and herself as "wild," "like a monster." Her coach put her in her place, first in subtle ways, like making her run through a sprinkler to get her T-shirt wet, and eventually by demanding sex.

While this is an extreme example of how girls are reminded that they are, in the end, "just girls," or "just bodies," coaches, parents, fans, and the media make other attempts to control the image of girls in sports. Athletic organizations as well as coaches limit girl athletes' aggression while similar aggression is many times supported or seen as essential to the game in boys' sports. In hockey, for example, when girls and women play, the official rules do not allow them to check, throw their body against another person to throw them off balance and get the puck. For better or worse, this is an integral part of men's hockey games.

People who believe in girls' essential goodness and cooperation think that the more women's sports are controlled by men (and there is a trend for girls' and women's sports teams to have male coaches more often than women), the more they reflect so-called male values such as hierarchy, competitiveness, and aggression. But these are people who think that aggression is not and shouldn't be a part of women's psyche and lives. Early on, the physical education establishment even said that girls didn't want highly competitive sports. This has not turned out to be true and is reminiscent of the politicians who argued that women were happy in the home and didn't want to vote.

Culturally speaking, Americans like to feminize our female athletes. Although the terms "lady" or "ladylike" are rarely used anymore in this culture to describe women, sports teams continue to take male team names and add the word "lady" to feminize them. At the college where I teach, the men's basketball team is the Knights; the women's is the Lady Knights. In Amherst, Massachusetts, there are the Hurricanes and the Lady Hurricanes, and in West Springfield High of Washington, D.C., the Spartans and the Lady Spartans.

The media also like to sexualize (and thus feminize) girls playing sports because sex sells. In 1999 *U.S. News and World Report* reported: "Women athletes—those who kick and shove and pant and grunt—have not traditionally held a lot of advertising appeal. Sequined skating outfits were sexy, smelly shinguards were not."

Sex appeal was also part of the magic of the 1999 World Cup women's soccer team. Although many women jog, play games, and exercise in sports bras, when Brandi Chastain tore off her jersey after scoring the winning goal of the World Cup, her sports bra was seen as an undergarment and her act was described as "provocative" by journalists. David Letterman called the whole team "babe city."

The media also make big news of female athletes' anger while at the same time feminizing it. Because anger isn't sexy, it isn't feminine. When Svetlana Khorkina showed her anger at the 2000 Olympics when the Russian team missed the gold because of a mistake in the placement of the vault, journalists called her a "diva." She wasn't just an angry athlete, as John McEnroe once was called the "bad boy of tennis"; instead, she was a "diva," "sullen," "petulant," and "pouty," all feminized, quasisexualized descriptors. Straight-talker Rosie O'Donnell relabeled her behavior accurately; she was "angry." Calling an angry woman athlete a prima donna or pouty demeans her and makes it seem as if when a woman gets angry she is getting too big for her britches (diva) or she is infantilized (pouty).

Girls who love and play team sports are not girl-like in one more important way: They seem to prefer to run with a group rather than preserve that hallmark of "femininity," the best friendship. Remember, most researchers report that girls prefer (even though such a so-called preference may be a second resort) to walk around hand in hand, disclosing secrets and sharing feelings, while boys play tag, football, and kickball on the playground. One recent study, however, funded by the Girl Scouts, asked 362 girls which activities they did made them feel good about themselves. Unfortunately, being in the Girl Scouts, an institution that has become increasingly "feminized," did not typically make the girls feel good. Athletics won. Girls responded that it was because sports made them feel competent. The researchers make the point that previously psychologists had agreed that girls derive their self-worth from relationships, but only 10 percent of the girls they interviewed said that they liked an activity because they got to be with other girls.

This research contests the idealized notion that girls prefer being in pairs, walking around the playground. Many studies have shown that girls are "better" at friendships and that "best friends" matter more to girls than boys, but this doesn't have to mean that there is some kind of natural inclination in girls to bond, to nurture, to take care of others. Instead, Valerie Hey's concept of "performance of friendship" operates here as a certain girl-based "performance of femininity." Girls like best friendships for the intimacy and connection they provide, but girls also *feel the need to create* best friendships because they are trying to be girls, trying to be normal, and doing what their mothers and the culture expect them to do. Parents of daughters and researchers alike glorify best friendships for girls as almost a requirement of normality, whereas team or group membership is practically ignored. Few parents feel that it is important for their girls to learn to be part of a team. In fact, it may be more threatening to the culture when girls team up with each other rather than stay in small, cozy dyads or triads. Many adult women I spoke to complained about mothers forcing them to play with another girl, to be nice to her, and their desire to resist this imposition. Not one woman or girl complained, as perhaps some boys might, that they were forced to play a sport, or forced to be a part of a team they didn't like.

Some might argue that even though I write from a feminist perspective, I am, like male authors before me, putting down girls' specific competence in friend-making and friend-keeping (relationships) and elevating a male competence (the ability to play on teams), but I am not. I am only looking at opportunities and how the approval of certain kinds of experiences and disapproval of other kinds of experiences shapes and restrains girls' development. And while if this book were about boys I might be saying that we as a culture ought to be promoting best friendships among boys, this book is about girls, and we ought to look at what participation in sports affords them.

What Do Girls Say?

Many of the girls I spoke to play soccer. None of the adult women I interviewed identified themselves as athletes, preferring to call themselves tomboys if they played sports in youth, thus confirming that they bought into the idea of their time that girls should not play sports.

When I asked the girls about getting aggressive, Avery wanted to reassure me that she was still nice and kind. She said:

> I get aggressive, but if I do and it really hurts somebody, I feel bad and I help them and stuff. Like the most, the worst I've ever done was stepped on somebody's toe, you know, and like, "Are you okay?"

She sees aggression and skill as two different methods in sports and told me "boys are a lot more aggressive than girls, but the girls have a lot of skills that the boys can't do. And the girls are a lot smaller so they can." Keeping in line with girl mythology of the present (that girls are not aggressive), she heard my question about aggression as a girls versus boys question and told me how girls are "better."

Maya, however, owned the aggression. When I asked her what she likes about the aggression, the pushing and shoving, she answered, "It's just the way I play." When I pushed her to find out what it feels like for her to be aggressive, she said,

> Well, I like it more than just being a little meek soccer player, 'cause then you just get walked all over. . . . Yeah, normally I just like, if people are insulting me during school I just ignore it. And on the soccer

field, if people are taking the ball away from me I get to stand up for my-self then. That's what I like about it.

Good girls can't fight back in school, but on the soccer field, if someone pushes you you don't have to take it, you can push back.

One twelve-year-old girl, Mia, asked that her alias in my book be "Mia" after Mia Hamm. When she openly admitted, "In soccer I'm rough, I'm, like, physical," I asked her if she ever purposely hurt someone in soccer or took it a bit too far. Mia answered honestly, "Probably. Like, well, I do. I push people and stuff." Her aggression doesn't bother her immensely. She told me:

I feel good! I like it, especially after it's, like, you just scored a goal or something. Or like when someone pulls my shirt, I feel like I've got to get them back, and I push them really hard. Even in front of the ref, but it makes me feel like, "Don't mess with me!" And I love doing that. So I'm really rough in soccer and stuff. That's why I love that so much.

What a statement for a girl to make! "Don't mess with me!" a statement that they can't make in the halls of the school. How could anyone deny a girl that kind of forthright feeling of power and self-respect? On the soccer field it feels right; off the field, it is often interpreted as masculine or too much.

Mia readily admitted to a time when she lost control on the field. In her last soccer tournament, when her team wasn't very good and only scored one goal all season:

So it was like our last game in the season, and we were playing this team that was like really good, because they had been playing for a while. They were like making passes, and they had scored like ten goals on us, and I got a breakaway kind of, and I think I would have scored in the end, but these two girls came and like tripped me, and I went flying, and my mom, luckily my mom and the other parents were right there, or I think I would have like punched them, I was so mad at them. I was like crying 'cause I was so mad at them. It hurt, but I was like crying more and screaming and yelling because I was so angry. . . . I think I was about to like go over the edge. I went over the edge. I was on the verge a lot of other times, because you know they had scored so many times, plus then being tripped. I just lost it. And my

*mom and my friend like had to like hold me back . . . and I'm, like
"Let go!"*

Appropriately her mom and other parents held her back, but she wanted to
punch the other team members. Still angry in retrospect, she said, "They
didn't deserve to win. I deserved to win!"

In another game, a girl kept grabbing Mia's wrist. She said to me in the
interview, "I just lost it, I think, and said, We'll show them that we can play
better or that we can get them back. . . . I just was really mad, so I just
started like pushing them, playing their game." I asked her how she felt
about that, and she said, "I thought it was pretty fun to do that. I probably
wouldn't mind doing it again."

Some Girls Like the Aggression

What is the secret about girls and aggression in sports? That they like it.
Where else can they stand up for themselves like that? Mia, in school, gets
straight As, and at home, obeys her parents. She is a very good girl. But on
the soccer field, in her own words, she can "lose it." When people lose control, they usually don't feel good, although it allows them to abdicate responsibility for their actions; but what Mia calls loss of self-control is not
entirely self-control. It makes her feel good, although she others the response, in a sense, by disconnecting herself from it. But because she responds with pleasure, it seems that by losing control she may be giving
herself permission to act out aggressively on the field, to show her anger, to
push back, and to seek revenge for unfairness. We allow boys to have those
feelings on and off the field, and we can do that for girls.

In team sports girls get approval simply by being able to be aggressive
en masse, in the company of other girls. While a girl who plays an individual sport may be aggressive in her pursuit of excellence or against her op-
ponent, alone she can be dismissed as a "freak." When a team of girls is
aggressive together, they support one another and create an acceptable
space for this aggression.

And they love it. Most are not trying to "prove something," although
there is an antifeminist contingent who seems to want to read girls'
achievements in this way. They ask girls and women who are good at sports
whether they are trying to "prove something" about what girls or women
can do. And when they do, girls look back cross-eyed and say, "I play be-

cause I love to play." A reporter asked Laila Ali, Muhammad's daughter, before a boxing fight whether she was promoting feminism, then added, "Hey, you're pretty, how can you do this kind of sport?" She answered, "It has nothing to do with looks." Katie Downing, wrestler for the University of Minnesota–Morris team, said to a reporter, "All the girls I know that wrestle are there because they love to wrestle."

Girls who have found pleasure in sports have found something many other girls haven't: a culturally approved of space to get to know themselves physically and in terms of their potential for and limits to aggression. They have found an area where they are allowed to take up space. Iris Marion Young, a philosopher and social theorist, writes in her book *Throwing Like a Girl* that girls and women in sexist society are physically handicapped. She argues that when society aims at physically inhibiting, confining, and objectifying women, through means such as rape, pornography, lower wages, and other forms of diminishment, women and girls come to represent that oppression physically. "As lived bodies," she writes, "we are not open and unambiguous transcendences that move out to master a world that belongs to us, a world [made by] our own intentions and projections." The social confining of women gets enacted physically when women stand with their legs closer together and girls carry their books close to their chests. It is enacted when women "throw like a girl," "run like a girl," and "swing like a girl," all of which have in common the fact that women confine themselves by not putting their whole body into a fluid and directed motion. Women's bodies tend not to "reach, extend, lean, stretch, and follow through." Indeed, she writes, "I have an intuition that the general lack of confidence that we frequently have about our cognitive or leadership abilities is traceable in part to an original doubt of our body's capacity."

Is it no wonder, then, that girls who participate in sports are more likely to be leaders in their high schools and careers later? Sports can give girls the exhilarating opportunity to get to know their body's potential in a different way. When there is a safe space for the expression of aggression and a girl can push herself to break society's limits on aggression and the female body, and yet still do so within the confines of play, which is, we should remember, the foundation of all sports, girls can soar.

Chapter 21

Class, Clothes, and Cutting Her Down to Size

"She used to think she was the best. She used to wear nice clothes. So one day I picked a fight with her: 'You think you're better than me?' "
—Camelia, Puerto Rican, 31

When girls get angry or aggressive with each other for no apparent reason, more often than not it's over issues of social class. It may be disguised in phrases like, "She's such a snob," or "She thinks she's better than every-body," but when you pick apart these phrases, you'll often find that these girls are referring to socioeconomic class. It can go in either direction: Sometimes they beat up other girls because the other girl has nice clothes; sometimes they are cruel and distant because the girl is poor and wears dirty clothes or clothes that are out of fashion. In the grade school years, not just in high school, clothing is the marker of social class among girls, an impetus for hatred and sometimes aggression.

Social scientists have analyzed class and the association of good girls with middle class and bad girls with lower or working class. (Upper-class girls are almost too few to analyze, and rarely appear in studies.) Some-times these social scientists have looked at what class means to the girls themselves, how they themselves measure it, and what they do about it, because middle-class shaping of difference and superiority depends on class distinctions. These distinctions are made on the basis of dress, self-restraint, and how femininity is portrayed. But how girls need to dress, what they need to do to restrain themselves, and what exactly is feminine change by the decade.

Class and Clothes

Cora, who grew up in the thirties and forties and never had new dresses, was judged by her peers as an outcast; Josephine, who grew up in the fifties and sixties, said a good girl "kept her clothes clean"; those who grew up in the seventies and eighties depended on having the right style of clothes; and in the nineties, wearing "cheap" clothes was a sign of being lower class.

Wini Breines, in her book *Young, White, and Miserable*, suggests that the fifties was a time when girls began to be bombarded with advice about how to be popular. "Girls' popularity was based on attractiveness and 'good clothes' and a certain kind of poise more characteristic of middle-class girls than lower-class girls," she writes. But above all, white, middle-class girls were to conform to a single idea of what to wear. Postwar America was a melting pot and differences were supposed to be invisible. Breines also notes the invisibility of African-American girls and the lack of influence from African-American culture on the lives of white middle-class Americans.

One would think that the girls who don't dress well, who don't have the money to buy expensive clothes, might be the ones who are teased or most vulnerable to others' aggression. And this is true some of the time. For example, Chanelle, a teenager who goes to a public school near her home in the projects, admitted to insulting other girls by saying, "You ugly and your clothes look cheap." And then, she said, she starts flinging her hair around. The idea of flinging her hair around seems to be a marker of superiority that emerges directly from a white ideal. (*New York Times* journalist Lena Williams notes in her recent book, *It's the Little Things: The Everyday Interactions That Get Under the Skin of Blacks and Whites*, that when a white person does this in an elevator with a black person, it can be considered offensive.)

But more often than not it is the girl who thinks she's better than the rest, or who other girls perceive is putting on airs, who gets cut down to size. This cuts across race and class and is encapsulated in the phrase "she's a snob." While girls outwardly imply a desire for equality among all girls, that no girl should think she's better than any other, this disguises a deeper and sometimes hidden competition between girls that our culture supports and nurtures.

Nine-year-old Madeleine, who is white and lives in an apartment building just outside of a big city, talked about how she and her friends made fun of a girl, Wanda, in her grade school. She justified it by saying, "She's Polish; she's snobby; she thinks she's perfect." Remember that for many white girls, "perfection" is an ideal; thus, her hatred of Wanda may have more to do with her resistance against the ideal of perfection or her jealousy of Wanda's perfection than with the American belief that everyone in a democracy is equal.

Kezia, who is eleven, said she hates Nina, a girl in her fifth-grade class, because she's "stuck up." Ten-year-old Courtney said that a bad girl was "someone who is just Miss Popular."

Often another girl's snobbiness is used as a justification for aggression. Danielle, a seventeen-year-old African-American girl, remembered playing a prank on a girl because "she had this look like she didn't want to get to know any of us." And Aidee, a nineteen-year-old Puerto Rican girl, remembered pushing a girl in the mud simply because "she was prissy." Aidee, the tomboy whose mother called her a devil child, had particular reason to hate the girl who embodied girlish perfection.

Some women admitted to themselves, looking back, that their aggression in grade school was about personal jealousy. For example, Cora used to fight all the time because of "jealousy; they had a better life than me 'cause they ate. I would rather dress than eat." Kids had made fun of her for the "sacks" she wore, and she saved her money to buy new dresses rather than to buy treats and lunches.

Jealousy is not only a quality of those girls growing up in poverty. It is cultivated in all girls. Elyse, a middle-class white girl growing up in the Northeast in the eighties and nineties, picked on a girl in third grade because "she was like one of these perfect little girls who . . . had everything she wanted . . . and I think I really resented that."

This hatred of girls who thought they were better than the rest seemed particularly strong in the low-income Puerto Rican community of women I interviewed, growing up as they were with immigrant parents and varying job opportunities that depended on their language skills, training, and ability to adapt to an urban environment. Camelia, a child of the seventies, described her aggression as jealousy of a girl who dressed nicely: "She used to think she was the best and she used to wear like nice clothes . . . and I was sorry I couldn't have it like that. So one time I got a fight with her: 'You think you're better than me?' and started pulling her hair."

Pilar, a thirty-eight-year-old woman who grew up part-time in Puerto Rico, fought other kids "every day." And why? She said, "For nothing, because the other kids wanted me to fight the new one who wanted to be higher, more intelligent. They don't want to be seen with poor people." Corazon, too, a forty-nine-year-old woman, had dogs chasing her because a girl who owned them was jealous of her:

> A girl, she don't like the way I was dressed. When you have a little bit of money, you know, more than the other one? People are jealous . . . and my mother used to comb my hair nice . . . and for some reason, that girl, she don't like me.

This desire to put down those who have a little more may be more a function of class than ethnicity. Researchers who have studied girls' friendships have found that working-class black and white adolescents didn't compete for status or popularity as much as middle-class girls, but worked at socializing others into group behavior and norms. When girls didn't comply with a group norm, other girls would be angry at them.

Angela McRobbie, in her studies of working-class girls in England, showed how the automatic response of working-class girls when in contact with middle-class girls was competitiveness and antagonism: They called them snobs. However, Lyn Mikel Brown, in her book *Raising Their Voices*, shows middle-class white girls acting much the same way with respect to their view of the popular girls. They see the popular ones as thinking they are "better than everyone else." But instead of fighting, they compete in their minds, attempting to convince themselves of their superiority through studying hard and having better, more caring, values.

Girls Hating Girls

What is girl infighting about? Sharon Thompson, in her interviews with over four hundred adolescent girls, remarks on how girls often define themselves against other girls when they talk about sexual and social relations. Others propose this as a kind of "horizontal violence" akin to what educator and activist Paolo Friere talks about in *Pedagogy of the Oppressed*: Girls who struggle to exist within a male-dominated culture align themselves with dominant voices. For example, while dominant society might use the term "slut" to keep women in their place and allow greater freedom to men, girls adopt this name-calling of other girls in order to set themselves apart from other girls and to presumably be seen in a more favorable light to boys, men, or some monolithic, imaginary (male-controlled) other called culture.

But it's not all planned out in any conscious way. This other, the voice of dominant society, becomes an internal voice to which the girl responds and which polices her. Lyn Mikel Brown uses the word "ventriloquation," borrowed from philosopher Mikhail Bakhtin, to convey what girls do when they start talking about others, especially other girls, as if they themselves were white male authority figures judging them. This also could be the source of comments that girls make that get called "catty" and prompt adults to exclaim, "Girls are much worse than boys" in terms of verbal aggression. This cattiness is a form of spectacle, or public entertainment, for adults, as women's anger is minimized and contained through adult jokes such as, "Oooh, cat fight!" when women disagree.

In an article called the "The Meaning of Meanness," one researcher studied popularity and isolation in a group of junior high school girls. Girls who weren't "supernice" in an *egalitarian* sort of way risked being called "stuck-up." But popular girls who actually *were* mean to others protected their position as popular. Because they weren't aloof, they couldn't be called "stuck up," and other girls didn't feel like competing with them because then they would risk being treated meanly.

Back-stabbing is so salient in girls' relationships, Brown argues, because it is really the converse of a group ideal of loyalty. The constraints of being "supernice" and superloyal backfire on them, producing the opposite kinds of behavior. Whether it's too tough to keep up the "good" work because girls long for a bit of the power or respect that outspoken, more aggressive girls command, girls find ways to speak in mean ways without challenging the male-dominated institutions they rely on. In addition, girls have a particular power to wound one another because the cut comes from a supposed ally.

Some support for the idea that girls are imitating ways of thinking that male-dominated society produces comes from looking at the way girls attack each other. Girls don't become mean to each other about what we think of as girl-centered kinds of issues (disloyalty, for example, or caring) but about how appealing a girl looks (how appealing to a boy, that is) or how she is dressed.

Girl-to-girl solidarity does exist. There are girl groups, girl gangs in the high school years, and girls' athletic teams. Many researchers have noted working-class white adolescent girls' tendency to support one another against teachers and out groups as well. But as girls become adolescents, and teacher authority diminishes, I wonder if the only remaining way that girls can secure power (if they secure it at all) is through becoming someone's girlfriend. Then the competition that begins as who's dressing better in grade school becomes a contest about who's the best heterosexual girl, the most desirable one.

By asking girls to be nicer to one another, less exclusive and more inclusive in their cliques and playground talks, teachers and parents are asking for girl-to-girl solidarity. They want girls to be more caring and egalitarian. Doesn't society want this of all its children? But those appeals can never be entirely successful, because girls feel the anger and unfairness of class differences and, quite simply, they also feel competitive. These feelings are not to be denied. The cattiness and exclusivity, more indirect forms of expressing anger, don't do them justice and give girls a bad name for being underhanded and sneaky about their aggression. Unless proposed solutions to girls' cattiness and exclusivity acknowledge and find more direct ways to honor girls' anger and self-righteousness as well as their very human feelings of competition, rather than covering them over with "good girl" values of caring and sympathy, the girl-to-girl solidarity will have a falseness to it.

A real solidarity can be built through shared anger. Helping girls to identify common enemies can help, whether they are "the media" or "advertising" or "the system of inequality" or "poverty." If girls fight against these forces together, they can build solidarity while integrating feelings of anger with caring. Is this too much to ask of grade school girls? How young is too young to educate about class difference and unfairness in life's opportunities? If we start early, and examine it within our own lives and relations to one another, girls will be in a much better place in relation to one another when they hit high school.

Zeroing In On: Language and Loudness

It is that act of speech, of "talking back," that is no mere gesture of empty words, that is the expression of our movement from object to subject—the liberated voice.

—*bell hooks, in* Talking Back

Kerri, a middle-class white girl growing up on the West Coast, called a girl a "piece of shit" in the fourth grade. The teacher wrote a note home to her parents. Shaping her class-related behavior, her parents let her know how embarrassed they were: "How could you do such a low-class thing? Do you want to be a good person and make people think highly of you? Don't curse in front of them." That was her parents' fear given the circumstances when they grew up, that by using those particular words, Kerri would indicate she was "low class."

Cursing and loudness are associated with being lower class. Yet they're as associated with girls described as "white trash" as with African-American girls who "tell it as it is." Wendy Luttrell, a professor at Harvard's graduate school of education, talks about an image of white working-class femininity that conveys characteristics such as tough-talking, feminine, and responsible nurturer all at the same time. This ideal was embodied most recently by Julia Roberts in the film *Erin Brockovich*.

Loudness in this film, as well as in the ideal of the working-class white woman, is associated with telling the truth. It also speaks of a lack of division between private and public life. On the one hand, it has been true historically that people who have less power have less privacy from those who do have the power. On the other hand, loudness and telling it like it is are seen by those who cultivate a more private life as a lack of class or restraint. What people forget is that those who have the luxury of cultivating a private life can do so without fearing that their beliefs, their visions, their opinions will go unheard, because these opinions already are preserved in the dominant society. For other girls, being good means suppressing disagreements; the louder one disagrees with what's going on, the harder it is to be viewed as good.

Lyn Mikel Brown writes about loudness in the working-class, junior high school girls she observed and interviewed in Maine. The "Mansfield girls" insist on "bringing their loud, direct selves to school." They "speak their mind" and disrupt the boundaries between private and public lives, private and public speech; their aggressiveness disrupts what teachers hope to find in class in the name of the good girl. Brown says their teachers label the loudness as "impulsive, childish behavior," while in reality it is an attempt to be "heard and understood."

White middle-class girls also care about loudness, although it is not as salient an issue. Many of them have mastered the quiet of the good girl. Heather, now a college student, looked back to her grade school years and visualized the bad girl as "girls who were loud and drew a lot of attention to themselves in, I thought, a way that I thought was disrespectful to other people, especially like a teacher in a classroom setting. And I think it bothered me more than boys who were disrespectful like that." It's interesting to see how she holds girls to a higher standard of quiet than boys.

In African-American girls, the loudness means something in addition to "telling the truth with little regard for the consequences," because such loudness occurs in the context of a historical and institutional silencing. Even more than working-class whites, African-American women in our culture have been silenced from the beginnings of slavery through educational systems that continue to be oppressive.

Grace Evans, an author in Dale Spender's anthology about girls and education called *Learning to Lose,* coined the phrase "Those Loud Black Girls" to describe African-American girls who refused to stay in the background of white girls' lives in high school. Building on this work, Signithia Fordham, an anthropologist at the University of Connecticut, says that this loudness announces "I am here and I will not be made invisible." Fordham's observations at a high school in the D.C. area showed her that academically successful black girls became so in part because of their willingness to silence themselves. Calling these girls "phantoms of the opera," she worries that they silence themselves too much. One Asian-American "good girl," Vicky, was punished by being sent to the closet in the third grade; so invisible was she to her teacher that her teacher forgot she was there for the whole day.

Fordham also notes that sometimes silence can be an act of resistance. The silent girl protects herself from others' reactions and preserves a sense of her wholeness for her home environment. It is a "controlled response to their evolving, ambiguous status." Felicia, now a forty-five-year-old African-American woman, became silent for two years in adolescence. Today she says she doesn't know why, but she snapped out of it and "was fine."

The American Association of University Women's finding that African-American girls generally maintain a personal sense of self-worth yet disconnect from school may follow from Fordham's observations. Fordham's research with John Ogbu, a professor of anthropology at the University of California at Berkeley, showed that high-achieving African-American girls are ostracized by peers for "acting white"; meanwhile, low-achieving girls are asked or made to be quiet because of disruptive comments.

African-American girls describe a good girl in terms of voice; they say that good girls are not loud. Two of the middle-class African-American women I spoke to talked about loudness in this way. Both Marissa and Robin are high-achieving and soft-spoken college students. Marissa defined herself in contrast to the girl across the street who swore and played rock music loud. She was in Marissa's mind, and in the perceptions of their middle-class mixed-race neighborhood, the quintessential bad girl. Robin extends the idea of the good girl to someone who doesn't talk back to her parents or other adults.

The idea of loudness is associated with badness, but for African-American girls who are loud, it means presence. The paradox for African-American girls is that the louder they are, the more visible, yet the more they risk being seen as bad, wild, unruly, or simply unacceptable.

Loudness is a way of taking up space and garnering attention. As such it is an important form of resistance. But when women and girls take up space, Dana Jack explains in *Behind the Mask*, they are considered male and stigmatized as pushy and unfair. In fact, middle-class girls' goodness often has been defined against boys' messiness and loudness in schools.

In a society that puts you down, being pushy, loud, taking up space, and making oneself known can be a form of self-protection. Janie Ward, in her book *The Skin We're In,* says she likes bell hooks's phrase "tongues of fire" to describe talk between African-American mothers and their daughters as a sort of a rehearsal for the real world, a way of toughening them up. Ward, who interviewed middle-class African-American parents around the country, says "bold, unreserved, 'in-your-face' truth telling in the service of racial socialization" is a part of African-American tradition. Standing one's ground and "speaking one's mind" is a resistance strategy to being lost in the system. In another study of teens of color, Niobe Way found that "speaking one's mind" and showing anger were essential to keeping relationships. Without the social glue of confrontation, friendships and family relationships would lose their sense of closeness.

Although an important strategy of resistance, there are some problems with simply equating loudness with standing one's ground. By romanticizing loudness as a way for girls to be heard, the complexity of girls' intents is lost. Many, in their loudness, make wisecracks and insult those with power or advantage, using such noticeable acts of performance as a form of revenge. Furthermore, in choosing this individual style of becoming loud and "getting in people's faces," girls miss opportunities to join together. Peggy Orenstein, in her study of two junior high schools, points out that individualistic strategies of fighting male-dominated institutions take the place of joining together with other girls and thus changing the system. Another problem with choosing loudness as a strategy is the way it supports a disconnection of loud girls from the educational system and their teachers who could be role models and mentors. Middle-class girls look for power in the school through identification with teachers, and loud girls look for a personal power that can never quite reach the level of power to change the environment that they deserve to have and deserve to change. In one important study, Latina and African-American girls who were depressed had the best understanding of racism, sexism, and classism. This study could suggest that when girls don't get loud, they get depressed.

Loud girls also make themselves more "masculine" in the eyes of their teachers and the culture when they are loud, and this may make them more vulnerable later to proving their femininity in stereotypical ways. Does the girl who is seen as loud and pushy prove to herself and her peers that she is also a "woman" through reckless or early involvement in heterosexual romance or sex? When she reaches adolescence might she be more prone to look for acknowledgment of her "girl-ness" through stereotypical girl dress or getting a boyfriend?

In some ways, loudness, while it may serve some girls in terms of their self-worth, may also serve middle-class girls in creating an other to define themselves against. In adolescence, loudness projected onto the working-class white or African-American girls is conflated with sluttiness, serving as another opportunity for the middle-class girl to paint herself as the keeper of purity—as the good girl.

What's important here is to understand the complexities of loudness as completely as we can. It's not only a form of resistance but also plays into a white middle-class othering of girls who do not fit into this narrow, exclusive category. Parents and teachers would do well to pay attention to loudness, as it serves not only as a celebration of girls' voices and truth-telling, but also as a kind of vengeance that emerges from being excluded, from being hurt. It is a way of connecting to other people rather than letting oneself disappear, a way of assuming masculinized power. It has strengths, although girls who use this individualized bid for power may be at risk. Bringing loud girls' voices into the fold of all girls' voices and not permitting the othering or misreading of this voice as bad or "trashy" or "slutty" serves all girls of all classes. When all girls get loud, these single voices won't stand out quite as much.

Chapter 22

"I'm No Sucker":
Fighting and Fighting Back

"I know I'm bad, but I'm not the baddest one."
—Kiara, African American, 14

Some girls like to fight and some girls have to fight. Until recently, television and other forms of media have ignored girls' aggression, implying that the actions are so deviant they can't even be discussed. But recent headlines have proclaimed that girls are getting more violent, and more violent at a faster rate than boys. In 1986 girls constituted 22 percent of all juvenile arrests, and in 1997, 26 percent. The Violent Crime Index indicates that the arrest rate for girls rose 102 percent between 1981 and 1997, while it rose only 27 percent for boys; however, it's important to note that the greatest increase was for drugs and curfew violations. Still, personal offenses were also up, up 146 percent for females versus an increase of 87 percent for males. The National Council on Crime and Delinquency (NCCD) report shows that a disproportionate two thirds of those girls arrested are African American or Latina. Researchers ask whether girls really are getting more violent or whether counting strategies have changed; that is, previously police may not have arrested or brought into the system girls who were violent. Interpretations tend to blame the new statistics on either the women's movement or the victimization of girls.

When we worry about girls getting too aggressive, it often stems from the pacifist assumption that it is better not to be so, that it is better to resolve arguments and injustice through talk, or when talk won't work, through avoidance. This assumption, however, applies only loosely to boys, who are permitted some forms of aggression as shows of masculinity and pride. When a girl acts aggressively, the public responds as though she has breached her proper role. For example, when Carol, a white middle-class girl growing up in the suburbs of New York, got so angry that she ripped the blouse of a girl, a neighbor saw and "he was like appalled that two girls would be fighting like that."

Middle-class girls and women experience their aggression as a surprise, an eruption, as coming out of nowhere. Anne Campbell, in her book *Men, Women, and Aggression*, calls this the expressive view; aggression comes from no longer being able to hold one's anger in. But women and girls who grow up in low-income neighborhoods, who face so many more stresses (illness, drugs, poor schools, and lack of safety), typically use an instrumental view, one that corresponds with the way men and boys view violence. The instrumental view sees aggression as useful; in such environments, the "coercive power" that aggression brings with it operates as a tool for survival. It is difficult to persuade girls to rely on the so-called pacifist responses of talking or avoidance when they live in the center of such injustice with little outside protection. The place in which girls grow up, thus, is enormously important in understanding the usefulness of aggression as well as the meaning of it in their lives. The interaction of neighborhood, home environment, and peer group plays a primary role in influencing the way girls act out aggressively, in the acceptance of aggression in girls, and in the shamefulness or lack of shame they feel when they are aggressive.

The majority of the women and girls I talked to, whether from middle-class suburbs or low-income neighborhoods, had at least one experience where they hurt someone else; where they became aggressive; where they punched or kicked and did it so it would hurt. "Good girls" did it maybe once or twice and felt ashamed; "bad girls" did it more frequently, with righteous anger. While good girls handle this guilt as a secret worry, the bad girls dismiss the guilt and experience the aggression as a part of their lives, a part of themselves.

Revenge and Self-Protection

Revenge and self-protection go hand in hand for many girls who fight. Dana Jack, who interviewed only adult women for her book *Behind the*

Mask, sees her most aggressive subjects as putting up a "wall of self-protection." But attacking others is not only about protecting oneself, it's about revenge against those who have harmed you. Many girls and women cite examples of getting even or fighting back when someone provoked them. Fighting back is a matter of survival. Corazon, a fifty-year-old Puerto Rican, describes fighting between kids in low-income neighborhoods: "If the kids fight they fight together, and the parents they don't get, how you say, messed up in any of the fights of their kids. No. We had to defend ourselves. That we call 'survival.' "

Acts of revenge show the attacker that he or she can't pick on you, that you are a person to be reckoned with, even that you are a person to be respected. For example, a boy tripped Corazon in grade school, so she waited for him after school "with a rock in my hand, and I hit him in the head. . . . After that he never bothered me. I make a hole in his head." Tanisha, ten, African-American, and living in a housing project, said, "I hurt other people when they hurt me." Kezia, who is eleven and currently negotiating the different rules of her home life in the projects and her private, mostly white school life, won through scholarships, is still ready to interpret accidents as an opportunity for revenge. A boy hit her in the head with a tennis ball, so she "got mad, and I pushed him into the wall. I do bad things, very bad things." When asked why she thinks this is a bad thing, she says she should have waited to see if it was an accident, but that "if someone hits me, I hit them back real fast. It comes out of nowhere." Though Kezia says these impulses come from nowhere, they likely spring from reflexes she uses to protect herself in her home neighborhood.

Girls also fight when they are teased. Karen, a white girl growing up in a rural area, wore hand-me-downs; when one girl started making fun of her, she "punched her in the face." Cora, the fifty-two-year-old African-American woman from the South, was also teased about her clothes: "I think that made me very, very angry and mean. I would fight all the time." Josephine, from a working-class African-American family, responded when a boy called her a bitch: "You remember clogs?" she asked. "I took my clogs, and because I felt irritated, I started hitting him, it was so irritating." And her response worked: Every time he saw her coming "he was going the other way." Josephine was the first of her friends to ever attack back: "I guess they was scared of him, but I had to be the bold one." Felicia, from a working-class African-American family, was teased constantly by a girl for being fat. In home economics she asked the mean girl for a pincushion and, when the girl threw it at her, Felicia "was so frustrated, I picked up a pair of scissors and, just like, . . . stabbed her in her butt and she jumped." The girl never teased her after that.

The explanations girls and women give for these acts prove their aggression to be instrumental, or useful, to them. Their stories show that when you stand up to teasing with a show of aggression, people leave you alone. There are other situations where a show of aggression comes from a deeper sense of injustice and a broader need for revenge, revenge on the system and representatives of the systems that have caused deep and individual hurt. One such system is the schools.

Several Puerto Rican women recall the prejudice of New York City teachers toward immigrants in the sixties, seventies, and eighties. Many of them put thumbtacks on teachers' chairs. Dolores remembered becoming so angry at a teacher that she tore an old wooden schooldesk out of the floor to which it was nailed and held it over her head, threatening the teacher. Cora remembered a teacher "beating her" because she wouldn't apologize to another child.

Racial prejudice was and is a system worth fighting, but it is hard for schools to recognize when combativeness comes from standing up for oneself specifically as an African-American girl or a Puerto Rican girl. Shamika claimed that even now she fights at school "like, every day" because the kids call her "blackie." She said simply, "They irritate me. They deserve it."

Toni, three decades ago, also felt prejudice acutely and responded violently. She would beat up her little cousin just "because he was light-skinned." Toni remembered the day Martin Luther King was shot:

> I was a young girl, and I wasn't in school, and I was enraged. I didn't even know who Martin Luther King was, to tell you the truth, but I remember sitting in class and it came over a loudspeaker that Martin Luther King had died, and I knew that he was a Black person, and all I know is, a white person did it. And I remember going on the street just looking for white people, and in my community there was very little white people, so any light-skinned person who had long straight hair got beat up. . . . I remember yanking a girl who did nothing to me, just by her hair, for no reason at all. Just because she was white.

Kiara, who is fourteen, remembered how, when she was younger, an act of aggression arose from a feeling that all whites were racists. She told of picking on a little white boy simply because he was white. She told me, "I play with whites now. I'm used to them now. I play on a white basketball team, so I'm used to them."

Sometimes life was so bitterly unfair for a girl or woman, and racism appeared to pervade all environments from school to playground, that all she could do was hit and fight and make trouble. The NCCD study of juvenile female offenders found that 92 percent of them had been subjected to some form of abuse. By age thirteen to fourteen they were likely to have been beaten, stabbed, shot, or raped. Such overwhelming factors are a key to becoming aggressive, and yet the revenge isn't aimed necessarily at the person who has committed the harm, but at anyone, anyone in their path.

Sometimes anger is so immense with nowhere to go that it simply feels good to hurt someone else, Cora told me. Although she constantly beat up other children, even stuck a pencil into a girl's face for revenge, she said she feels most ashamed of the day she killed a cat. "I said that if you scratched me, why can't I do something to you? So I killed the cat. . . . I was a evil little child for my age. . . . I think what made me so angry was because of the way I was treated." Cora had been beaten for years by her stepfather and sexually abused by an uncle. This was a revenge killing misdirected.

Protection of Others

Having been abused themselves, many girls also show extraordinary sympathy for others who are vulnerable and fight on their behalf, especially their little brothers and sisters. O'Brishia, for example, got in one fight "because this girl slapped my brother, the one that I be fighting." And even though she fought her brother at home constantly, when this other girl said her brother had big lips, she was on her: "I was, like, 'My brother does not have big lips.'" Kiara protected her sisters: "One of my sisters might get hurt, really, really hurt. Then I would jump in." Stella, a white woman in her fifties who grew up in a poor neighborhood, remembered:

I beat up a girl because she hit my baby brother, and I chased her for half a block. I chased her into a store. She didn't think I was going to go after her. I went in the store and I beat the hell out of her, and I said, "If you ever hit my brother again I'll come back and kill you."

LaShauna saw someone picking on her sister and beat her up: "I felt that I did the right thing protecting my sister. . . . I knew that my sister couldn't take this girl on." Roxanne, having no sisters, made friends with a bully: "She looked after me 'cause I had no sister, and the girls used to always beat me up."

Girls do look after one another. Jessie, a white girl from a rural area, got into "a hell of a fight in the fifth grade." There was a black girl from Africa in her class, and the kids called her "black widow." She stuck up for her African friend one day, so the other girls started beating Jessie: "All I remember is I smashed her head into the sink because she was beating me up. I got really ugly. . . . I almost broke her nose." Chrissie also took pride in her role as protector: "Not only was I the aggressor, hurting people, but lots of times I was the protector too. . . . I was always the sort of the girl that would somehow be able to defend or protect or whatever."

Some girls learn to protect others at home. Toni would see her father beat up her mother for drug money, and she and the other kids would join in, trying to beat their father off. LaShauna grew up in a household where she observed many strong women getting beaten down by their boyfriends and husbands. She remembered how her aunt Lena was beaten so badly that it was in the newspaper: "And I'm like, 'Oh my gosh!' And I was little. I was like six." She continues to describe how her aunt couldn't take care of herself because of the beatings, and her mom would send her over to her aunt's house to help her wash up and take a shower.

> And when her boyfriend hit her I be right there. I wanted to see every-thing, you know. I just felt that I had to . . . but after a while I didn't take it any more, so when he started hitting her I was like, "You are dead wrong." And I started getting into it. When he get in my face, I was like, I felt really proud. . . . I was kind of scared because . . . his face was whenever I moved, he would move too, and I didn't like that, so I pushed him out of my way because he wanted to hit me. But he didn't, though, and my aunt came in, and she was like, "No, don't put your hands on her. Don't put your hands on her."

The courage of that little girl is quite amazing. And one can imagine that this experience of protecting adult women beaten by adult men might make a difference in the kinds of relationships she will become involved in later in life. While we might wish that a little girl did not have the responsibility, or take on the responsibility, to stand up to a grown man, we hear pride and power in her stance: "You are dead wrong."

Teach Your Children Well

In some households, girls are taught to fight back, and why not? Girls need to. Teaching a daughter to fight back can be akin to teaching her to stand up for herself. As Rosa's mother said to her, if Rosa didn't fight back she would give her a beating herself when she got home. With her mother's past in mind, a past in which she was exploited and hurt many times, it's no wonder that she didn't want her daughter to grow up to be similarly exploited. It is understandable how vehemently she felt that Rosa must learn to fight.

Mothers teach their daughters to fight simply so that they are ready for anything. Realistically, their daughters will face times when someone wants to hurt them, and being able to fight back is a necessary skill. Some readers may think that fighting doesn't get anyone anywhere, that violence begets more violence, and that girls put themselves at greater risk when they fight back. This also used to be the wisdom of rape counselors, until the last few years, when research showed that women who fight a rapist have a much greater chance of getting away; furthermore, if they don't get away, they still have a much quicker recovery. Fighting back works instrumentally as well as psychologically.

O'Brishia, who fought off her brother constantly, finally was allowed to beat him up. He was two years younger than she and wanted her blue crayon. When she said no,

> he bit me on my back and I had the teeth marks. I cried and cried and cried. But the next day we was in the backyard and I beat him down. My mother tried to stop me. [But] my aunt said [to her mother], "Uh uh. You not going to stop her. All that he's been doing to her, you is not going to stop her." And they let me beat him up. Ever since then we still fight, but he cannot beat me at all.

Carol's middle-class white mother told her to fight back: "If she's going to pick on you every day, then you have to fight back." Gail, although a "goody-two-shoes," learned to fight back by wrestling with her father and other sisters: "He'd toss us around and would allow us to hit him as hard as we could." Once, when she came home crying, he said to her, "The next time you come home crying, as hard as you hit me when we play, you should be able to knock somebody out. . . . We were always basically told to do what is best for yourself. And when he gave me permission, when this girl came to us . . . I fought like I had never fought before. . . . I came out of it unscathed, and she was the one who was crying." Rosa also appreciated her mother's lessons:

> She used to tell me that if anybody hits you and you stay hit, when you get home I'm going to give you a beating, So if anybody picked on me I made it my business to hit back. . . . She made me a strong person in that sense, where I didn't let nobody bully me.

Fighting with brothers was also good practice. Susan, raised in a large Catholic family, said that kids would "try to bully me, and maybe because I was always fighting with my two brothers, I was not intimidated. . . . So we would start hitting, and I would break this kid's glasses, you know, or give someone a black eye. . . . I wasn't afraid to do it." Valerie's older brothers would tease her, hide her books, take the heads off her doll babies. She and her brother started fighting one day on the way to church—"I was kicking and everything, you know?"—and it suddenly dawned on her, "Hey! I can fight these boys!" Rather than serving as a merely destructive ability, knowing how to fight was a route to empowerment and protection.

The Tougher They Are

Sociologists for decades have seen boys' aggression in the "underclass" as a plea for respect and a show of masculinity that society has denied them through lack of opportunity to prove themselves in more mainstream and middle-class venues. The rise in aggression in women and girls might also stem from a rise in feelings of injustice and a desire for more agency and power in the world outside the home. While girls and women aren't fighting to prove their masculinity, they are certainly fighting to gain respect among their peers.

Anne Campbell, in *Men, Women, and Aggression*, describes this kind of proving oneself among girl gang members. Her girls enjoy "image-promoting" and, through bragging, even seek to earn the label of "crazy bitch." She points out how the girls reassure themselves of their own toughness, and even begin to use aggression preemptively.

Toni used to be a member of the group the Sweet Six, six girls who would go around New York City beating people up just to beat them up. Tai remembered a group of girls "instigating" her. A boy she liked preferred this other girl and her friends would "light her up" to get her to fight. She remembered them saying to her, "Oh, if I were you I would knock her out. I would get her, 'cause she's always with your boyfriend," and "Look, she brought her mother to hit you." Tai said, "They would bring up things to kind of stir me up, and I guess I thought I had to prove something."

Proving something is important to girls who live in areas where fighting means toughness. LaShauna, twelve, agreed that "sometimes I fight to prove that I'm worthy of being a good fighter. Or sometimes I would fight just 'cause I want to . . . but it's been a long time since I fought, you know, almost a year." Sometimes fighting proves to other girls that a girl is tough enough to be avoided. Yvonne, who considered herself to be a "good girl," remembered a couple of girls trying to force her to fight with someone else, although she wasn't really a fighter. She said that "it was more or less like a truth-or-dare kind of thing, and they said, "Oh, we know you not gonna fight her. We know you're too scared to fight her." Lucy, in the fourth grade, was told by her girlfriend to go hit another girl: "I guess she dared me, told me to go hit her for no reason, and the girl was cool, too. And I just went up to her and I just hit her and I pushed her."

Proving you are tough earns you respect from peers. Chrystal, a white teen growing up in the projects, remembered, "I picked a fight with the wrong person, and she was bigger than me, and it started a lot of rumors that she was planning on having other people jump into the fight and that she was planning on having weapons, and I got nervous and brought a steak knife to school." When asked why she picked the fight, she said, "Because she was bigger than me and I thought I could take her. . . . If you lose the fight you get friends, they won't leave you alone about it. . . . And if you win the fight you've met their standards, and I was a typical kid. I wanted to be liked."

Traditional girl theorists might have a hard time fitting Chrystal's vying for position and status through aggression into their theories. They might interpret this aggression as an internalized "male" vision of how to win friends and influence people. But her feelings and actions are not less authentically female than are pacifist inclinations, unless the model for comparison is a white middle-class stereotype of femininity.

For these very real girls, their toughness means self-esteem and self-respect, not only from others, but from themselves. Cora saw herself as a "sweet bad kid. I had a lot of sweet intentions in me," and yet she knew that "if trouble came to me, I'm here to bank myself. . . . That's right. You treat me right!" Becca stood up for herself as early as in the first grade: "I don't care if you're eighteen feet tall, . . . I wasn't going to take it, like I hit back." Her mother had taught her to stand up for herself. When she was bullied by a bigger girl, she thought: "Just because she was big and she was using her size against me and I was like, screw you! I don't care how big you are, you know?"

Over and over girls said, "The fighting was something you needed to do because you had to prove that you wasn't gonna let anybody take advantage of you, number one." Another said quite simply, "I felt proud I could protect myself."

Toughness gives a girl a kind of freedom. Middle-class white Chrissie said it was "liberating to think of myself as tough: 'I am tough.' " She also confessed that, for better or worse, "once you admit that that's true of yourself, then you're not a good girl or a nice girl."

Fighting girls tell their stories with incredible pride and joy. This pride and joy, I think, speaks to a feeling of competence. The guilt about hurting another person is simply not present. As Chrissie said, "I remember I got such a rush. . . . There was this one boy. I can't remember why I got mad at him, but I kicked him in the balls. I was a big fan of kicking boys in the balls. You knew they were so vulnerable there. You were such a stud if you could just completely knock a guy out. . . . It was really fulfilling to kick that guy in the balls and feel like I'd really hurt him."

Other girls spoke in this free way about accepting their aggressive sides. Lillian said, "I was a fighter to the heart. [And why?] Because I could. 'Cause I was old enough. 'Cause I was big enough. 'Cause I was bad enough. [How did you feel about it?] Good. . . . Because I could do it. Just 'cause I could do it." Even if it was just in the area of aggression, Lillian was competent.

LaShauna, the girl who defended her aunt, didn't even understand the interviewer's question about whether or not she felt any guilt when she was aggressive. Her fighting was about protection, and sometimes about revenge. She fought a girl and fought hard, ending up in the principal's office, and even though she said to Bev, my assistant, "I felt guilty," when Bev asked her why, she said, "Because I didn't win."

The Meaning of Aggression

Aggression is about self-respect and not letting others take advantage of you. Through aggression girls not only protect themselves but show pride in their competence, their ability to protect themselves. Knowing that so many of these girls are also victims, we have to ask whether their aggression is a defense against their vulnerability, and of course it is that too. But not solely. Through aggression they make an angry statement to the world about their abuse, the prejudice of schools, of whites, and the harm done to them by family members.

Denitra, who is twenty-two and has three children, said that as a child she was "stuck in the house" while her mother did drugs. Even today she has many secrets and few friends. She also sees herself as a "good girl:" responsible, doesn't smoke, doesn't drink, and is "kind-hearted." But when asked if she ever got into a fight as a child, she answered, "Oh my gosh! Almost every week [with] basically anybody." She explained that "basically it made me feel good. I got a lot of anger out, and you know that was that. I was happy." For one eight-year-old African-American girl, fighting is part of who she is. To her a good girl is someone who doesn't pick on "*too* many" people (my italics). But fighting? Well, "it's one of my favorite ways to let my anger out."

These are girls. They "should" be playing house or school or pet shop or some relational game with their best friend in the privacy of their bedroom. They should "tell the teacher" when someone threatens them so she will protect them. They should "walk away" if someone says a nasty remark to them, content in the superiority that they don't have to fight.

But what a luxury that would be. "Devil" children, like Aidee, whose mother called her that, are devil children because they have to be. Warlords, as Lillian dubbed herself, are warlords because there is a war out there. Fighting is a way a girl who is unprotected can stand her ground, feel some power, battle injustice, and seek revenge. Sure it's compensatory, in part. Compensatory because it is too threatening and horrible to feel the real lack of protection and vulnerability. Sure it's at times all bluff and bravado. And unfortunately so, because these tough girls are still likely to be victimized. But I wouldn't take this form of power away, coercive or not, until we can afford them better protection.

I also want to say that we should be careful not to normalize white middle-class girls who seek to mask or control their aggression as "real girls" or "natural girls" while making these mostly lower-class, but some middle-class, girls the "problem girls." Instead, we should see whether or not a girl is aggressive as a function of her need to be so. One might even argue that middle-class girls go unarmed into colleges and bars where men will grope and acquaintances might rape. Perhaps more of them should go to college better trained.

Chapter 23

Raising Aggressive Girls?

"[A fourteen-year-old girl] fought off a would be kidnapper as she walked home from school in La Crescenta California . . . she was able to break free of the attacker by administering a swift kick to the groin area which caused him to fall to the ground."
—Los Angeles Times, November 23, 1993

Parents could learn a little from those "bad girls," the ones who curse and fight and grow up to raise their own daughters to know and understand their potential for aggression and be able to use it if the situation calls for it. While pointless violence is always wrong, don't we want girls to be able to fight if they need to? How many among us know that we could or would be able to fight back in a rape attack? Some of us would think of relying on our intelligence to talk the rapist out of it, or on our ingenuity to escape. Few of us have taken our daughters to a self-defense course. Teachers of self-defense always meet up with women's resistance to using their body to defend themselves, their fear of bringing all of their anger and aggression to bear on a situation. Sometimes it's necessary. Colette Dowling, author of *The Frailty Myth*, writes that most violence against women has a point: "to reaffirm that women are incapable of responding." We have taught our daughters to not respond.

Some theorists have suggested that girls developed higher levels of conflict resolution because they *couldn't* fight as well as the boys. But any of the "bad girls" I interviewed could tell you with pride about which boy they clobbered on the playground. I think, instead, that the ladylike behavior expected of middle- or upper-class white girls, from the Deep South of the nineteenth century to the suburban homes of the fifties, was cultivated much to girls' detriment.

The trouble with the so-called bad girls is not that they've learned to be aggressive and that this is now an unnatural part of who they are, nor is it the fact that they take pride in their strength and ability to fight. The trouble is more one of judgment. Other methods of conflict resolution would help them in the long run, and they do turn to violence too readily, even when nonaggressive approaches would yield better results. But in the short run we ought not to disarm these girls who live in dangerous places, among dangerous people. Instead, we ought to first work with them on choosing ways in which they want to use their aggression, join with them in their pride in this ability, and help them to understand to not turn immediately to aggression. All this while working on longer-term solutions to poverty and violence in neighborhoods.

We need to help girls to understand and feel angry, justifiably angry, when the situation calls for it. Today, though there's a lot of "in your face" advertising about girl power and supposed girl assertiveness, anger is never discussed as a part of this right to exist. Jeffrie Murphy, a philosopher and author of many books and essays on virtue, argues that anger and resentment are the proper response when one's rights have been violated. But even in the shocking pink, wild, and wonderful teen guide *Deal With It*, advertised as a "whole new approach to your body, brain, and life as a gurl," including chapters on boobs, masturbation, and zits, there are no entries on aggression. Even in these authors' attempts to be subversive, they leave out the parts that just don't fit with being a girl. Anger is found under the topic of "Those Sucky Emotions," and in this section, girls are given advice from other girls on how to cope with it: "cry"; "count to 10 and wait for the feeling to go away"; and think about whether your anger could really be about "loneliness" or "poor self-esteem." Is anger only a "sucky" emotion? Is it *never* justified in the life of a girl? And why cry or wait for it to go away when you might actually do something about it?

Anger is one of a palette of emotions, all of which are rich resources to all girls. Middle-class girls need encouragement to be angry when they are justified to be so, to be heard out loud, and to develop ways of expressing it. They need to be taught about their own potential for aggression, to develop fighting back as a skill, and to know when they might use this power and when it is better to negotiate or walk away.

Girls who grow up in rougher neighborhoods ought to learn about other means of conflict resolution, but they also need better protection. We need to protect these children as well as we protect middle-class girls who grow up in suburbia. When they can relax their aggressive stance, they will be better able to reach out to others in solidarity and use their aggression on issues of fairness, justice, and protection of others.

It is quite interesting that one of the girls who felt the most pride for her aggression was the one who grew up among a lot of aunts who were beaten by husbands and boyfriends. At the age of seven, LaShauna stood up to a grown man to protect her aunt, and she backed him down. What a dangerous and courageous act.

Parents, teachers, neighbors:

- Don't let girls grow up afraid of their own aggression. Teach them to use it wisely: to learn to walk away when it is important, negotiate verbally when they can, and stand up physically for injustice and self-respect when it is needed.
- Realize that anger and aggressive feelings can be the impetus for creative and productive acts. It can lay behind the ambition to achieve, the desire to win, the urge to create and express oneself in art or by writing. These forms are not hidden forms of expression such as diaries but ways in which women have creatively and productively integrated their anger when they could.
- Don't let girls feel utterly helpless in the face of someone else's aggression. Teach them how to fight back or resist the aggression in all different ways, some physical, some not.
- Every girl should be given the opportunity to participate in an aggressive sport—to learn karate for example, or a team sport like soccer, or even how to box. These kinds of opportunities teach girls to feel their bodies are competent, and that they deserve to take up space.
- Remember that education about aggression doesn't undo empathy and caring. They can exist simultaneously in everyone's lives. Empathy, caring, and fairness are always important.

Conclusion

Chapter 24

Welcoming Sex, Power, and Aggression into the Lives of Girls

"The aim of each thing we do is to make our lives and the lives of our children richer and more possible."
—Audré Lorde

People are always afraid that if you drop the bar a little bit, all hell will break loose. Pandora just took a little peak into the box and, whoa, all the troubles of the world emerged. But this myth, like our current myths, is used to police girls and women.

That is why all "good girls" lead a double life. In public they are sweet, innocent, lovely, and well-behaved. They define their image in opposition to the "bad girl" who is sexual, mean, aggressive, loud, or simply just other by virtue of race or class. In private, these good girls still play sexual games, write angry passages in their diaries, and act out aggressively.

These private acts can be seen as a form of resistance against the pressures of being good; they also can be seen as examples of their real selves erupting beyond their control. Neither and both capture all of what is happening because the differences among girls are vast and irreducible.

When good girls act out sexually, they both conform and resist. We see in the midriffs, the stripteases, and the enactment of rape scenes that girls are picking up a form of adult sexuality that objectifies them and teaches them that in a man's world they are to be desired, ogled, and ravaged. But as they pursue their own sexual feelings, arrange to play games in which they explore the boundaries of what is right and what is them, they resist becoming objects and come to understand desire as a rich and possible seed within.

When good girls are aggressive they both conform and resist. Especially for girls of color, when they act out aggressively, they conform to expectations that emanate from a culture more ready to label them violent and dismissable. But they also resist this by proclaiming they are not invisible, that they are strong enough to stand up for themselves. When good girls are aggressive, they conform by calling such aggression other or alien and describe it as coming out of nowhere. They also conform by subscribing to versions of being a girl that mean being catty and mean rather than forming sisterhoods. But they resist such notions if they take on a powerful stance as a girl that incorporates aggression as a form of self-protection, a form of protecting those close to you, or a delightful and appropriate exercise of power, as in sports.

Whether daughters are resisting or conforming, the first step for parents is to recognize that girls do get angry and aggressive, that they do have sexual feelings and interests, and that this is as true for the good girl as it is for the bad. Girls need to acknowledge both of these forces in themselves, and we as a culture need to honor this struggle.

First, girls need to know and understand erotic energy, which can be translated into knowing one's body, understanding the potential for pleasure, seeing oneself as someone with desires and not just desirable. All of these make a girl complete. Many an adult woman I interviewed sighed, as if it were too late to see herself in an erotic way. But these women also claimed that if they could not see themselves in this way, at least they would like to know how to make this a part of their daughters' lives. Erotic feelings are powerful feelings that can sometimes overwhelm, especially when they are experienced as coming from outside oneself, unexpected, and not in one's control. When a girl has control of her body, of her fantasies, of her pleasures, and gives herself some permission to explore, to educate herself, or even to lose control for a bit in a safe place, she will grow up into an adult who has and gives pleasure without shame or fear.

Girls also need to understand themselves as potentially aggressive beings. This realization is also crucial to growing up whole. When a girl gets permission to be angry, she is taught self-respect. When parents address their daughter's aggression, it is important and necessary that they deal not only with feelings such as distress or frustration, but also with anger and the desire for and pleasure in power. Aggression can be harmful, but it can also be the foundation for ambition, for fighting for social justice, and for acts of creativity. With maturity, girls can begin to use their aggressive potential in creative and socially laudatory ways. Think of the anger and aggression in the work of lawyers who fight in the courts, or in artists who push against social expectations and laws, or even in authors who write with bite. When this aggressive potential is suppressed, there is less chance that it can mature and be shaped in these particularly important ways.

Guilt may be one of the foundations of morality, inspiring us to do good and make amends, but too much guilt is not good. Too much guilt for playing sexual games and for aggressive acts undermines self-confidence, interferes with making reparations, and makes girls restrain themselves in activities in which they need to grow. Giving girls some slack is not the same as making excuses for bad behavior.

Going into the twenty-first century, the two most important prohibitions for girls are against sex and aggression. These differentiate girls from boys most emphatically, and also "good" girls from "bad." Truthfully, problems of sex (such as rape and abuse) and aggression (murder, shootings) abound in our culture, and the control of these two areas is important to our society and to personal development. But repression, denial, and ignorance do not take away the potential for sexuality and aggression in all of us. We deny these feelings in ourselves at our peril. For girls to develop in life-affirming, constructive ways demands that these feelings be invited into childhood, brought out into the open, made unsecret.

To grow up to be healthy sexual adults, able to have and give pleasure, able to be women with desires they are not ashamed of, girls need practice. To grow up to protect themselves against abuse, feel their physical strength, and use this strength wisely, they need practice. To be fully emphatic and fight for fairness, they need their anger. Our girls need to practice these feelings and emotions in spaces where adults acknowledge them and help shape their development. We diminish girls when we restrain them in conventional ways, preserve a fake ideal of goodness, and force them to lead secret lives. We don't want to do that anymore.

Notes

Acknowledgments

"Practicing," from *What the Living Do* by Marie Howe. Copyright © 1997 by Marie Howe. Used by permission of W. W. Norton & Company, Inc.

Introduction: Good Girls versus Real Girls

3   *we shouldn't even use the word "normal"*: For a good discussion of this, see Michael Warner, *The Trouble with Normal: Sex, Politics, & the Ethics of Queer Life*. NY: Free Press, 1999.

5   *the rebellious lost teens of* Reviving Ophelia: Pipher, M. *Reviving Ophelia: Saving the Selves of Adolescent Girls*. NY: Ballantine Books, 1995.

5   *the voices of caring, nurturing women who were ignored*: Gilligan, C. *In a Different Voice*. Cambridge, MA: Harvard University Press, 1982; see also Brown, L. M., and Gilligan, C. *Meeting at the Crossroads: Women's Psychology and Girls' Development*. Cambridge, MA: Harvard University Press, 1992.

8   *but Valerie Walkerdine, a British sociologist and feminist, points out that the image of the supergirl*: Walkerdine, V. Project 4-21; Transition to womanhood in 1990s Britain. Talk given at the 27th International Congress of Psychology in Stockholm, Sweden, July 25, 2000.

9   *as William Pollack asserts about "real boys"*: Pollack, W. *Real Boys: Rescuing Our Sons from the Myths of Boyhood*. NY: Random House, 1998.

Part I: The Sexual Lives of Girls

11   *the cultural theorist Ken Plummer tells us:* Plummer, K. *Telling Sexual Stories: Power, Change, and Social Worlds.* NY: Routledge, 1995.

12   *The African-American poet feminist Audré Lorde wrote, "[K]nowledge is power":* Lorde, A. *Sister Outsider: Essays and Speeches by Audre Lorde.* Freedom, CA: The Crossing Press, 1984.

12   *Marie Howe, in her poem "Practicing":* Howe, M. *What the Living Do: Poems.* NY: W. W. Norton, 1999.

Chapter 1: "I'll Show You Mine If You Show Me Yours"

16   *In a study of over three hundred professionals, Jeffrey Haugaard:* Haugaard, J. J. Sexual behaviors between children: Professionals' opinions and undergraduates' recollections, in *Families in Society: The Journal of Contemporary Human Services* (February 1996), 81–89.

20   *Freud thought that girls, when they looked down at their bodies:* Freud, S. *Three Essays on the Theory of Sexuality.* Vol. VII, in Freud, S. *The Standard Edition of the Complete Psychological Works of Sigmund Freud,* trans. and ed. J. Strachey. London: The Hogarth Press, 1961/24.

20   *Karen Horney, laughingly pointed out in her essay, "Womb Envy":* Horney, K. *Feminine Psychology.* NY: W. W. Norton, 1967.

20   *The French feminist writer Irigaray has since pointed out:* Irigaray, L. *This Sex Which Is Not One.* Ithaca, NY: Cornell University Press, 1985.

Zeroing In On: Play. What is Play? What is Sexual Play?

25   *D. W. Winnicott, the famous English psychoanalyst, describes certain special qualities about play:* Winnicott, D. W. *Playing and Reality.* NY: Basic Books, 1971.

Chapter 2: Just Practicing: It's in Her Kiss

28   *The sociologist Barrie Thorne sees a copy of the imbalanced gender relations of adulthood:* Thorne, B. *Gender Play: Girls and Boys in School.* New Brunswick, NJ: Rutgers University Press, 1994. See also Thorne, B., and Luria, Z. Sexuality and gender in children's daily worlds. *Social Problems* (1986) 33, 176–90.

30   *for kissing the girl next to him at lunch:* Sanchez, R. In School, Early Lessons on Sexual Harassment. *Washington Post,* October 4, 1996.

33   *Candace Feiring and Michael Lewis . . . call it the "birthday party effect":* Feiring, C., and Lewis, M. The child's social network: Sex differences from three to six years. *Sex Roles* (1987) 17, 621–36.

Chapter 3: Feminine Ideals: Make-up, Midriffs, and the Pleasures of Being Objectified

39   *"One is not born a woman—one becomes one"*: Beauvoir, S. *The Second Sex*, 1953.

39   *Few have analyzed the appeal of these images for women:* Few authors who publish for the general reading public, that is, and none who write on girls. Many postmodern feminist theorists have analyzed this very issue. And I take my argument most generally from their work.

41   *Church fathers from medieval times onward have argued:* Tseelon, E. *The Masque of Femininity: The Presentation of Woman in Everyday Life.* London: Sage, 1995.

41   *One church father, Clement of Alexandria, wrote:* For the original, look to *The Writings of Clement of Alexandria*, Ante-Nicene Christian Library, 1867. *Translations of the fathers down to* A.D. *3325*, ed. by A. Roberts and J. Donaldson. Vol. 4, London: Hamilton. Cited in Tseelon, 1995, p. 36.

42   *manipulate the items they truly do want to wear:* The idea that dress codes encumber girls more than boys is also found in Smith, L. Sexist assumptions and female delinquency: An empirical investigation. In Smart, C., and Smart, B. (eds.), *Women, Sexuality, and Social Control.* London: Routledge, 1978; pp. 74–86.

43   *has already begun with Christina Hoff Sommers's new book:* Hoff Sommers, C. *The War Against Boys: How Misguided Feminism is Harming Our Young Men.* NY: Simon & Schuster, 2000.

44   *Joan Riviere, one of the early American female psychoanalysts, used the word masquerade":* Riviere, J. Womanliness as masquerade. *The International Journal of Psychoanalysis* (1929) 10, 303–13.

44   *The psychoanalytic literary theorist Lacan also understands:* Lacan, J. The signification of the phallus. In *Ecrits: A Selection*, trans. A. Sheridan. NY: W. W. Norton, 1966, 1977.

44   *Their gaze can't be reduced to a male's gaze:* See Mary Ann Doane's influential 1982 piece called, "Film and Masquerade: Theorizing the Female Spectator," in *Screen*, 23, 74–87, for an understanding of how women "appropriate" the male gaze for their own pleasure. See also Sue-Ellen Case, "Toward a Butch-Femme Aesthetic" in Henry Abelove, Michele Barale, and David Halperin, *The Lesbian and Gay Studies Reader*, NY: Routledge, 1993, for a discussion of how women hold femininity at a distance through masquerade.

45   *a sharp differentiation in the way men and women dress:* Tseelon, pp. 22–23.

Chapter 4: Naked Barbies

48   *Ruth Handler, who masterminded the creation and marketing of its biggest seller: Barbie:* The information in this paragraph and the following comes from Stern, S. *Barbie Nation: An Unauthorized Tour.* New Day Films/El Rio Productions, 1998.

49 quoted in Mary Rogers's book, Barbie Culture, agrees: Rogers, M. F. Barbie Culture. Beverly Hills, CA: Sage, 1999.

49 In a 1964 issue of The Nation magazine one man wrote (and also the quote from Ramparts): Stern.

49 will be ruled by the superior judgment of her husband: Dijkstra, B. Evil Sisters: The Threat of Female Sexuality and the Cult of Manhood. NY: Knopf, 1996.

49 by exaggerating what is "actual, possible, or conceivable": Rogers, p. 3.

49 "Barbie was intentionally crafted to invoke a specific kind of imaginary role playing": Kline, S. Out of the Garden: Toys, TV, and Children's Culture in the Age of Marketing. London: Verso, 1993, p. 251.

52 Barbie is a female doll that excites girls: Rand, E. Barbie's Queer Accessories. Durham, NC: Duke University Press, 1995.

52 what she called the "lesbian continuum": Rich, A. "Compulsory Heterosexuality and Lesbian Experience." In Stimpson, C. R., and Person, E. S. (eds.), Women: Sex and Sexuality, Chicago: University of Chicago Press, 1980, pp. 62–91.

52 and turn it into fun, glamour, and excitement: Rogers, p. 36.

Zeroing In On: Childhood Innocence and the Shaming of Sexuality

54 "fundamentally conveys who we hope to be": Warner, M. Six Myths of Our Time: Little Angels, Little Monsters, Beautiful Beasts, and More. NY: Vintage, 1995.

55 "and revengeful as young as they are" as well as information in two paragraphs following: Cox, R. Shaping Childhood: Themes of Uncertainty in the History of Adult-Child Relationships. NY: Routledge, 1996.

56 The famous sex researcher Alfred Kinsey: Kinsey, A. Sexual Behavior in the Human Female. Philadelphia: Saunders, 1953.

56 In a study of Irish parents: Fitzpatrick, C., Deehan, A., and Jennings, S. Children's sexual behavior and knowledge: A community study. Irish Journal of Psychological Medicine (1995) 12, 87–91.

56 In another study, William Friedrich: Friedrich, W. N., Grambsch, P., Damon, L., Hewitt, S. K., et al. Child Sexual Behavior Inventory: Normative and clinical comparisons. Psychological Assessment (1992) 4, 303–11.

56 Gail Wyatt and her colleagues at UCLA: Wyatt, G., Newcomb, M. D., and Riedale, M. H. Sexual Abuse and Consensual Sex: Women's Developmental Patterns and Outcomes. Beverly Hills, CA: Sage, 1993.

56 Anthropologists have learned that children can have orgasms: This and the anthropological information that follows in this paragraph and the next are from Bagley, C. Children, Sex, and Social Policy: Humanistic Solutions to the Problems of Child Sexual Abuse. Brookfield, VT: Avebury, 1997.

57 Today, Sweden is the first country to require a comprehensive sex education program and following in that paragraph: Martinson, F. M. The Sexual Life of Children. Westport, CT: Bergin and Garvey, 1994.

58   *Diana Gittins writes in* The Child in Question: Gittins, D. *The Child in Question*. NY: St. Martin's Press, 1998.

Chapter 5: Bodies and Pleasure: If It Feels Good, Why Is It So Bad?

59   *in the late 1970s when anthropologist Gilbert Herdt returned:* Herdt, G. *Guardians of the Flute:* Vol. 1, *Idioms of Masculinity.* Chicago: University of Chicago Press, 1981. Note that the name of the tribe, the Sambia, is a name Herdt invented to protect the anonymity of the tribe.

60   *For example, an anthropologist studying Hawaiian cultures was amazed:* Diamond, M. Cross-generational sexual behavior in traditional Hawaii. In Feierman, J. (ed.), *Pedophilia: Biosocial Dimensions*, pp. 422–44. NY: Springer-Verlag, as cited in Bagley.

60   *In Africa, among the Baganda, an anthropologist, to his embarrassment, observed:* Bagley.

64   *permission to lose control:* Thorne and Luria.

Chapter 7: Wanting It and Not Wanting It

70   *"We won't have sex unless we are seduced, driven, out of control":* Cassell, C. *Swept Away: Why Women Confuse Love and Sex . . . and How They Can Have Both.* NY: Simon and Schuster, 1984, p. 6.

75   *ambivalences about things called "date rape" or "sexual abuse":* For an excellent discussion of this, see Phillips, L. *Flirting with Danger*, NY: New York University Press, 2000.

Chapter 8: Two Kinds of Guilty Pleasure

77   *especially important to Puerto Rican girls:* Most of the interviews I did with Latina women were with women whose parents had come or who themselves had come at an early age to the United States from Puerto Rico. I also interviewed a Chicana woman; however, I regret not finding a more diverse group of Latina women to include in the book.

77   *live under the "cult of the virgin" and among "macho men":* This kind of information about women, and especially Puerto Ricans, comes from several sources: Espin, O. *Women Crossing Boundaries: A Psychology of Immigration and Transformation.* NY: Routledge, 1999; Espin, O. Traumatic historical events and adolescent psychosocial development: Letters from V. In Franz, C., and Stewart, A. (eds.), *Women Creating Lives: Identities, Resilience, and Resistance.* Boulder, CO: Westview Press, 1984, pp. 187–98; and Fontes, L. Disclosures of sexual abuse by Puerto Rican children. *Journal of Child Sexual Abuse* (1993) 2, 21–35.

Chapter 9: African-American Girls and Their Secrets

85   *African-American women:* I sometimes use the terms African-American and
      Black interchangeably. The term "Black" seems appropriate because the
      girls themselves use that word to describe their race, and in certain phrases
      the word seems to capture the feel of the expressions used by the Black
      women and girls I interviewed. Also, the term African American seems not
      to apply to some girls, who consider themselves Black and Caribbean. The
      phrase "people of color" would not differentiate the Latina women I inter-
      viewed from the African-American women. Still, "African-American"
      seems to denote a kind of respect I want to show to the women and girls
      whom I interviewed, and so that is why I switch back and forth.

85   *Hortense Spillers, a scholar who writes about Black women and fiction:* Spillers,
      H. Interstices: A small drama of words. In Vance, C. S. (ed.), *Pleasure and
      Danger: Exploring Female Sexuality,* Boston: Routledge & Kegan Paul, 1984,
      78–79.

85   *an African-American girl's ability to control her sexuality:* Wyatt, G. *Stolen
      Women: Reclaiming Our Sexuality, Taking Back Our Lives.* NY: Wiley, 1997,
      pp. 3–4.

85   *disproportionately profiling Black girls who are "out of control" and at high risk for
      early pregnancy:* The idea that the media and researchers only recognize de-
      viance rather than development in their work on African-American ado-
      lescents and sexuality is found in Tolman, D. Adolescent girls' sexuality:
      Debunking the myth of the urban girl. In Leadbetter, B., and Way, N. (eds.),
      Urban Girls: Resisting Stereotypes, Creating Identities. NY: New York Univer-
      sity Press, 1996. See also Vera, E. M., Reese, L. E., Paikoff, R. L., and Jarrett,
      R. L. Contextual factors of sexual risk-taking in urban African-American
      preadolescent children. In Leadbetter and Way.

92   *strictness and straightness in African-American families who have close ties with
      their church:* Ward, J. *The Skin We're In: Teaching Our Children to be Emotion-
      ally Strong, Socially Smart, and Spiritually Connected.* NY: Free Press, 2000.
      Here Janie Ward describes the emphasis in black baby-boomers' upbringing
      on appearances and respectability in order to instill a sense of personal dig-
      nity. "White people," Ward writes, "black children were warned, were often
      wild and crazy, undisciplined. But they could behave that way. The same be-
      havior exhibited by black kids would be considered much worse. Whites
      think we are wild and undisciplined already." (p. 16) See also Fordham, S.
      Blacked Out: Dilemmas of Race, Identity, and Success at Capital High. Chi-
      cago: University of Chicago Press, 1997: "The central lesson the mothers of
      high-achieving females taught them was the value of behaving in socially
      appropriate ways (conformity)—most important, *not* bringing shame on the
      family by acting on their developing sexuality." (p. 146)

92   *the taboo against homosexuality:* This taboo has been discussed more fre-
      quently in literature on male homosexuality, beginning perhaps with Amiri
      Baraka's poetry and 1969 piece "Black Aesthetic," and more recently in

Stokes, J. P., and Peterson, J. L. Homophobia, self-esteem, and risk for HIV among African-American men who have sex with men. *AIDS Education and Prevention* (1998) 10, 278–92, and in Gayfield, D. R. On the periphery of manhood: The African-American community's marginalization of black male homosexuality. *The Berkeley McNair Research Journal* (2000) 8, www.mcnair-berkeley.edu. On the taboo against black lesbians, Evelyn Hammond writes of the ease with which heterosexual black women can cast them as "traitors to the race." Hammond, E. Toward a genealogy of black female sexuality: The problematic of silence. In Alexander, J., and Mohanty, C. T. (eds.), *Feminist Genealogies, Colonial Legacies, Democratic Futures*, NY: Routledge, 1997.

94 *The strictness in African-American families can be a source of pride:* Fordham.

94 *"We lose sight of the way in which the ability to experience and know pleasure is an essential ingredient of wellness":* hooks, b. *Sisters of the Yam*, Boston: South End Press, 1993, p. 116.

95 *Janie Ward, educator and author of* The Skin We're In, *a book for African-American parents:* Ward.

95 *Elijah Anderson's street sociology of an African-American urban community:* Anderson, E. *Streetwise: Race, Class, and Change in an Urban Community.* Chicago: University of Chicago Press, 1990.

Chapter 10: Periods, Pubic Hair, Boobies, and Bodily Torture

96 *Most children around the world do not get their sex education from their parents:* Bagley.

96 *and research shows that African-American and Puerto Rican girls get even less than Caucasian girls:* Wyatt.

98 *Both feminist author Sharon Thompson, in* Going All the Way, *and feminist professor of education* and author *Michelle Fine, in "The Missing Discourse of Desire," suggest:* Fine, M. Sexuality, schooling, and adolescent females: The missing discourse of desire. In Fine, M. (ed.), *Disruptive Voices: The Possibilities of Feminist Research*. Ann Arbor: University of Michigan Press, 1992, pp. 31–60; Thompson, S. *Going All the Way: Teenage Girls' Tales of Sex, Romance, and Pregnancy*. NY: Hill and Wang, 1995.

99 *Author Karin Flaake wrote these wise words in her essay "A Body of One's Own":* Flaake, K. A body of one's own: Sexual development and the female body in the mother-daughter relationship. In van Meus-Verhulst, J., Schrews, K., and Woertman, L. (eds.), *Mothering and Daughtering*. London: Routledge, 1993, pp. 7–14.

101 *girls negotiate the forces of adult femininity:* Thorne.

101 *Researcher Janet Lee, in her study of forty women's narratives:* Lee, J. Menarche and the (hetero)sexualization of the female body. *Gender & Society* (1994) 8, 343–62.

102 *As psychiatrist Harry Stack Sullivan wrote, having a chum:* Sullivan, H. S. *The Interpersonal Theory of Psychiatry*. NY: Norton, 1953.

103   *Anne Stirling Hastings, in* Body and Soul, *writes about how children learn to cut off awareness:* Hastings, A. S. *Body and Soul: Sexuality on the Brink of Change.* NY: Plenum Press, 1996, p. 3.

Chapter 11: Guilty Minds and Sexual Obsessions

108   *The psychiatrist Harry Stack Sullivan, in* The Interpersonal Theory of Psychiatry, *now a classic, wrote:* Sullivan.

Chapter 12: Too Sexual Too Soon

117   *Look at the new trends for oral sex in junior high school. When journalists have investigated this:* Jarrell, A. The Face of Teenage Sex Grows Younger. *New York Times,* April 2, 2000, sec. 9, pp. 1, 8f.

117   *was eight when she began developing breasts:* Lemonick, M. Teens Before Their Time. *Time* (Oct. 30, 2000).

117   *Until recently researchers believed that African-American girls are more likely to:* Alan Guttmacher Institute. *Sex and America's Teenagers.* NY: Alan Guttmacher Institute, 1994. See also Brooks-Gunn, J., and Paikoff, R. L. Sex is a gamble, kissing is a game: Adolescent sexuality and health promotion. In Millstein, S. P., Petersen, A., and Nightengale, E. (eds.), *Promotion of Health Behavior in Adolescence.* NY: Oxford University Press, 1993; Udry, J. R. Biological predispositions and social control in adolescent sexual behavior. *American Sociological Review* (1988) 53, 709–22, and several CDC reports as cited by Phillips, L. *The Girls Report: What We Know and Need to Know About Growing Up female.* NY: National Council for Research on Women, 1998.

118   *Tolman, . . . writes that when race and class are not confounded, differences between whites and Blacks almost disappear:* Tolman, p. 257. Wyatt (1989) has also shown that blacks' experience of first intercourse at a younger age has more to do with family income and single-parent homes than race. Research on "The Impact of African American Fathers on Adolescent Sexual Behavior" by Dittus, P. J., Jaccard, and Gordon, V. V. *Journal of Youth and Adolescence* (1997) 26, 445–65, supports this.

118   *In* Streetwise, *the sociologist Elijah Anderson writes about the game young African-American teen and preteen boys play:* Anderson.

118   *It has long been known that children (of any race) in homes with only one biological parent are:* Dittus, Jaccard, and Gordon. See also Hogan, D. P., and Kitawaga, E. M. The impact of social status, family structure, and neighborhood on the fertility of black adolescents. *American Journal of Sociology* (1985) 90, 825–55.

118   *"unprotected nest":* Anderson.

120   *As Sharon Thompson writes . . . , the association of sex with love may be girls' biggest vulnerability:* Thompson.

120   *The southern white girl was training to become a lady and discussion follow-*

ing from Caraway, N. *Segregated Sisterhood: Racism and the Politics of American Feminism*. Knoxville: University of Tennessee, 1991. See also Carby, H. *Reinventing Womanhood: The Emergence of the Afro-American Woman*. Oxford: Oxford University Press, 1987; Davis, A. Reflections on the black woman's role in the community of slaves. *Black Scholar* (1971) 3, 3–15; Fox-Genovese, E. *Within the Plantation Household*. Chapel Hill: University of North Carolina, 1988; Lerner, G. *Black Women in White America*. NY: Vintage, 1973.

121 *A significant number of them have been sexually touched or exploited at young ages:* Wyatt et al.

121 *bell hooks warns that white feminists have ignored the impact of abuse:* hooks.

121 *"reticent about discussing sex and birth control with their children":* Anderson, p. 135.

121 *not hemmed in by prudery and constriction:* Rainwater, L. *And the Poor Get Children*. Chicago: Quadrangle Books, 1960.

122 *Luce Irigaray, wrote about a powerful form of women's sexuality that celebrates its womanliness:* Irigaray.

122 *into a positive view of herself?:* hooks, cited in Tolman.

Chapter 13: Unwelcome Intrusions: Sexual Coercion in the Lives of Girls

124 *Research documents boys taking over use of hands-on science equipment in coed classes:* Jovanovic, J., and Steinbach, S. Boys and Girls in the Performance-Based Science Classroom: Who's Doing the Performing? *American Educational Research Journal* (1998) 35, 477–96.

124 *It records mothers of preschoolers making their little girls:* Ross, H., Tesla, C., Kenyon, B., and Lollis, S. Maternal intervention in peer conflict: The Socialization of principles of justice. *Developmental Psychology* (1990) 26, 994–1003.

126 *to master what happened to them by modeling themselves after the aggressor:* Freud.

Chapter 14: Raising Sexual Girls: A Few Words to Parents

134 *What Every Girl Should Know:* This information about Margaret Sanger's series of articles came from a *New York Times* article, "When nice girls didn't," November, 16, 1999, Health & Fitness section.

Part II: Aggression, Destruction, and Being Mean

Chapter 15: Aggression in Girls

141 *an interview . . . on 20/20, a newsmagazine television show:* Barbara Walters interviews Naomi Campbell, *20/20*, aired June 17, 2000.

142   *punish girls . . . for aggression and decreasingly punish boys:* Mills, R. S., and
      Rubin, K. H. A longitudinal study of maternal beliefs about children's social
      behaviors. *Merrill-Palmer Quarterly* (1992) 38, 494–512.

144   *likely to be in a position subordinate to the person she is angry at:* Tavris, C.
      Anger: The Misunderstood Emotion. NY: Simon and Schuster, 1982.

144   *"aggression can be a positive, enhancing act":* Burbank, V. *Fighting Women:
      Anger and Aggression in Aboriginal Australia.* Berkeley: University of Califor-
      nia Press, 1994.

145   *making a display of strength rather than hiding in supposed weakness:* Haaken, J.
      Battered Women's Refuge as Social Symbolic Space. Talk given at Saint
      Michael's College, Colchester, VT, November 12, 1999.

145   *are fundamentally about connection and loss of connection:* Jack, D. Behind the
      Mask: Destruction and Creativity in Women's Aggression Cambridge, MA:
      Harvard U. P., 1999.

145   *women's aggression occurs in relationships, but she prefers to call it a form of com-
      munication:* Burbank.

Chapter 16: A Good Girl Doesn't Do That

147   *"tyranny of the nice and kind":* Brown and Gilligan.

150   *African-American adolescents seem to succumb much less frequently to anorexia
      and bulimia:* For a review of this literature see Striegel-Moore, R. H., and
      Smolak, L. The role of race in eating disorders. In Smolak, L., Levine, M.,
      and Striegel-Moore, R. J. (eds.), *The Developmental Psychopathology of Eating
      Disorders.* Mahway, NJ: Erlbaum, 1996, pp. 259–84. See also Kumanyika, S.,
      Wilson, J. F., and Guilford-Davenport, M. Weight-related attitudes and be-
      haviors of black women. *Journal of American Dietetic Association* (1993) 93,
      416–17.

150   *so that they often "act nice and feel mean":* Jack.

Zeroing In On: Tomboys

155   *half of all adult women remember themselves as tomboys:* Carr, C. L. (1998)
      Tomboy resistance and conformity: Agency in Social psychological gender
      theory, *Gender & Society,* 12, 528–553

156   *to conform to more stereotypical images of girlhood as they approached adoles-
      cence:* Carr.

157   *afforded some girls the opportunity to be closer to distant dads:* Ibid.

158   *Female executives of Fortune 500 companies.* www.womenssportsfounda
      tion.org.

Chapter 17: Dear Diary, I Hate Her! Secret Anger in Girls

159   *"anger is a molten pond at the core of me, my most fiercely guarded secret":*
      Lorde, A. *Sister Outsider: Essays and Speeches by Audre Lorde,* p. 145.

159   *girls are masters of indirection when it comes to anger:* Pearson, P. *When She Was
      Bad: Violent Women and the Myth of Innocence.* NY: Viking/Penguin, 1997.

159   *"go underground to reach others through hidden channels, while surface behaviors mask the intent"*: Jack, p. 188.

159   *at an early age girls more than boys learn to mask anger in their facial expressions*: Underwood, M., Coie, J., and Herbsman, C. Display rules for anger and aggression in school-age children. *Child Development* (1992) 63, 366–80.

159   *contain themselves more in the presence of an adult*: Cole, P., Zahn-Waxler, C., and Smith, D. Expressive control during disappointment: Variations related to preschoolers' behavior problems. *Developmental Psychology* (1994) 30, 835–46.

160   *The reverse is true of mothers speaking to their sons*: Cross, S. E., and Madson, L. Models of the self: Self-construal and gender. *Psychological Bulletin* (1997) 122, 5–37.

160   *includes gossiping, excluding, and withdrawal*: Crick, N. R., and Grotpeter, J. K. Relational aggression, gender, and social-psychological adjustment. *Child Development* (1995) 66, 710–22.

160   *that the culture cannot accept female anger* and following: Jack.

160   *girls were treated badly by those around them when they were angry*: Cox, D., Stabb, S., and Bruckner, K. *Women's Anger: Clinical and Developmental Perspectives*. NY: Brunner/Mazel, 1999.

160   *boys more anger*: Birnbaum, D. W., and Croll, W. L. The etiology of children's stereotypes about sex differences in emotionality. *Sex Roles* (1984) 10, 677–91.

160   marianisma *require martyrdom and quiet suffering rather than anger*: Jack.

160   *seen by whites as "uppity" or dangerous when they get angry*: Cox, Stabb, and Bruckner. See also hooks; Lorde; Ward.

161   *demanding woman gone to extremes*: Becker, D. *Through the Looking Glass: Women and Borderline Personality Disorder*. Boulder, CO: Westview Press, 1998.

161   *"self-clarification to a weapon of self-destruction"*: Cox, Stabb, and Bruckner, p. 9.

162   *subordinate position that makes them mask their anger*: Tavris.

162   *receive permission to feel, display, and act on anger than those with less authority*: Averill, J. The emotions: An integrative approach. In Hogan, R., Johnson, J., and Briggs, S. (eds.), *Handbook of Personality Psychology*. San Diego, CA: Academic Press, 1997, pp. 513–43.

162   *one of the major tasks of her life*: Lorde.

165   *rage is like a foreign language over which they have no control*: Valentis, M., and Devane, A. *Female Rage: Unlocking Its Secrets, Claiming Its Power*. NY: Carol Southern Books, 1994.

165   *threatens annihilation*: Lorde, p. 130.

Chapter 18: The Aggressive Acts of Good Girls

167   *calls this "unfamiliar territory"*: Jack.

Zeroing In On: Pranks, Mischief, and Little Meannesses

175   *working-class girls' anger is a form of resistance:* L. M., Brown *Raising Their Voices: The Politics of Girl's Anger,* Cambridge, MA.: Harvard (1999).

177   *boys like to play in groups and girls like to play one-on-one:* Many researchers have pointed out the phenomenon of boys playing in groups and girls playing one-on-one, from more mainstream perspectives to more feminist perspectives. See Beutel and Marini. Although, see M. H. Goodwin's 1994 study, Social differentiation and alliance formation in an African-American children's peer group. In Stevenson, M. (ed.), *Gender roles through the lifespan.* Muncie, IN: Ball State University Press, showing African-American girls forming larger coalitions. See also Lever, J. Sex differences in the games children play. *Social Problems,* 23, 478–87, and Thorne.

177   *courage as a virtue we should promote in boys:* Courage has been considered a manly ideal for centuries. In the early 1900s, at the beginning of the Boy Scouts, it was promoted as a virtue. See Hantover, J. P., 1989. The boy scouts and the validation of masculinity. In Kimmel, M. S., and Messner, M. A. (eds.), *Men's Lives,* NY: Macmillan, 1976, pp. 158–66. Robert Bly complained that after the women's movement, men became afraid to develop courage. Bly, R. *Iron John.* NY: Addison-Wesley, 1990. Recent boys' authors like Pollack and Gabarino, J. *Lost Boys,* NY: Free Press, 1999, don't always include "courage" as a value we need to help boys develop.

Chapter 19: Feeling the Power

178   *I've been striving for it all my life:* Madonna Live, BBC 2, 1991, as cited in Lees, S. *Ruling Passions: Sex, Violence, Reputation, and the Law.* Buckingham, England: Open University Press, 1997.

178   *our victimization rather than on our strengths:* I have written about this in Lamb, S. *The Trouble with Blame: Victims, Perpetrators, and Responsibility.* Cambridge, MA: Harvard University Press, 1996, as well as in Lamb, S. Constructing the victim: Popular images and lasting labels. In Lamb, S. (ed.), *New Versions of Victims: Feminists Struggle with the Concept.* NY: New York University Press, 1999. See also Haaken, J. *Pillar of Salt: Gender, Memory, and the Perils of Looking Back.* New Brunswick, NJ: Rutgers University Press, 1998, and Wolf, N. *Fire with Fire.* NY: Random House, 1993.

179   *love to prove "Girls Rule":* Dahl, R. *Matilda.* NY: Puffin Books, 1988.

186   *the need to be aggressive comes from a failure of relationship:* Jack.

Chapter 20: Getting Physical: Girl Athletes

189   *revealed something few previous researchers have realized:* Jaffee, L., and Sickler, H. Boys' and girls' choices of equipment and activities on the playground. *Melpomene* (1997) 17, 18–23.

190 *a time when girls largely had been excluded from participation:* Sklover, B. Women and sports: The 25th anniversary of Title IX. *AAUW Outlook* (1997) 90, 12–17.

190 *dangers of physical activity for women and girls:* Cahn, S. K. *Coming on Strong: Gender and Sexuality in Twentieth-Century Women's Sport.* NY: Free Press, 1994.

190 *physical self-esteem:* Dowling, C. *The Frailty Myth: Women Approaching Physical Equality.* NY: Random House, 2000.

190 *and a lower school dropout rate:* Sabo, D. F., and Women's Sports Foundation. *The Wilson Report: Moms, Dads, Daughters, and Sports.* East Meadow, NY, 1988. President's Council on Physical Fitness and Sports. *Physical Activity and Sport in the Lives of Girls.* Washington, D.C.: President's Council on Physical Fitness and Sports, 1997.

191 *wear before they start looking too unfeminine:* Dworkin, S. L., and Messner, M. A. Just do . . . what? Sport, Bodies, and Gender. In Ferree, M. M., Lorber, J., and Hess, B.B. (eds.), *Revisioning Gender.* Thousand Oaks, CA: Sage, 1999, pp. 341–61.

191 *flowing hair, and "spectacular outfits":* Messner, M. A. Theorizing gendered bodies: Beyond the subject/object dichotomy. In Cole, C. L., Loy, J., and Messner, M. (eds.), *Exercising Power: The Making and Remaking of the Body.* Albany: State University of New York Press, forthcoming (as cited in Dworkin and Messner).

191 *fans and the media may do it for them:* Bolin, A. Flex appeal, food and fat: Competitive bodybuilding, gender, and diet. *Play and Culture* (1992) 5, 378–400. See also Bolin, A. Vandalized vanity: Feminine physique betrayed and portrayed. In Mascia-Lees, F. E., and Sharpe, P. (eds.), *Tattoo, Torture, Mutilation, and Adornment: The Denaturalization of the Body in Culture and Text.* Albany, NY: State University of New York Press, 1992, pp. 79–90.

191 *femininity rather than on their athletic success:* Daniels, D. Gender (body) verification (building). *Play and culture* (1993) 5, 370–77.

191 *Girls who participate in sports often have a double identity:* Jack.

191 *Leslie Heywood writes what it was like in high school to be marked as a good athlete:* Heywood, L. *Pretty Good for a Girl.* NY: Free Press, 1998.

192 *this is an integral part of men's hockey games:* Theberge, N. It's part of the game: Physicality and the production of gender in women's hockey. *Gender and Society* (1997) 11, 69–87.

192 *they reflect so-called male values such as hierarchy, competitiveness, and aggression:* Hall, M. A. *Feminism and Sporting Bodies: Essays on Theory and Practice.* Champaign, IL: Human Kinetics, 1996.

192 *didn't want highly competitive sports:* Festle, M. J. *Playing Nice: Politics and Apologies in Women's Sports.* NY: Columbia University Press, 1996.

192 *"Sequined skating outfits were sexy, smelly shinguards were not":* Ackerman, E. She kicks. She scores. She sells. *U.S. News & World Report.* Business & Technology section, July 26, 1999, Vol. 127, ISS. 4, p. 42

192   *Letterman called the whole team "babe city":* Anonymous. Dec. 31, 1999. Brandi Chastain. *People Weekly*, 52, 100–101.

192   *she was a "diva," "sullen," "petulant," and "pouty":* See Barnes, S. (September 22, 2000). Khorkina Fails to Find Saving Grace. *Times* (London); and Glauber, B. (September 25, 2000), Sports, section 15E Russia's Khorkina Balances Her Gloom on Uneven Bars Gold. *Baltimore Sun,* for two examples.

193   *because they got to be with other girls:* Erkut, S., Fields, J. P., Sing, R., and Marx, F. Diversity in girls' experiences: Feeling good about who you are. In Leadbetter and Way.

193   *certain girl-based "performance of femininity":* Hey, V. *The Company She Keeps: An Ethnography of Girls' Friendships.* Buckingham, England: Open Universities Press, 1997.

197   *"it has nothing to do with looks":* Anonymous: Win Some and Lose Some. *Newsweek,* May 1, 2000, p. 71.

197   *"All the girls I know that wrestle are there because they love to wrestle":* Slaughter, J. Post-Feminist Smackdown. *In These Times,* July 10, 2000, p. 30.

197   *Iris Marion Young, a philosopher and social theorist:* Young, I. M. *Throwing Like a Girl and Other Essays in Feminist Philosophy and Social Theory.* Bloomington, IN: Indiana University Press, 1990.

Chapter 21: Class, Clothes, and Cutting Her Down to Size

199   *"of poise more characteristic of middle-class girls than lower-class girls":* Breines, W. *Young, White, and Miserable: Growing Up Female in the Fifties.* Boston: Beacon Press, 1992, p. 111.

199   *it can be considered offensive:* Martin, J. Everyone behaving badly: Review of L. Williams's *It's the Little Things: The Everyday Interactions That Get Under the Skin of Blacks and Whites.* NY: Harcourt, 2000. *New York Times Book Review,* October 15, 2000.

201   *worked at socializing others into group behavior and norms:* Eder, D. *School Talk: Gender and Adolescent Culture.* New Brunswick, NJ: Rutgers University Press, 1995.

201   *competitiveness and antagonism: They called them snobs:* McRobbie, A. *Feminism and Youth Culture.* Boston: Unwin Hyman, 1991.

201   *convince themselves of their superiority through studying hard and having better, more caring, values:* Brown.

201   *themselves against other girls when they talk about sexual and social relations:* Thompson.

201   *within a male-dominated culture align themselves with dominant voices* Brown, L., Way, N., and Duff, J. L. The others in my I: Adolescent girls' friendships and peer relations. In Johnson, N., Roberts, M. C., and Worrell, J. (eds.), *Beyond Appearance: A New Look at Adolescent Girls.* Washington, D.C.: APA Press, 1999.

202   *Brown uses the word "ventriloquation":* Brown.

202 *one researcher studied popularity and isolation in a group of junior high school girls:* Merten, D. The meaning of meanness: Popularity, competition, and conflict among junior high school girls. *Sociology of Education* (1997) 70, 175–191.

202 *converse of a group ideal of loyalty:* Brown.

202 *one another because the cut comes from a supposed ally:* Hey.

202 *support one another against teachers and out groups as well:* Brown; Hey.

Zeroing In On: Language and Loudness

205 *tough-talking, feminine, and responsible nurturer all at the same time:* Luttrell, W. The Edison School struggle: The reshaping of working-class education and women's consciousness. In Bookman, A., and Morgen, S. (eds.), *Women and the Politics of Empowerment.* Philadelphia: Temple University Press, 1988.

205 *Being good means suppressing disagreements:* Hey.

205 *teachers label the loudness as "impulsive, childish behavior":* Brown, p. 205.

206 *refused to stay in the background of white girls' lives in high school:* Evans, G. Those loud black girls. In *Learning to lose: Sexism and Education.* London: The Women's Press, 1988, as cited in Fordham, S. "Those loud black girls": Women, silence, and gender "passing" in the academy. *Anthropology and Education Quarterly* (1993) 24, 3–32.

206 *"I am here and I will not be made invisible":* Fordham. See also Fordham, S. *Blacked Out: Dilemmas of Race, Ethnicity, and Success at Capitol High.* Chicago: University of Chicago Press, 1996.

206 *"phantoms of the opera," she worries that they silence themselves too much:* Fordham, S. Phantoms in the opera: Black girls' academic achievement at Capitol High. Paper presented at the annual meeting of the American Anthropological Association, New Orleans, November, 1990, as cited in Fordham, 1993.

206 *"controlled response to their evolving, ambiguous status":* Fordham, 1996, p. 17.

206 *maintain a personal sense of self-worth yet disconnect from school:* AAUW. *Shortchanging girls, shortchanging America.* Washington, D.C.: AAUW, 1991.

206 *or made to be quiet because of disruptive comments:* Fordham, S., and Ogbu, J. Black students' school success: Coping with the "burden of acting white." *Urban Review* (1986) 18, 176–206.

207 *associated with badness:* Smith in Smart and Smart.

207 *they are considered male and stigmatized as pushy and unfair:* Jack.

207 *"tongues of fire":* hooks, b. *Sisters of the Yam: Black Women and Self-recovery.* Boston: South End Press, 1993, as cited in Ward.

207 *"bold, unreserved, 'in-your-face' truth-telling in the service of racial socialization" is a part of African-American tradition:* Ward, J. Raising resisters: The role of truth-telling in the psychological development of African-American girls. In Leadbetter and Way, 1996, pp. 85–99.

207 *showing anger were essential to keeping relationships:* Way, N. "Can't you see the courage, the strength I have?" Listening to urban adolescent girls speak about their relationships. *Psychology of Women Quarterly* (1995) 19, 107–28.

207 *take the place of joining together with other girls and thus changing the system:* Orenstein, P. *Schoolgirls: Young Women, Self-esteem, and the Confidence Gap.* NY: Doubleday, 1994.

208 *look for power in the school through identification with teachers:* Walkerdine, 1987.

208 *best understanding of racism, sexism, and classism:* Pastor, J. Possible selves and academic achievement among inner-city students of color. Master's thesis, City University of New York, 1993, as cited in Pastor, J., McCormick, J., and Fine, M. (1996). Makin' homes: An urban girl thing. In Leadbetter and Way.

208 *another opportunity for the middle-class girl to paint herself as the keeper of purity:* Hey.

Chapter 22: "I'm No Sucker": Fighting and Fighting Back

209 *topic is so deviant, it can't even be discussed:* Campbell, A. *Men, women, and aggression.* NY: Basic Books, 1993, p. 37.

209 *personal offenses were also up, up 146 percent for females versus an increase of 87 percent for males:* Sickmund, M. Offenders in Juvenile Court, 1995. Bulletin. Washington, D.C. U.S. Department of Justice, Office of Justice Programs, Office of Juvenile Justice and Delinquency Prevention, 1997.

209 *report shows that a disproportionate two thirds of those girls arrested are African-American or Latina:* Acoca, L., and Dedel, K. *No Place to Hide: Understanding and Meeting the Needs of Girls in the California Justice System.* San Francisco, CA: National Council on Crime and Delinquency, 1998.

210 *she has breached her proper role:* Campbell, p. 52.

210 *aggression comes from no longer being able to hold one's anger in:* Campbell.

210 *the "coercive power" that aggression brings with it operates as a tool for survival:* Tedesci, J. T., Smith, R. B., and Brown, R. C. A reinterpretation of research on aggression. *Psychological Bulletin* (1974) 81, 540–62.

211 *putting up a "wall of self-protection":* Jack.

213 *were likely to have been beaten, stabbed, shot, or raped:* Acoca and Dedel.

215 *if they don't get away, they still have a much quicker recovery:* Bart, P., and O'Brien, P. *Stopping Rape: Successful Survival Strategies.* NY: Teachers College Press, 1985. This finding was also presented at the Association of Women in Psychology Conference in April 1999, Providence, RI, by Dr. Patricia Rozee in her presentation, "Psychology of Rape Resistance."

216 *this kind of proving oneself among girl gang members:* Campbell, p. 137.

Chapter 23: Raising Aggressive Girls?

221   *area which caused him to fall to the ground:* Li, T. Special to the *Los Angeles Times,* November 23, 1993, found in Snortland, E. *Beauty Bites Beast: Awakening the Warrior Within Women and Girls.* Pasadena, CA: Trilogy Books, 1998.
221   *"incapable of responding":* Dowling, p. 253.
222   *the proper response when one's rights have been violated:* Murphy, J. G. Two cheers for vindictiveness. *Punishment and Society* (2000) 2, 131–43.
222   *the shocking pink, wild and wonderful teen guide:* Drill, E., McDonald, H., and Odes, R. *Deal With It.* NY: Pocket Books, 1999, p. 168.

Index